KEY
for Schools
TRAINER 2

SIX PRACTICE TESTS
WITH ANSWERS AND TEACHER'S NOTES

Cambridge University Press
www.cambridge.org/elt

Cambridge Assessment English
www.cambridgeenglish.org

Information on this title: www.cambridge.org/9781108401678

© Cambridge University Press and UCLES 2017

First published 2017

20 19 18 17 16 15 14 13 12 11 10 9 8 7 6 5 4 3 2

Printed in Dubai by Oriental Press

A catalogue record for this publication is available from the British Library

ISBN 978-1-108-40167-8   Student's Book with answers with audio
ISBN 978-1-108-40165-4   Student's Book without answers with audio

Contents

Introduction

If you are aged between 11 and 15 and want to take **Key for Schools**, this book is for **YOU**!

This book is called '**Trainer**' because it is full of exercises to help you get better and better at doing each part of **Key for Schools**.

So, complete all the exercises then do all the practice papers! If you train and work hard, you'll soon be ready to take **Key for Schools**!

First, do the grammar and vocabulary exercises on each **Training** page.
Then do the task on the **Exam practice** page and check your answers.

On Training pages, you will find:

 Cambridge Learner Corpus

This shows information about mistakes that some **Key** candidates make. If you do these useful exercises, you will learn <u>not</u> to make these mistakes when <u>you</u> do **Key for Schools**!

Tips!

These are ideas to help you do well in the exam. For example: *Look at the words before and after the space.*

Remember!

These are quick reminders about grammar points or vocabulary that you should learn. For example: ***its*** *goes with a noun: The cat broke **its** leg.*

On Exam practice pages, you will find:

- a **Key for Schools exam task** for you to try and complete
- **advice** to help you with different parts of the task

Tests 3, 4, 5 and 6:

When you finish Tests 1 and 2, you will be ready to do complete **Key for Schools practice tests**.

Tests 3, 4, 5 and 6 are just like real **Key for Schools** Reading and Writing, Listening and Speaking papers. Doing these will help you even more to prepare for the exam.

Keep a record of your scores as you do the tests. You may find that your scores are good in some parts of the test but you may need to practise other parts more. Make simple tables like this to help record your scores:

Paper 3 Listening

	Part 1	Part 2	Part 3	Part 4	Part 5
Test 3					
Test 4					
Test 5					
Test 6					

Other features of the *Key for Schools Trainer*

- **Visual material**

  In the Speaking test the examiner will give you an information booklet. The visual material on pages 228–235 will help you practise and become familiar with the type of information you will be given and help you increase your confidence.

- **Teacher's notes and Key**

  You will find all the answers to the exercises and practice tests in this part of the book. The teacher's notes also explain why some answers are wrong. You will find more CLC information here too.

- **Answer sheets**

  Look at these to see what the *Key for Schools* answer sheets in the test look like and learn how to complete them. Ask your teacher to photocopy them so that you can use them when you do practice tests.

- **Downloadable Audio online**

  Listen to these to practise the Listening paper. You will need to listen to these to practise some parts of the Speaking paper too.

- **Audioscripts**

  Read the audioscript after you have done a listening exercise. Find the answers and the information that is wrong. This should help you hear the right answers the next time you practise.

The Key English Test for Schools

Contents

Key for Schools has three papers:

Reading and Writing: 1 hour 10 minutes

You will need to able to read and understand simple information that you might see on signs or read in brochures, newspaper or magazine articles. You will also have to choose words to fill gaps in sentences, understand some definitions and spell their words. You will have to write a short message or note that is between 25 and 35 words long too.

Listening: 30 minutes

You will need to be able to listen and understand people who are talking together or people who are giving information about something. You will have to choose or write answers to questions which are about what these people say. Don't worry! The people talk very clearly and they don't talk fast!

Speaking: 10 minutes

You will need to be able to listen and understand what the examiner is saying. You will have to answer some simple questions about yourself. You will also be given some information to look at. You will ask and answer questions about the information with another candidate. You usually take the Speaking test with just one other candidate, but sometimes candidates take the Speaking test in groups of three.

Frequently asked questions:

What level is Key for Schools?

Key for Schools is A2 level. At A2 level, **Key** students can:
- understand simple instructions and questions
- write, talk or ask about simple information, opinions or ideas
- complete forms
- write short, simple letters, messages or emails about personal information.

For more information on 'Can Do' statements go to:
http://www.cambridgeesol.org/exams/exams-info/cefr.html

Note that some candidates might be better than others (at speaking or writing, for example) but still get the same final **Key** grade. The A2 'Can do' statements therefore help teachers and employers to understand what a candidate can generally do at this level.

What percentage grade do we need to get to pass Key for Schools?

The percentage of marks that candidates need to get for each grade may change from test to test. This is because tests cannot always be exactly the same. Some might be a little more difficult than others. However, the ranges of percentages for each grade of **Key for Schools** are:
- Pass with Merit 85% i.e. 85 out of 100 marks
- Pass 70% — 84%
- Narrow Fail 65% — 69%
- Fail 64% and below.

This information is included on your Statement of Results.

What marks do we need to pass each paper, and to pass the exam?

Candidates do not have to get a certain mark to pass each section of the test. The final mark for **Key for Schools** is the total number of marks from all three papers Reading/Writing, Listening and Speaking. There are an equal number of possible marks for reading, writing, listening and speaking at **Key for Schools**.

> Is Key for Schools suitable for candidates of any age?

Key for Schools is more suitable for students who are at school and aged from 11–15. To make sure that the material is not too difficult or too easy for this age group, all the parts of the reading, writing and Listening papers are pre-tested. This means that different groups of students try each part of the tests first. The parts will then only be used in real exams if the results of the tests show they are suitable for candidates who want to take **Key for Schools**.

> Can we use pens and pencils?

In **Key** and **Key for Schools**, candidates must use **pencil** in all papers.

> What happens if I don't have enough time to finish writing?

You can only be given marks for what you write on your answer sheets so if you cannot complete this, you will lose marks. Watch the clock, plan your time carefully and do not waste time by writing answers on other pieces of paper first. If you want to change an answer, just rub it out, write your correct answer then quickly move to the next question.

> If I write in capital letters, will this affect my score?

No. You do not lose marks for writing in capital letters in **Key for Schools**.

In this part, you:

- **read** eight notices and five sentences
- **choose** one notice to match each sentence

Vocabulary Focus on meaning

1 Match words 1–9 with words from the box.

> | price | competition | guest | coach | mobile |
> |---|---|---|---|---|
> | photo | door | woods | ~~bike~~ | class |

Tip! In Part 1, there are different ways to say the same thing. Often there is a word in a notice that matches the meaning of a different word in one of the sentences.

Example: bicycle ....bike......

1	entrance	....	4	bus	....	7	phone	....
2	forest	....	5	race	....	8	picture	....
3	lesson	....	6	cost	....	9	visitor	....

2 Who CANNOT do each activity? Use two words from the box for each notice.

Tip! Words about age, like **adult**, **child** and **teenager** are often tested in Part 1.

> children   teenagers   adults

Example: This film is for adults only. ....children...... and ....teenagers......

1 Playground for under 10s only   .... and ....
2 Course for 13–19 year olds   .... and ....
3 This club is for people over 20.   .... and ....
4 Kids disco. No-one over 12 please!   .... and ....

3 Read the notices. Choose the words so the sentences match the notice.

Tip! Notices and matching sentences often use words such as **can**, **will**, **must**, **might** and **should**. Make sure you know what they mean.

Example: This area is for under 5s only.   Small children **can** / ~~must~~ use this area.

1 Please take off shoes at the door   You *will not / should not* wear shoes in this place.
2 Adults only after 9 p.m.   Children *must not / might not* be here after 9 o'clock.
3 Cash only!   You *cannot / should not* pay by credit card here.
4 This machine does not give change.   You *may have / need to have* the right money.
5 Discounts for those with student cards. Students *will / might* pay less here.

Questions 1–5

Which notice (**A–H**) says this (**1–5**)?
For questions **1–5**, mark the correct letter **A–H** on your answer sheet.

Example:

0   You can't cycle here at the moment.   *Answer:*

1   Those who enjoy cycling can try this activity.

2   Adults cannot do this activity.

3   You must never use your bike here.

4   You can choose what time you go and listen to this.

5   You should not bring pet animals here.

Advice

1 What do you ride if you enjoy cycling?

4 What can you listen to?

5 What type of animal do people take out with them?

A
> **Talk – 'Forest Animals'**
> **Every two hours**
> **Children must be with an adult**
>

B
> **Keep your bike safe!**
>
> **Leave it here, at the Bike Park**
>

C
> **Park Zoo**   **Please do not give food to any of our animals.**

D
> **No cycling**
> **in this area of the park**

E
> **After-school football course**
> **(for 11–15s only)**
> **Tuesdays at 4 p.m.**
>

F
> **Entrance to the woods**
> **Please stay on the paths**
> **No dogs**
>

G
> **BIKE RACES**
> on Sunday
> Adults ⋯⋯⋯⋯⋯⋯ 10 a.m.
> Ages 11–16 ⋯⋯⋯⋯ 2 p.m.

H
> **CYCLE PATH CLOSED**
> for two months.

Test 1 Training Reading and Writing Part 2

In this part you:

- **read** five sentences
- **choose** one word (A, B or C) to complete each sentence

Vocabulary Focus on meaning

1 **Cross out the wrong word in each sentence.**

> **Tip!** Think about the meaning of each of the words you have to choose from.

Example: I **lost** / ~~missed~~ *my phone yesterday.*

1 There weren't many people at the party, but it was really *busy / noisy*.
2 I like most animals, but I think my *favourite / best* is the horse.
3 Have you seen Pamela since her family *changed / moved* to their new house?
4 I'm going shopping for some new *dress / clothes*.
5 I haven't finished the homework *yet / already* – it's not easy!
6 I don't really like being in the house *alone / only*.
7 My grandfather *grows / makes* lots of different vegetables in his garden.
8 I've *packed / made* up my bags ready for my holiday.

2 **Choose the best word (A, B or C) for each space.**

> **Tip!** Look at the words before and after the space in the sentence.

Example: I ....hope.... *everyone can come to my party on Friday.*

   A decide   **B** hope   **C** want

1 My parents are .... of buying me a bicycle for my birthday.
   A hoping   **B** thinking   **C** wanting
2 I .... to be an engineer when I'm older.
   A think   **B** want   **C** decide
3 I'm going out with my mum to .... some new shoes.
   A pay   **B** spend   **C** buy
4 Those jeans are great, but they .... a lot of money.
   A cost   **B** pay   **C** spend
5 I .... too much money yesterday, so I'm not going shopping today!
   A spent   **B** cost   **C** bought
6 I'm going to .... my little brother some money to buy Mum a present.
   A borrow   **B** spend   **C** lend

> **Remember!**
> to **think** about / of
> to **want** to be, to do, to have, etc.
> to **buy** something
> to **pay for** something
> to **spend** money, £5, a lot, etc.
> to **borrow** means to give
> to **lend** means to receive

Grammar Verbs plus prepositions

Some *Key* candidates make mistakes with the words that come after particular verbs.

3 **Correct the mistakes in these sentences.**

Example: I *'m looking* at my pen – have you seen it? ....looking for....

1 I'm helping to <u>look to</u> my baby brother. ....
2 <u>Look after</u>! You're going to fall! ....
3 <u>You look</u> like nice today! ....
4 <u>Look up</u> that beautiful painting! ....
5 I love <u>looking out to</u> the window on planes. ....
6 I'm <u>looking forward for</u> seeing you. ....

Questions 6–10

Read the sentences about a girl who lives on a farm.
Choose the best word **(A, B or C)** for each space.
For questions **6–10**, mark **A, B** or **C** on your answer sheet.

Example:

0 Marcia's father .... on the farm.

    A growed up   **B** grew on   **C** grew up

Answer: | 0 | A B **C** |

---

6 Marcia .... likes spring on the farm, when the animals have babies.

    A exactly   **B** especially   **C** already

7 If an animal gets ...., Marcia helps to look for it.

    A lost   **B** alone   **C** missing

8 As well as keeping animals on his farm, Marcia's father also ....
vegetables.

    A brings   **B** grows   **C** makes

9 When Marcia was a small child, the farm .... to her grandfather.

    A belonged   **B** borrowed   **C** bought

10 Marcia .... the farm will be hers when she's older.

    A decides   **B** wants   **C** hopes

Advice

6 Exactly means something which is completely accurate e.g. He arrived at exactly 3 o'clock.

Already is used to talk about something which happened before now, or before a particular time e.g. I've already eaten breakfast, and it's only 6.30 a.m.

8 What does a farmer do with vegetables?

9 Look at the word after the space.

In this part you:

- **read**   what someone says
- **choose**   one answer (A, B or C) to complete the conversation

Completing Conversations

1   **Why is the person speaking? Match each sentence with a reason from the box.**

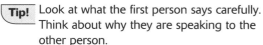

> **Tip!** Look at what the first person says carefully. Think about why they are speaking to the other person.

> **a** to say 'yes'   **b** to ask for something
> **c** to offer something   **d** to suggest something

Example: *Can I borrow your pen?* .....**b**......

1 Why don't we go to the cinema? ....
2 I'd love to come!   ....
3 Would you like a drink?   ....
4 Shall I take that for you?   ....
5 Have you got any money?   ....
6 Let's go for a walk.   ....

2   **Look at the first half of the conversations carefully. Cross out the wrong answer.**

> **Tip!** When you have decided why the person is speaking, think about the correct way to answer.

Example: *Would you like a drink?*   *~~Sorry, I have got one.~~ / Thanks, that's kind of you.*

1	Can I borrow your pen?	*Here you are. / Where did you leave it?*
2	I'd love to come!	*That's great! / Where is it?*
3	Let's go for a walk.	*Why will you do that? / Where shall we go?*
4	Have you got any money?	*Do you need to borrow some? / No, that's not mine.*
5	Shall I take that for you?	*Not really. / Thanks very much.*
6	Why don't we go to the cinema?	*Great idea! / I didn't see it.*

> **Remember!** You can sometimes answer a question with another question.

3   **Cross out the two wrong answers**

Example: *I'm really sorry, I can't come to your party.* **That's okay**. / ~~**You're right.**~~ / ~~**So do I.**~~

1	I have to go home now.	I'm not sure yet. / That's a pity. / No, I'm fine thanks.
2	Could you help me with my homework?	Could you? Thanks! / Yes, you do. / Yes, of course.
3	This is my cousin, Zara.	Nice to meet you. / Oh, is she? / What does she look like?
4	I don't think you should buy that.	Yes, it's nice, isn't it? / You're probably right. / I'll try again later.
5	Let's go to the park after school.	I'm afraid I can't. / I don't know when. / I'm sure we won't.
6	You look very nice today!	That's better! / Thank you! / I'm okay.

Questions 11–15

Complete the five conversations.
For questions **11–15**, mark **A**, **B** or **C** on your answer sheet.

Example:

0

How are you?

A   Fine, thanks.

B   I'm 14.

C   My name is Mario.

Answer: | **0** | A̲ B C |

---

11   Have you been to the new pool yet?

   A   Sorry about that.

   B   Not before Monday.

   C   I'm going now.

12   I'll really miss my friends during
         the school holidays, Mum.

   A   Well, ask them round then.

   B   So, how do they do that?

   C   OK, it won't take them long.

13   Are you sure the concert is free?

   A   It finishes at 9 o'clock.

   B   That's what I heard.

   C   I'm quite busy then.

14   We've got football practice after school.

   A   Oh yes, it's Wednesday today.

   B   Fine, what about you?

   C   All right, I'll look for it again.

15   Have you got a dictionary with you?

   A   That's better.

   B   Here you are.

   C   I know it is.

Advice

12 What can you do if you miss someone?

13 Be careful! It's the concert which is free, not a person, and the speaker isn't asking about time.

15 The speaker is asking to borrow something.

In this part you:

- **read**   what the first person says in a conversation
- **choose**   the second person's replies

Completing conversations

1   **Look at the responses to the questions. Cross out the wrong one.**

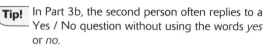

> **Tip!** In Part 3b, the second person often replies to a Yes / No question without using the words *yes* or *no*.

Example: *You wanted a new bike for your birthday, didn't you?*
That's right. / ~~That's what I did~~.

1   Have you been to the beach this year?   *I didn't always go. / Only for a few hours.*

2   Shall we meet in the park?   *OK – at the café. / It's near the station.*

3   Can you be ready by ten?   *I think so. / I'm going then.*

4   Will 6 o'clock be too early?   *OK. I will. / It's fine.*

5   Did you see that nature programme on TV yesterday?   *I was out. / I'm sure it was.*

6   Do you know the bookshop near my house?   *Of course! It's on the corner. / I found it really easily.*

2   **Match the first part of each conversation with one of the answers.**

> **Tip!** Check that the pronouns match with the people and things in the conversation.

Example: Is your bike still broken?

1   Do you think your sister would like to come?

2   Can I borrow your sunglasses?

3   I saw you and your mum at the shops.

4   Where does your brother work?

5   Have you finished your homework?

6   I'm not sure where to get the bus.

a   Yes, they're in the drawer.

b   We were getting some milk.

c   At the theatre. He loves it.

d   *My brother fixed it for me.*

e   I gave it to the teacher yesterday.

f   It stops right outside your house!

g   I'll ask her later.

3   **Complete the conversations. Read the sentences before and after the space and choose a reply A–G from the box.**

> **Tip!** Make sure you read the words that go before and after the gap. This will help you choose the correct answer.

> **Tip!** The speakers in Part 3b often make suggestions. Think of the different ways you can respond to a suggestion.

A Good idea!   **B** Maybe my sister.   **C** It's too busy there.
D Not yet.   **E** Don't worry.   **F** ~~I'm busy then~~.
G I'd rather go home.

Example: *Shall we go on Monday?*   ......**F**......   *Let's go later in the week.*

1   Let's meet at the station.   ....   The café is better.

2   Why don't we go into town?   ....   Shall we take the bus?

3   We could have lunch there too.   ....   It's less expensive.

4   Shall I ask Mum to take you home?   ....   I don't want to bother her.

5   Have you been to the new shopping centre?   ....   Shall we go there?

6   Shall we invite anyone else?   ....   She likes shopping.

Questions 16–20

Complete the conversation between two friends about a bike.
What does Paolo say to Freddie?
For questions **16–20**, mark the correct letter **A–H** on your answer sheet.

Example:

Freddie: Hello Paolo. Did you enjoy your birthday?

Paolo: **0** ....F.........

Answer:

Freddie: You wanted a new bike, didn't you?

Paolo: **16** ....

Freddie: Fantastic! Have you been out on it yet?

Paolo: **17** ....

Freddie: My brother helped me repair it. We should go out together.

Paolo: **18** ....

Freddie: I'm busy today. But maybe this Saturday?

Paolo: **19** ....

Freddie: Me too! Do you want to meet in the park?

Paolo: **20** ....

Freddie: Outside the café. See you there at about two o'clock.

A   A bit, but I'd like to go for a longer ride. Is your bike still broken?

B   My brother went there on Saturday.

C   Fine. Where's a good place?

D   Yes, I'll bring some money.

E   OK, that's probably better. I'm free after lunch.

F   Yes, it was fun. I got some great presents.

G   That's right – and my parents got it for me!

H   Great idea! How about this afternoon?

Advice

*16 How can you answer **didn't you?** without saying **yes** or **no**?*

*18 Which reply goes with the suggestion ´**We should go out together.**´?*

*20 ´**Outside the café**´ is an answer. What is the question?*

In this part you:

- **read** a text
- **choose** the correct answer (Right, Wrong or Doesn't say or A, B, C) to seven questions.

Vocabulary Focus on meaning

1 Match words 1–12 with words in the box which mean the opposite.

 Tip! Sometimes the question will use a word which has the opposite meaning to a word in the text.

~~lose~~	before	start	sad	always	best	large
same	enter	love	heavy	nothing	alone	

Example: win ....**lose**....

1 worst	....	5 after	....	9 different	....
2 everything	....	6 finish	....	10 hate	....
3 small	....	7 light	....	11 never	....
4 leave	....	8 happy	....	12 together	....

2 Read about Ethan. Are sentences 1–6 Right, Wrong or Doesn't say?

Tip! If you see information in the question which is not in the text at all, the correct answer is *Doesn't say* (C).

Right (the information is the same) – write **A**.
Wrong (the information is different) – write **B**.
Doesn't say (the information isn't in the text) – write **C**.

> Ethan lives on a large farm in the USA with lots of other families. Ethan and his friends study together. Their parents teach them. Sometimes they go outside for lessons. They have a timetable, but they can also ask their parents to teach them about things which they are interested in.

Example: The farm Ethan lives on is big. ......A......

1 The farm belongs to Ethan's parents. ....
2 Ethan's parents grow vegetables on the farm. ....
3 Ethan has his lessons alone. ....
4 Ethan's parents studied to be teachers. ....
5 Ethan and his friends always have lessons inside. ....
6 Ethan's favourite subject on the timetable is maths. ....
7 Sometimes Ethan and his friends choose what to learn about. ....

Questions 21–27

Read the article about a boy called Ethan.
Are sentences **21–27** 'Right' **(A)** or 'Wrong' **(B)**?
If there is not enough information to answer 'Right' **(A)** or 'Wrong' **(B)** choose 'Doesn't say' **(C)**.
For questions **21–27**, mark **A**, **B** or **C** on your answer sheet.

Learning at home

Fourteen-year-old Ethan Cosgrove lives on a very large farm in West Virginia, USA. Because the farm is so large, several families work on it together. Each family has its own small house on the farm, and in total there are ten children and teenagers, including Ethan. None of them has ever been to school. Instead, they have lessons at home, or at the home of a neighbour.

Lessons are taught by the students' parents. Students who are the same age learn together, so Ethan doesn't study with his little sister. Some of the subjects that they study are the same as the ones in normal schools, but they also go outside to learn. For a science class they might go into the woods, and for maths they may visit a local business. Another difference is that students can ask the teachers for lessons on subjects that they are interested in.

There is a timetable, but if the students are enjoying a lesson, and the teacher thinks they are learning, they don't have to stop when the timetable says. Ethan says, 'Studying at home makes us grow up because we often study alone. It's not like a normal school, because adults don't do everything for us'.

Example:

0 The farm is too big for one family.

  A Right   **B** Wrong   **C** Doesn't say   *Answer:*   **0**   A B C

---

21 The families who work on the farm live together in the same house.

  A Right   **B** Wrong   **C** Doesn't say

22 The teachers are members of the students' families.

  A Right   **B** Wrong   **C** Doesn't say

23 Students of all ages study together in one group.

  A Right   **B** Wrong   **C** Doesn't say

24 The students spend more time outside than inside.

  A Right   **B** Wrong   **C** Doesn't say

25 Sometimes Ethan and his friends choose what they want to study.

  A Right   **B** Wrong   **C** Doesn't say

26 A teacher can make a lesson longer if the students like what they are doing.

  A Right   **B** Wrong   **C** Doesn't say

27 Ethan wants to go to university when he's older.

  A Right   **B** Wrong   **C** Doesn't say

Advice

21 Find the word **house** in the article. What information does the article give?

26 Is there a word in the article which means the same as **like**?

27 Is there any information in the article about what Ethan wants to do in the future?

In this part you:

- **read**   some information
- **find**   eight missing words (choose from A, B or C)

Grammar Form of tenses

1 **Cross out the <u>two</u> wrong words in each sentence.**

| **Tip!** | In Part 5, you often have to find the correct form of a verb. Read the text carefully to help you choose the correct answer. |

Example: I **was** / ~~am~~ / ~~were~~ *born in Spain.*

1 Have you *see / saw / seen* my photograph in the newspaper this week?

2 My younger sister *love / loves / loved* drawing when she was little.

3 My grandfather has lots of different fruit trees *grow / grows / growing* in his garden.

4 My cartoon *was / am / been* published in the school newspaper yesterday!

5 I like lots of different sports, but *swim / swims / swimming* is my favourite.

6 About eight million people *live / lives / living* in my city.

Grammar Prepositions

2 **Correct the mistakes. Write the correct preposition.**

| **Tip!** | Prepositions are often tested in Part 5 |

1 Charles M. Schulz was born <u>in</u> November 26th, 1922. ....

2 Schulz's mother was <u>of</u> Germany. ....

3 Schulz spent a lot of time <u>among</u> his father when he was a child. ....

4 Schulz started drawing cartoons <u>with</u> his dog. ....

5 Soon, Schulz's cartoons started to be published <u>on</u> the newspapers. ....

6 <u>In</u> the time Schulz died, his cartoons were famous all over the world. ....

Remember!

In March
On March 15th
In 2014
On Saturday
I come **from** China.

Grammar Adverbs

3 **Complete the sentences with words from the box.**

| **Tip!** | Adverbs are also often tested in Part 5. Make sure you know what each one means and how it is used. |

| yet   even   before   ~~soon~~   quite   well   just |

Example: How ......**soon**...... *can you get here? We need to leave in an hour!*

1 Everyone came to my party – .... Mikael!

2 Haven't you finished that book .... ? It's only short!

3 We take photographs in our art classes, as .... as drawing pictures.

4 I've .... spoken to my mum. She says she can give us a lift.

5 Peter is .... tall, isn't he!

6 I've never seen that picture .... Where did you find it?

Questions 28–35

Read the article about a famous artist who drew cartoons.
Choose the best word (**A, B or C**) for each space.
For questions **28–35**, mark **A**, **B** or **C** on your answer sheet.

Charles M. Schulz

Charles M. Schulz was born in the USA **(0)** .... 26th November, 1922. His father was German and his mother was from Norway. When Charles was a child, he liked **(28)** .... Sunday mornings with his father. Together, they read the cartoons in all the newspapers. Charles started drawing cartoons **(29)** .... his dog, Spike. He found he **(30)** .... do this really well. When Charles was 14, a national newspaper printed **(31)** .... of those cartoons. Charles was so happy about this **(32)** .... he decided to be an artist.

When Charles was nearly 30, a cartoon of his called 'Peanuts' started to be printed in seven US newspapers. The cartoon, **(33)** .... included a dog called Snoopy, became very famous. **(34)** .... the time Charles stopped working, in 1999, the Peanuts cartoon was in 2,600 newspapers **(35)** .... the world.

Example:

0 **A** in	**B** on	**C** at	*Answer:*	0 A **B** C

28	**A** spending	**B** spend	**C** spent
29	**A** from	**B** to	**C** of
30	**A** need	**B** shall	**C** could
31	**A** one	**B** other	**C** everything
32	**A** than	**B** as	**C** that
33	**A** who	**B** where	**C** which
34	**A** For	**B** By	**C** In
35	**A** around	**B** along	**C** among

Advice

*28 What form of the verb comes after **like**?*

30 All of the information in the article is in the past. Which of these words can we use in the past?

33 A cartoon is a thing, not a person or a place, so which word do we need here?

In this part you:

- **read** five sentences that each describe a word
- **write** five words, spelling them correctly (you see the first letter and the number of letters in each word)

1 Read the text. Molly is going for a walk with her family. Where are they?

> Molly and her family are walking along a path, and they can see lots of different plants and some flowers. They can hear birds, and sometimes they see birds flying high above their heads. There are other animals too, and lots of insects. Molly's father says that there are snakes, but they haven't seen any yet. There's a small lake in front of them, and they have to cross a bridge to get over it. They're going to sit down soon to eat their picnic. Molly wants to read her book, and her little brother wants to climb a tree.

   A in a town   **B** at the beach   **C** in the forest

Which words helped you to get the answer? Underline them.

Vocabulary Spelling

2 Look at these words from the text about Molly.

> **Tip!** In Part 6, you must spell all of the words correctly.

hear   heads   eat   read

We spell them all with the vowels *ea*.
Complete these sentences about Sam's day. All of the words in the answers have *ea* in them.

Example: *When Sam got up in the morning, he had a big* b<u>r e a k f a s t</u>.

1 It was a b _ _ _ t _ f _ l, sunny day, so Sam and his older brother decided to go for a walk in the forest.

2 It was bit a cold, so they didn't wear shorts. Their mum told them to wear j _ _ n _.

3 Sam's brother wanted to take some fruit to eat, so they took some p _ _ r _.

4 There was a lot of b r _ _ _ in the kitchen, so they made some sandwiches too.

5 The forest is quite n _ _ _ to Sam's house, so they didn't have far to go.

6 In the forest, they saw lots of birds and plants and climbed some trees. They had a g r _ _ _ time!

Vocabulary Double letters

3 Some words in English have double vowels, for example *book*. Look at the text below. <u>Underline</u> the 12 words which have double vowels.

> On our school trip, we went camping in the woods. We took all of the food that we needed for the two days that we were there, and we had to cook everything on a fire. We wore boots because the weather wasn't very good. I hoped to see some bears, but I don't think they live in those woods. I did see insects, and one of my friends saw a green snake.

4 Now match some of the words which you underlined in Exercise 3 with the correct definitions.

Example: *You can see lots of trees in this place.* ....*woods*........

1   You do this if you want something hot to eat. ....

2   Grass is usually this colour. ....

3   This is the opposite of bad. ....

4   This is a place where children go to learn. ....

5   People often wear these on their feet in winter. ....

6   This is a word for things that we can eat. ....

5 Read the descriptions below. Underline the verbs in the description. Complete the answers.

Tip! There are often verbs in the Part 6 descriptions which help you to get the answer. For example, if you see *wear*, you know that you need a word about clothes.

Example: *If the weather is too hot for trousers, people often* <u>wear</u> *these instead.*   s*horts*..............

1   This is a place where people can swim, or maybe go fishing.   l _ _ _

2   This is a tall plant which children enjoy climbing.   t _ _ _

3   You can walk along this small road in the forest or through fields.   p _ _ _

4   You can play this team game on ice or on grass.   h _ _ _ _ _

5   In the forest, you might collect this and use it to make a fire.   w _ _ _

6   This is a meal which you can eat when you are in the countryside, or at the beach.   p _ _ _ _ _

Vocabulary Homonyms

⊙ Some *Key* candidates make mistakes in Part 6 because there are words in English which sound the same but have a different meanings and spelling. For example, **wood** and **would**.

6 Cross out the wrong word in each sentence.

Example: *We need to get some more* **~~would~~** / **wood** *for the fire.*

1   Is the fire ready? We need to start cooking the *meat / meet*.

2   I've bought a new *pair / pear* of boots for our trip to the forest.

3   Can you *sea / see* any snakes?

4   I'm going for a walk. Do you want to come *too / two*?

5   We should *buy / bye* some food to take on our walk.

6   Look at that beautiful bird over *there / their*!

7 Read the descriptions of animals and birds. Complete the words.

Example: *This is long and doesn't have any legs.*   s<u>n</u> <u>a</u> <u>k</u> <u>e</u>

1   This is an animal which people can ride, or use to carry things.   h _ _ _ _

2   These are small, they have six legs and many of them can fly.   i _ _ _ _ _ _

3   You probably shouldn't get too close to this very big animal.   b _ _ _

4   Children often have these small animals as pets.   r _ _ _ _ _ _

5   This is a bird which can swim and fly and often lives on lakes.   d _ _ _

6   A lot of people eat the eggs from this bird.   c _ _ _ _ _ _

Grammar Singular and plural

8 Read the descriptions below. They describe nouns. Decide if the noun they describe is singular or plural.

> **Tip!** The answers in Part 6 are often nouns. They will usually be singular, but sometimes they are plural. You need to read the description carefully to decide.

Example: *These grow in the forest, they're small, often brown, and you can eat them.* **singular /plural**

1 This long area of water often starts in the mountains and ends at the sea.   *singular / plural*

2 If you want to cook food in the forest, you will need to start one of these.   *singular / plural*

3 These grow on plants and usually have pretty colours.   *singular / plural*

4 This is a large round star which gives us light and keeps us warm.   *singular / plural*

5 These are often white, but they may be darker if it's going to rain soon.   *singular / plural*

6 Farmers usually keep their animals in these, or grow vegetables in them.   *singular / plural*

Which words in the definitions helped you to decide whether the answer was singular or plural?

9 Now complete the words that match the descriptions in Exercise 8.

Example: m ushrooms

1 r _ _ _ _   3 f _ _ _ _ _ _   5 c _ _ _ _ _

2 f _ _ _   4 s _ _   6 f _ _ _ _ _

10 Look at six words from this training section. Use the prompts and write descriptions.

Example: **sandwich:** *make / this / bread / cheese*

You can ...... make this with bread and cheese. ......

1 **books:** borrow / these / library
   You can ....

2 **bridge:** walk / over / this / cross / river
   You can ....

3 **pet:** keep / this / type / animal / house
   You can ....

4 **fruit:** find / this / food / growing / trees
   You can ....

5 **shorts:** wear / these / when / weather / hot
   You can ....

6 **stars:** see these / sky / night
   You can ....

Questions 36–40

Read the descriptions of some things you can see in a forest.
What is the word for each one?
The first letter is already there. There is one space for each other letter in the word.
For questions **36–40**, write the words on your answer sheet.

Example:

0 People collect these in autum and often put them in omelettes or risottos.   m _ _ _ _ _ _ _ _

	Answer:	**0**	m u s h r o o m s

---

36 This animal can be 2 metres tall and lives in forests all over the world.   b _ _ _

37 It is often possible to swim in this, or go fishing or sailing.   l _ _ _

38 Some people go to the forest to collect this for a fire.   w _ _ _

39 If you go camping, you may sleep in this.   t _ _ _

40 These have six legs, and many different kinds live in the forest.   i _ _ _ _ _ _

Advice

38 Don't forget the double letter.

40 Does the description use **this** or **these**? Is the word singular or plural?

In this part, you:

- **read** texts that are usually one or two messages
- **write** the ten missing words

Grammar *be* and *have*

1 Complete the sentences with the correct form of **be** or **have**.

> **Tip!** Look out for gaps which need the verbs **be** and **have**. Think about which form of the verb you need.

Example: *My brother is older than me. I ......was...... born in 2002.*

1 We .... lived in this town for the last three years.

2 I .... really pleased that you can come to stay with us.

3 We can go on a city tour – it .... not expensive.

4 My friends .... going to come round to meet you on your second day here.

5 There .... a really big park near my house where we can play football.

6 The new sports centre in our town .... got a swimming pool.

Vocabulary Focus on meaning

2 Cross out the wrong word in each sentence.

> **Tip!** In Part 7, the missing word is part of a phrase, such as **give me a ring**.

Example: *A **lot** / ~~group~~ of tourists come to my town in the summer.*

1 *Let / Make* me know where you want to go.

2 *Why / How* about going to a concert in the park one afternoon?

3 We can go to the beach at the weekend, *if / so* you like.

4 There are lots of places to go, *for / in* example the castle, or the museum.

5 I really can't *stop / wait* to see you! We're going to have so much fun!

6 I *will / would* love to visit your country one day.

Grammar Pronouns

⊙ *Key* candidates often make mistakes with words such as *me, you, her* and *us* in Part 7. Remember to read the whole sentence before you fill in the gap.

3 Complete the message using words from the box. Use each word only once.

> us   she   they   ~~you~~   mine   him   we

| From: | |
| To: | |

Hi Olga.

Did **(0)** ......you...... get the message from Maria? **(1)** .... is going ice-skating on Monday. Her dad is taking her, and he says **(2)** .... can go too! It's really nice of **(3)** .... to invite **(4)** ...., isn't it? Maria and her dad are really good at ice-skating, so I'm hoping **(5)** .... can teach me! Maria says it's a good idea to take gloves. I've lost **(6)** .... – have you got any I can borrow?

Questions 41–50

Complete the email to a friend who lives in a different city.
Write ONE word for each space.
For questions **41–50**, write the words on your answer sheet.

Example:

0	*am*

From:	Meg
To:	Sam

Hi Sam,

Thanks for your last email. I **(0)** .... really pleased you

can come and stay with **(41)** .... this summer. Try and

come in July **(42)** .... you can.

(43) .... gets very hot here in August!

I can't wait **(44)** .... show you all the famous buildings

in my city. But, as well as sightseeing, **(45)** .... are

lots of other things we can do too. **(46)** .... example, a

fantastic sports centre opened **(47)** .... my home last

month. It **(48)** .... got a pool, a gym and two basketball

courts. It's not expensive, so we'll probably go there a lot.

Don't **(49)** .... to bring your swimming costume! You'll

also need a pair **(50)** .... trainers.

See you in the summer!

Meg

Advice

45 lots *is used to talk about plural things, so which word goes before* **are**?

46 *When we want to give an example, which preposition goes before the word* **example**?

49 *What is the opposite of* **remember**?

In this part you:

- **read**   two short texts to find five pieces of information
- **write**   five pieces of information (words and numbers)

Vocabulary Focus on meaning

1   Match each phrase below with a word or phrase from the box.

level	date	~~price~~	phone number	place
start time	bring	number of people	how we'll travel	

Tip! The words in the texts are usually different from the words on the form which you have to complete.

Example: it'll cost .....price.....

1   Let's go by   ....
2   You'll need   ....
3   We'll go on   ....
4   It's near the river ....

5   It begins at   ....
6   Call me on   ....
7   We're beginners.   ....
8   . . . just four of us ....

Looking at dates and times

2   Look at the short notices below. Read the information in the email and cross out the wrong answer.

Tip! In Part 8, you often have to choose between two possible times, dates, etc.

Notices	Emails	Important information
Example:	*Entry £10 (£8 for students)*	*We pay less because we're at college. Price for us: £10 / £8*
1 Tuesdays and Fridays only	It'll have to be Friday as I have football on Tuesday.	Day we'll go: *Tuesday / Friday*
2 We run courses from 13th June and 21st July	I'm on holiday in July, so let's go in June.	Start date: *13th June / 21st July*
3 Price: £4 per person	It'll be £8 in total – £4 each.	Cost for me: *£4 / £8*
4 We sell drinks only	Let's take sandwiches – we can get water there.	What to bring: *water / sandwiches*
5 Saturday film 'My life' Sunday film 'Places'	I've seen the film they're showing on Sunday, so we'll go on Saturday.	Name of film: *My life / Places*
6 Boats for hire for 2, 4 or 6 people	Let's hire a boat. There'll be 8 of us. So we'll need two.	Number of boats: *1 / 2 / 8*
7 Open from 9 a.m. to 4.30 p.m. (last entry 3.30 p.m.)	I can get there by 3.30 and we can skate until 4.30, so that's fine.	Time we'll finish: *3.30 p.m. / 4.30 p.m.*
8 New sports club behind the train station	Let's go to that new sports club. I'll meet you there – we can go by train	Where to meet: *station / sports club*

Questions 51–55

Read the advertisement and the email.
Fill in the information in Milo's notes.
For questions **51–55**, write the information on your answer sheet.

 Club One

For 11–15 year olds
at Summerside School
Tuesday and Friday
6 p.m. – 9 p.m.
Basketball, Dance, Painting
and starting next week, Cooking!
£3.00 for Summerside School
students £7.00 for others

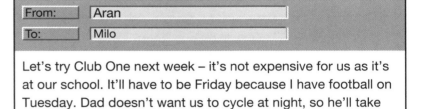

From: Aran
To: Milo

Let's try Club One next week – it's not expensive for us as it's at our school. It'll have to be Friday because I have football on Tuesday. Dad doesn't want us to cycle at night, so he'll take us by car. We'll be at your house at 5.40 p.m.

Milo's notes

Trip to club with Aran

Name of club:	Club One
Day we'll go:	51
How we'll travel there:	52
Time club finishes:	53 p.m.
Price I'll pay:	54 £
New activity:	55

Advice

51 There are two days in Aran's email. On which day is he free?

53 There are times in the advertisement AND the email. Which is the time when the club *finishes*?

55 There are four activities in the advertisement and two in the email. Look for the words which tell you which activity is *new*.

In this part you:
- **read**   three requests for information
- **write**   three pieces of information in a short message

Answering three questions

1 Look at this example of a Part 9 task. Underline the three pieces of information that you will need to write in the answer.

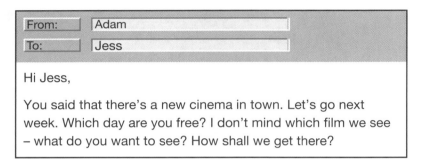

From: Adam
To: Jess

Hi Jess,

You said that there's a new cinema in town. Let's go next week. Which day are you free? I don't mind which film we see – what do you want to see? How shall we get there?

2 Read the three short messages. Match each message with one of Adam's questions from Exercise 1.

1
Dear Adam,
My father says
he can drive us
to the cinema.
It's not far.

2
Hi Adam,
Great idea! I
don't have any
plans for Friday
– let's go then.

3
Hi,
I would really
like to see the
movie about
fast cars.

1 ....

2 ....

3 ....

⊙ *Key* candidates often make mistakes with past and future in their answers. Remember to read the question carefully. Is it asking you about something you've already done, or something you're going to do in the future?

3 Read the questions and answers. Decide if each answer is correct for that question. If the answer is right, put a tick (✓). If it is wrong, put a cross (✗).

Example: *Which film would you like to see?*   *I went to see 'Silver Moon'.* | X |

1 Which day are we going to play tennis?   We're playing tennis on Thursday.   ☐
2 Where did you go on holiday?   We're driving to the mountains.   ☐
3 Who do you think will be there?   All of our friends are going.   ☐
4 Why did you like the book?   The story was really exciting.   ☐
5 What time do we need to be at Frank's house?   I got there at about 8 o'clock.   ☐
6 What did you do in the city centre?   I usually go shopping there.   ☐
7 What time can you get to the park?   I think I'll be there by 3 o'clock.   ☐
8 How are we going to get there?   We'll go by bus.   ☐

👁 *Key* candidates often make mistakes with the spelling of *-ing* forms.

4 The sentences below all have a spelling mistake. Underline the
word which is wrong. Then write the word correctly.
Use *Remember!* to help you.

Example: *I usually go* <u>danceing</u> *on Friday evenings.* ......*dancing*......

1 Are you going swiming at the weekend? ....
2 How are we geting to the party? ....
3 My brother is driveing me to the cinema. ....
4 Shall we go shoping at the weekend? ....
5 What time is the party startting? ....
6 The band starts playying at 8'clock. ....

Vocabulary Spelling

5 Cross out the wrong word in each sentence.

Example: *We're going on* ~~Tusday~~ / *Tuesday.*

1 We usually go on holiday in *August / Agust.*
2 Let's go on *monday / Monday*, after school.
3 I start at my new school in *Setember / September.*
4 Are you coming with us on *Wednesday / Wendsday*?
5 What time shall we meet on *Saturday / Saterday*?
6 The course starts on *July / Guly* the first.
7 Kim's part is on *Thirsday / Thursday.*
8 My birthday is in *February / Febrary.*
9 I haven't seen Carla since last *Mai / May.*
10 I stayed with my cousins during *march / March.*

Grammar Prepositions

👁 *Key* candidates often make mistakes with words like *on*, *at*
and *in* when they're writing about times, days and dates.

6 Complete the sentences below using *on*, *at*, *in* or – (no preposition).

Example: *I always go running* ......*in*...... *the mornings.*

1 Are you free to play football with us .... Saturday?
2 The concert starts .... 8.30 p.m.
3 I'm going to the sports centre .... Friday evening.
4 I find it difficult to get to sleep .... night.
5 My aunt and uncle got married .... April.
6 I've got tickets for a show .... 2nd January.
7 I saw your brother .... Thursday morning.
8 I'll give you the book when I see you .... this afternoon.

Remember!

In Part 9, you always have to write 25–35 words.
You often have to answer **Wh**- questions, e.g.
What, **Where** and **Why**.

Remember!

When you add **-ing**, take off the **e** for verbs
ending in **-e**.
e.g. *dance → dancing, write → writing*
Verbs ending in a vowel and **-y** don't change
e.g. *play → playing, buy → buying*
Double the final consonant when a one syllable
word ends in consonant +vowel +constant
e.g. *stop → stopping, get → getting*

Tip! In Part 9, you often have to write days and
months. Make sure you know how to spell them,
and don't forget the capital letters!

Tip! When you have finished writing your message in
the test, check it for spelling mistakes.

Remember!

On Monday, Tuesday, etc
On March 15th, August 1st, etc.
In the morning, afternoon
In January, February, etc.
At night
At 6 p.m., half past three, etc.
No preposition with this morning, this evening, etc.

7 Cross out the wrong word in each sentence.

Example: I'll meet you **to** / **at** the cinema.

1 We're going *in* / *to* the beach at the weekend.
2 My best friend is *from* / *of* Romania.
3 I love going *in* / *to* concerts!
4 Should I bring some money *with* / *on* me?
5 We're going there *on* / *by* bus.
6 I often take photographs *to* / *in* the park.
7 I'm going *in* / *to* the capital city next weekend.
8 The party is *at* / *to* Adel's house.

8 **Read the sentences. If a sentence is right, put a tick (✓). If it is wrong, put a cross (✗).**

> **Tip!** In Part 9, you are often asked to write about what to take or bring somewhere. There are lots of different ways to give this information.

Example: **a** *Bring a jacket, as it gets cold at night.* ✓

          b *To bring a jacket, as it gets cold at night.* ✗

1 **a** Remember to bring your ticket, or you won't be able to get in! ☐
  b Remember to bring your ticket, or you can't get in! ☐

2 **a** I think you will bring some water with you. ☐
  b I think it's a good idea to bring some water with you. ☐

3 **a** You should need an umbrella, as the weather isn't good today. ☐
  b You might need an umbrella, as the weather isn't good today. ☐

4 **a** You should bring something to eat. ☐
  b You will bring something to eat. ☐

9 Read this Part 9 task and the messages to Toni written by three *Key* candidates, Anita, Bea and Cami. Then answer questions 1–8 below.

 Tip! Read the instructions carefully! Remember you must write all three parts of the message to get a good mark.

You went to the cinema yesterday. Write an email to your English friend, Toni.
Tell Toni:

- **who** you went to the cinema with
- **which** film you saw
- **why** you liked the film.

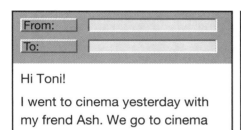

From:
To:

Hi Toni!

I went to cinema yesterday with my frend Ash. We go to cinema a lot. Yesterday we seen the film 'New Day' at cinema near my house.

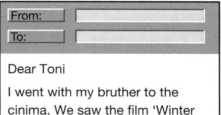

From:
To:

Dear Toni

I went with my bruther to the cinima. We saw the film 'Winter storm'. Why you did like this film?

Bea

From:
To:

Hello Toni

Last week I went to the cinema with my best friend Andrea. We watched 'The Cook'. We liked this film because it was very funny.

Cami

Which writer (Anita, Bea or Cami):

1 has included all three parts of the message?
2 has not understood one of the instructions?
3 has not made any grammatical mistakes?
4 forgot to put their name at the end?
5 has written fewer than 25 words?
6 has made a past tense mistake?
7 needs to check their spelling?
8 might get the best mark?

Test 1 Exam practice **Reading and Writing • Part 9**

Question 56

Your English friend Danni doesn't know anything about the party tomorrow. Write an email to Danni.

Say:

- **where** the party will be
- **what** Danni should bring
- **who** is going to be there.

Write **25–35** words.
Write the note on your answer sheet.

Advice

where – do you need to use **in**, **at** or **on**?
what – use *You should bring …*
who – do you need to tell Danni the reason for something, or tell her about people?

In this part you:

- **read**   five questions and **look at** three possible picture answers
- **listen to**   five short conversations and **choose** the right answer (A, B or C) for each

Listening for information

1 🎧 01 Listen and answer the questions about what Stella is doing this morning.

1   Who is Stella talking to?

2   Who is Stella going to visit?

3   How is Stella going to travel?

Tip! You'll hear something about all three pictures, but there's only one correct answer. Make sure you read the question very carefully!

Vocabulary Dates and times

2 🎧 02 Listen and choose the correct answer. When are Mia and her family flying to Australia?

Tip! In Part 1, you often have to answer questions about how someone is travelling.

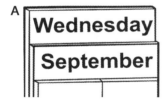
A 10th December

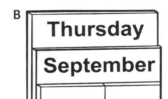
B 17th December

C 5th January

3 🎧 03 Listen and choose the correct answer. Which day will Leo and Tiana practise their song?

Tip! In Part 1, you often have to answer questions about days and dates.

A Wednesday September

B Thursday September

C Friday September

4 🎧 04 Listen and choose the correct answer. What is Luc doing <u>now</u>?

A

B

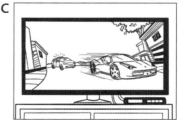
C

Tip! In Part 1, you often have to answer questions about what people are doing now, what they did, or what they're going to do. Pay attention to the verbs. Are they present, past or future?

5 🎧05 Listen and choose the correct answer. What is Sofia going to do this afternoon?

A    B    C

Vocabulary Places

6 🎧06 Listen and choose the correct answer. What has James lost?

> **Tip!** In Part 1, you sometimes have to answer questions about things you might see at home, or at school.

A    B 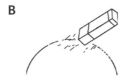   C

7 🎧07 Listen and decide which room Jasmine is in at the moment.

> **Tip!** Some Part 1 questions ask where someone, or something, is.

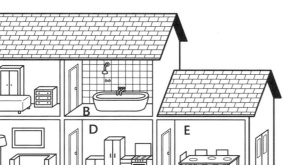

8 🎧08 Listen and choose the correct answer, A, B or C.

> **Tip!** Part 1 often tests numbers and prices.

1 How many pairs of earrings does Barbara have?   **A** 4   **B** 14   **C** 40
2 How many times has Anna spoken to her friend today?   **A** 2   **B** 4   **C** 5
3 How many people went to Billy's party?   **A** 12   **B** 20   **C** 22
4 How many ice creams does the man want to buy?   **A** 1   **B** 2   **C** 3

9 🎧09 How much are the shoes which Jonathan and his mother decide to buy?

      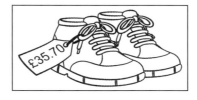

A   B   C

10 Questions 1–5

You will hear five short conversations.
You will hear each conversation twice.
There is one question for each conversation.
For questions **1–5**, choose the right answer.
For each question, choose the right answer (**A**, **B** or **C**).

Example: How many new T-shirts did Ellen get?   *Answer:*

2	**5**	**7**
A	B	C

---

1 Why didn't the boy buy an ice cream?

  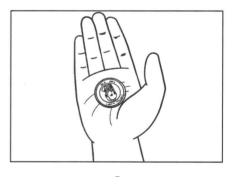

A   B   C

2 Who will Bella call on her phone next?

A   B   C

3 How will the friends travel to school tomorrow morning?

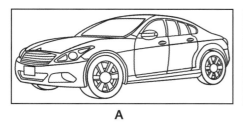

A

B

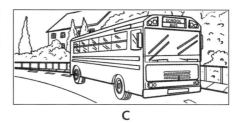

C

4 What day will Matt get his new tennis racket?

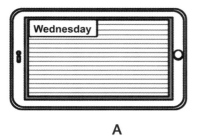

A

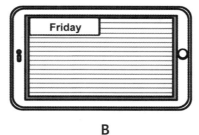

B

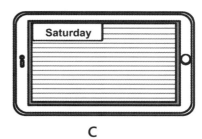

C

5 What's on TV this evening?

A

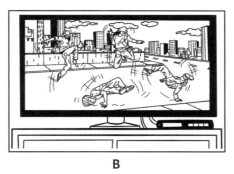

B

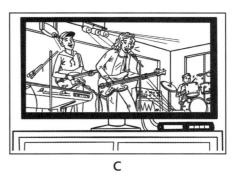

C

Advice

2 Make sure you listen for the person Bella says she is talking to now. Is it a man or a woman?

5 Listen carefully. Only one programme is actually on TV today.

In this part you:

- **read** two lists of information
- **listen** to a conversation and **match** the two lists of information

1 What are these people doing now? Match each activity 1–6 with another way of describing that activity.

> **Tip!** In the second list, the words you hear are often different from the words you read.

Example: *She's writing messages on her phone.*

1 He's going to see someone he knows from school.
2 She's putting clothes in suitcases.
3 He's having a tennis lesson.
4 She's working on her school project.
5 He's buying food for the party.
6 She's making dinner in the kitchen.

cooking
doing homework
learning a sport
packing
sending texts
shopping
visiting a classmate

2 🎧 11 Listen. Which activity did each person enjoy? Cross out the wrong words.

> **Tip!** You may hear more than one of the words or phrases on the list for one question, so listen carefully before you decide which one to choose.

Example: ~~watching birds~~ / *climbing trees*

1 *maths / history*
2 *looking at photos / shopping*
3 *watching a film / eating dinner*
4 *playing tennis / playing football*
5 *lying in the sun / swimming in the sea*
6 *making biscuits / making a cake*

> **Remember!**
> You can use an answer only once, and you don't need to use two of the answers.

3 🎧 12 Listen. How did each person in Karina's family help on the day of the party? Write one letter A – E next to each person. There is one extra answer.

KARINA'S FAMILY

1 mum ☐
2 sister ☐
3 Karina ☐
4 dad ☐

ACTIVITY

A preparing food
B finding music
C looking for something
D moving furniture
E shopping
F researching party food

Test 1 Exam practice Listening • Part 2

13 **Questions 6–10**

You will hear George telling his cousin about the first week of his school holidays.
What did George like best about each day?
For questions **6–10**, write a letter **A–H** next to each day.
You will hear the conversation twice.

Example:

0 Monday **A**

Answer:

0	A	B	C	D	E	F	G	H
	▬	▭	▭	▭	▭	▭	▭	▭

DAYS		BEST THINGS	
6 Tuesday	☐	**A**	going to the cinema
7 Wednesday	☐	**B**	going on a boat ride
8 Thursday	☐	**C**	going shopping
9 Friday	☐	**D**	learning a watersport
10 Saturday	☐	**E**	meeting a friend
		F	visiting a farm
		G	walking on the beach
		H	working on a computer

Advice

E *When did George see a friend? What's his name?*

C *Who went shopping?*

G *What do you use on a computer?*

In this part you:

- **read** five questions
- **listen** to a conversation and **choose** the correct answer (A, B or C)

Grammar Answering questions

1 🎧 **14** **Listen to the questions 1–6 and match each with an answer from the box.**

Tip! In Part 3, there are often questions about numbers.

| ten of us | three times a week | ~~number 102~~ | five metres wide and four metres long |
| six forty-five | fifteen pounds | an hour and a half | |

Example: number 102

1 .... 2 .... 3 .... 4 .... 5 .... 6 ....

👁 Most of the questions in Exercise 1 started with *How ...?* but not all of them. How did the other questions start?

2 🎧 **15** **Listen to a girl telling her mother about her new school. Cross out the wrong answer for each question.**

Tip! In Part 3, you sometimes have to answer a question, and sometimes you have to complete a sentence.

Example: Raquel's classroom is **6B / 8B**

1 Raquel's teacher is called *Mr Walters / Mrs Taylor*
2 Raquel sat next to *Jane / Emma*
3 The lunch time break is *an hour / 45 minutes*
4 For lunch Raquel had *soup and bread / salad*
5 Raquel's bus home comes at *quarter to four / three thirty*
6 Raquel will finish school early on *Tuesdays / Thursdays*

3 🎧 **16** **Listen to a boy telling his friend about a geography class. If the statement is right, put a tick (✓). If it is wrong put a cross (✗).**

Example: Today's geography class was about the sea ✓

1 The students got information from a video. ☐   3 For homework, the students must make a list. ☐
2 The students learnt about fish. ☐   4 Next week, the students need to take some food. ☐

4 🎧 **17** **Listen to Kira telling her friend about a TV programme. Choose the correct answer A, B or C.**

1 Which country is the TV programme about?
   A China   **B** India   **C** Japan
2 The programme is on at
   A 7 o'clock   **B** 8 o'clock   **C** 9 o'clock
3 Which channel will the TV programme be on?
   A Channel 2   **B** Channel 4   **C** Channel 5

🎧 18 **Questions 11–15**

You will hear Vincent telling his friend, Carla, about some homework.
For each question, choose the right answer **A, B** or **C**.
You will hear the conversation twice.

Example:

0 What homework do Carla and Vincent have to do?

   A science

   B English

   Ⓒ geography

Answer:

---

11 Carla must find out about a river in

   A India.

   B South America.

   C Africa.

12 Vincent will send Carla

   A a text message.

   B some photos.

   C a map.

13 The most Carla should write is

   A 200 words.

   B 300 words.

   C 500 words.

14 When must Carla give her homework to the teacher?

   A Tuesday

   B Thursday

   C Friday

15 What time will Vincent meet Carla?

   A 4.45

   B 5.15

   C 5.45

Advice

11 You'll hear Vincent say all of these places. Which one are they learning about at the moment?

13 Be careful! Only one of these is the total number of words to write.

15 There are other ways to say these times. What are they?

In this part you:

- **read**   a form that you must **complete** with words or numbers
- **listen to**   a short conversation and **write** the answers on the form

1 🎧 **19** Listen to two people talking about a new show on at the theatre. Which is the correct poster, A, B or C?

A	B	C
Sleep	Sleep	Sleep
Begins on: 30th April	Begins on: 2nd April	Begins on: 7th April
Name of theatre: Wilcott	Name of theatre: Wylcott	Name of theatre: Wlycot
Price of student tickets: £10	Price of student tickets: £8	Price of student tickets: £8

2 🎧 **20** Listen. Are these names of people and places spelt correctly? If the spelling is right, put a tick (✓). If it is wrong, put a cross (✗).

Example: Lycium Theatre   ☒ *X*

1	Mr Alsupp	☐	3	The Telos Centre	☐	5	Tom Akinto	☐
2	Ryedale Road	☐	4	Churmount	☐	6	www.gapes.com	☐

◎ **Key** candidates often make mistakes with vowels (**a**, **e**, **i**, **o**, **u**), so make sure you know how these are said in English. Remember that when someone says 'double **r**', it means that the letter **r** is written twice.

3 🎧 **21** Listen and complete the notes.

Tip!	You often have to write the name of a person or place in Part 4. You will hear someone spell it and you must write it correctly to get the mark.

Example: Town where Jack was born: ....Relwick....

1   Name of hotel: .... Hotel

2   Name of piano teacher: Mrs ....

3   Name of train station: .... Green

4   Who to call: Maria ....

5   Name of video game: ....

6   Find out about: The .... River

4 🎧 **22** Listen to people talking about time. If the time is right, put a tick (✓). If it is wrong, put a cross (✗).

Example: Hockey practice begins at: 3.45 p.m.   ☑

1	The bus leaves from school at:	9.15 a.m.	☐
2	The talk is at:	10.30 a.m.	☐
3	The train leaves at:	5.28 p.m.	☐
4	The TV programme begins at:	7.05 p.m.	☐
5	The concert ends at:	8:45 p.m.	☐
6	The shop opens at:	7:30 a.m.	☐

Remember!

Remember that **begin** and **start** mean the same, and **end** and **finish** mean the same.

5 🎧 **23** Listen to these questions, and write the times.

Example: *Party starts at* ......7.30 p.m.......

1 Shopping centre opens at: .... a.m.
2 Saturday opening time: .... a.m.
3 Penny arrives home at: .... p.m.
4 Course is from 10 a.m. to: .... a.m.
5 Pool opens at: .... p.m.
6 Film starts at: .... p.m.

Tip! When the answer is a time, you can write the time in words, but it's quicker to write numbers.

Remember! You will probably hear more than one time, so listen carefully for the right one.

Test 1 Exam practice   Listening • Part 4

🎧 **24** **Questions 16–20**

You will hear a student asking a dancer some questions for an article in his school magazine.
Listen and complete questions **16–20**.
You will hear the conversation twice.

Belinda Frenton – a famous dancer

Country where Belinda was born: .... Canada ....

Age Belinda began dancing: (16) ....

Name of show: (17) ....

Name of theatre: (18) ....

Time Belinda usually begins practising: (19) .... *a.m.*

Hobby: (20) ....

Advice

16 *Which word means the same as* **began**?

18 *When you see* **name***, you should listen carefully, as this often means you have to spell the word.*

19 *Listen carefully. You will probably hear more than one time. Which is the right one?*

20 *Think before you listen. How many hobbies can you think of?*

In this part you:

- **read** a form that you must **complete** with words or numbers
- **listen to** one person talking and **write** the answers on the form

Vocabulary Spelling days and months

1 Look at a *Key* candidate's answers. Correct the spelling mistakes in the answers.

Example: Next football practice: ~~fryday~~ .....Friday......

1	Day course starts:	Munday	....
2	Museum closed every:	wensday	....
3	School disco on:	saterday	....
4	Visit to castle on:	Choosday	....

2 🎧 25 Listen and write the correct day.

Example: Day of dance class next week: .....Thursday......

1 TV programme is on: ....
2 Swimming class is now on: ....
3 Party is on: ....
4 Return form by: ....
5 Day of hockey practice: ....

3 Cross out the wrong spelling.

Example: ~~Janury~~ / **January**

1 December / Dicember	5 February / Febrary	9 Juli / July
2 may / May	6 June/ Joon	10 Novembre / November
3 March / Martch	7 Oktober / October	
4 Aogust / August	8 Aipril / April	

4 🎧 26 Listen. Is the date right? If it is, put a tick (✓). If it is wrong, put a cross (✗).

Example: Date new shop opens: 20th September ☑

1 Date of school concert: 13th May ☐
2 Chess competition is on: 16 April ☐
3 Date of pop concert: 5th October ☐
4 Closing date for competition: 26th August ☐
5 Appointment for haircut on: 7th May ☐
6 Date of parents' meeting: 6 February ☐

5 🎧 27 **Listen and write the correct dates.**

Example: Date of art exam: .....28 May.....

Remember!
You will hear two dates. Listen carefully and write the right date.

1 Date of boat trip: ....
2 Festival ends on: ....
3 New café opens on: ....

4 Geography trip on: ....
5 Give in science project by: ....
6 Date of school quiz: ....

Test 1 Exam practice   Listening • Part 5

🎧 28 **Questions 21–25**

You will hear a woman talking about a one-day computer course for teenagers.
Listen and complete questions **21–25**.
You will hear the information twice.

One-day computer course

Place:	.....Park Hill College.....
Day:	(21) ....
For students aged:	(22) .... or older
Second part of course:	(23) learn to make a ....
Time course starts:	(24) .... a.m.
Cost for school students:	(25) £ ....

Advice

21 You need to write the name of a day. Make sure you spell it correctly and start it with a capital letter!

23 Think before you listen. This is a computer course, so what might you learn to make?

24 Which word means the same as **starts**?

In this part you:

- **speak**   to an examiner
- **answer**   questions about your name, school, your hobbies

Giving personal information

1 🎧 **29** Listen to Pablo talking to his new classmate, Marianne. Listen. If the statement is right, put a tick (✓). If it is wrong, put a cross (✗).

1 Marianne's surname is Dubois. ☐
2 Marianne is from England. ☐
3 Marianne doesn't have any brothers or sisters. ☐
4 Marianne is 14. ☐
5 Marianne likes her new school. ☐
6 Marianne's favourite sport is tennis. ☐
7 Marianne's favourite subject is maths. ☐
8 Marianne likes studying English. ☐

Understand the task

Tip! It's important to know what happens in Part 1 of the Speaking test. The information below will help you.

2 Put the information below in the correct order. Write 1–8 in the boxes. The first one is done for you.

There will be two examiners there. ☐

Someone will take you to the room where you will do the Speaking test. ☐

This examiner will ask you questions. ☐

Your partner will go to the room with you. ☐

You will give the first examiner your mark sheet. ☐

You will get a mark sheet with your name on it. ☐ 1

The second examiner will fill in your mark sheet. ☐

They will say *hello* and you will sit down. ☐

Tip! The examiner will ask you and your partner some questions about yourselves, such as your names and the subjects you study at school.

3 🎧 30 Listen to an examiner talking to a student. Complete the sentence with the words you hear.

1 Can you spell your .... for me?
2 How .... are you?
3 Where do you ....?
4 Are you a ....?

5 Do you like your ....?
6 What is your favourite ....?
7 Do you study any ....?
8 How many English .... do you have each week?

4 Listen again to the questions in Exercise 3 and give your own answers.

> **Tip!** The examiner will ask you some other questions, such as what your hobbies are and what you do in your daily life. Try to give more information than one-word answers.

5 Look at the questions and complete the students' answers.

Example: *What's your surname?*

........My surname is...... Andersson.

1 Where do you come from?
.... Sweden.
2 What do you like doing at the weekend?
.... shopping.
3 Who do you go shopping with?
.... with my friends, Ben and Lucia.
4 What are you going to do on Saturday?
.... swimming ....
5 What's your favourite hobby?
.... dancing.
6 Do you go to dance classes?
Yes, ...

6 Complete each *Tell me something about ...* answer. Add two more things for each one.

1 *Tell me something about your home.*
My home is in this town. It's ....
2 *Tell me something about your family.*
I've got a brother and a sister. My brother ....
3 *Tell me something about your country.*
I come from .... It's ....

> **Tip!** At the end of Part 1, the examiner will ask you to talk about something. He / She will say *Tell me something about ...* (e.g. your hobbies, friends, town, school).

7 🎧 31 Listen to a student answering one of the *Tell me something about ...* questions in Exercise 6. Which question is she answering?

Ask and answer the *Tell me something about ...* questions with a partner.

Test 1 Exam practice Speaking • Part 1

🎧 32 An examiner is talking to you and another student, Andrei. Listen to Andrei answering the questions. Then you answer them.

> **Tip!**
> • Try to answer questions using more than one word.
> • Try to think of three things to say when you answer the *Tell me about ...* question.
> • Don't worry if you don't know as much English as your partner.

In this part you:

- **read**   notes and **speak** to another student
- **ask and answer**   five questions

Looking at factual information

Sports classes

1   🎧 33   Look at the information below. Listen. Which activity is the boy asking about?

A

> ***Activity Days:***
> ***2–4 p.m.***
> from Monday to Friday.
> ***Wear comfortable trainers and come walking with us!***

B

> ***Activities for teenagers***
> ***Every weekday***
> ***from 3–5 p.m***
> Learn to play badminton and basketball. Don't forget your trainers!

Understand the task

> **Tip!**   It's important to know what happens in Part 2 of the Speaking test. The information below will help you.

2   Put the information below in the correct order. Write 1–8 in the boxes. The first one is done for you.

The examiner gives each student a new booklet with a different task. ☐

The other student (B) gets some information. ☐

The first examiner gives each student a question and information booklet. `1`

Student B asks questions about the new topic. ☐

Student A asks five questions, using the question words in their booklet. ☐

Student B answers each question, using the information in their booklet. ☐

One student (A) gets some questions. ☐

Student A finds the information in their booklet and answers the questions. ☐

3 Look at this information about swimming classes. What do you think the questions are? Complete them.

Swimming classes
Tuesday evenings
5 p.m.–6 p.m.
Hall Bank Swimming Pool
Races every week
Call Daniel on ✆ 01184960523
to book a place

1 When ....?
2 How long ....?
3 Where ....?
4 What ....?
5 Who ....?

4 Now answer the questions in Exercise 3. Use the words in the box to help you. Do not add any new information. Keep your answers short and clear.

> The classes are on ...   They are ... long.   They are at ...
> You can do ... every week.   You can call ... a place.

5 🎧 34 Listen to two students asking and answering questions about the swimming classes.

How many questions did Student A ask? ....
Did Student B answer all of Student A's questions? ....

Test 1 Exam practice Speaking • Part 2

CANDIDATE B Go to page 222

CANDIDATE A – your answers

> **Remember!**
> - The questions and the information are in a different order.
> - Remember to ask all five questions.
> - When you answer the questions, find the information in the booklet. Do not give any information which is not in the booklet.

Table tennis competition

at City Sports Centre

on 24 April

9 a.m. to 5 p.m.

Matches for all levels

Prizes: T-shirts for winners

Don't forget your bat!

Interested? Call Peter on 016 324 2981

CANDIDATE A – your questions

New gym

gym open weekends?

expensive for students?

close?

website? 🖱

staff / friendly?

- How many questions are there in Part 1?
- How many notices are there to choose from?

Vocabulary Focus on meaning

1 Match the words and phrases 1–6 below with the words from the box that have the same meaning.

> **Tip!** There are often words and phrases in the sentences that have the same meaning as words in the notices.

| bigger | closed | seat | movie |
| passenger | gift | ~~café~~ |

Example: place to buy a snack .....café.....

1 someone who is travelling ....   4 larger ....
2 not open ....   5 present ....
3 place to sit ....   6 film ....

2 Does the sentence match the notice? Write **yes** or **no**.

> **Tip!** The notices often have words about times, days and dates.

Example: 0 This place is only open in the morning.   Café open from 2 p.m. to 5.30 p.m.   .....no.....

1 This place is closed at the weekend.   Library. Open Monday – Friday   ....
2 You can learn tennis here on any day.   Tennis lessons. Monday – Saturday only.   ....
3 You can only have this meal in the morning.   Restaurant. All-day breakfast!   ....
4 This place will be open after this date.   Pool closed until April 30ᵗʰ.   ....
5 There are two days when you can see the show.   Show dates: Nov 3ʳᵈ – 16ᵗʰ.   ....

3 Look at the notices below. Choose **this** or **these** to complete each matching sentence.

> **Tip!** In the sentences you will often see words like **this** or **these** which match a word in the notices. Make sure you know which word is singular and which is plural.

Example:

Bus passengers must buy a ticket before getting on.

1 **Sale – football boots half-price today**
2 Bus leaves at 9 a.m. We won't wait!
3 No cash? Pay by credit card
4 *Castle shop – guidebooks available*
5 Tour starts in 5 minutes. Tickets still available!

You need (this)/ **these** if you want to travel.
You can buy *this* / *these* more cheaply at the moment.
Make sure you aren't late for *this* / *these*.
It doesn't matter if you don't have *this* / *these*.
Visitors can buy *this* / *these* here.
It's not too late to go on *this* / *these*.

Questions 1–5

Which notice **(A–H)** says this **(1–5)**?
For each question **1–5**, mark the correct letter **A–H** on your answer sheet.

Example:

0 This place has films for children.

Answer:

0	A	B	C	D	E	F	G	H
	▢	▢	▢	▬	▢	▢	▢	▢

---

1 This is now in a different place.

2 Go to this if you are interested in learning about these films.

3 This place has added new kinds of food to its menu.

4 You can come here again after this date.

5 It is possible to choose what time to watch this.

Advice

*1 What is another way of saying **is now in a different place**?*

4 Which place is offering food which it didn't serve before?

*5 Which notice gives two different times for you to **choose**?*

A

Only take food bought at this cinema into the film.

B
Cinema closed for repairs until 10 March

C

'Great 20th Century Movies'
Talk by Julia Lanza
July 4th 3.30 p.m. School Hall

D
KIDS' CLUB
Cartoons and animated films
Saturday 10 a.m.
Under 12a £5

E
CINEMA SHOP
Sweets, popcorn, drinks
New opening hours: 11 a.m. –10p.m.

F
CINEMA CAFÉ
Now selling burgers and chips as well as sandwiches

G
MOVIE HOUSE CINEMA HAS MOVED TO NORTHGATE STREET. BIGGER THAN BEFORE!

H
FILM CLUB
Dec 6: *Blue Mountain*
Showing at 4.30 and 6.30

Test 2 Training / Reading and Writing Part 2

- How many questions are there in Part 2?
- How many answers must you choose from?

Vocabulary Focus on meaning

1 **Cross out the wrong word in each sentence.**

Tip! Think carefully about the difference in the meaning of the two words.

Example: *I don't like playing baseball because I can't* **catch** / ~~take~~ *the ball.*

1 The *driver / pilot* of the plane spoke to some of the passengers.
2 Look at this *advertisement / notice* in the newspaper for a new computer game.
3 We have to work in *crowds / groups* for our school project.
4 What do you do in your *free / clear* time?
5 We *shared / joined* the birthday cake between all of us.
6 My sister *uses / spends* so much time on her phone!
7 My cousin lives a long *time / way* from my house.
8 I don't *mind / matter* which film we see.

2 **Write the correct word in each space.**

Example: *I need to* **choose** *a book to write about*
             for my homework

prefer / ~~choose~~ / agree

1 Shall I .... the bags to your car?   *hold /collect / carry*
2 Did you .... the postcard I sent you?   *receive / catch / collect*
3 Could you .... this box while I find my key? *get / have / hold*
4 I .... really good marks for my essay.   *took / got / put*
5 It .... a long time to learn to play the violin. *wants / uses/ takes*
6 Mum usually .... me from school in the car.   *collects / takes / catches*

> **Remember!**
>
> **collect** means to go to get
> **hold** means to have in your hands
> **carry** means to hold and take somewhere
> you can **take** something somewhere
> something can **take** time to do

Grammar to infinitive or *–ing*

⊙ Some *Key* candidates make mistakes with the form of the verb when it follows another verb.

3 **Cross out the wrong form of the verbs in each sentence.**

Example: *I really want to* **go** / ~~going~~ *to the party on Saturday.*

1 My brother really enjoys *to go / going* to football matches.
2 We decided *see / to see* the film at 8 p.m.
3 I love *go / going* dancing!
4 I prefer *play / playing* computer games with friends than alone.
5 I like *playing / play* tennis in the park.

> **Remember!**
>
> **like / love / enjoy / prefer** + verb + *-ing*
> **want / decide** + infinitive (to go)

Questions 6–10

Read the sentences about a horse-riding competition.
Choose the best word (**A, B** or **C**) for each space.
For questions **6–10**, mark **A, B** or **C** on your answer sheet.

Example:

0   Sonya .... in a horse-riding competition last week.

   A entered   **B** went   **C** competed

Answer: | 0 | A ▭ B ▭ C ▬ |

---

6   It .... Sonya three hours to travel to the competition.

   A used   **B** took   **C** needed

7   Before the competition started, Sonya was a bit ....

   A worried   **B** boring   **C** terrible

8   Sonya had to do a .... of different things in the competition.

   A variety   **B** group   **C** crowd

9   Sonya .... to remember everything her riding teacher taught her.

   A thought   **B** said   **C** tried

10   Sonya won the competition and .... a silver cup as a prize.

   A carried   **B** brought   **C** received

> **Advice**
>
> **6** A person needs time to do something, so you can say 'Sonya **will need** three hours to travel to the competition', but not '**it needed** Sonya ...'. For the time a person needs to do something, we use the verb **take**.
>
> **7** Is the sentence describing Sonya or the competition?
>
> **10** If you win a competition, someone gives you a prize. Which word means Sonya was given something?

- How many questions are there in Part 3a?
- How many answers must you choose from?

Grammar Wh- questions

1 Complete the first part of each conversation with a word from the box.

Tip! The first part of the conversation in Part 3a often has a question word in it. Make sure you know what type of answer each question word matches.

why   what   ~~which~~   when   where   whose   who

Example: ....Which.... film would you like to see?   *The one about animals.*

1   Do you know .... coat this is?   I think it's Robert's.
2   .... are those people laughing?   They're watching a funny video.
3   .... shall I meet you tomorrow?   How about at the library?
4   .... is your brother's football match?   Tomorrow, after school.
5   .... is that standing in the playground?   Our new science teacher.
6   .... is your book about?   Animals that live in Australia.

Vocabulary Agreeing and disagreeing

2 Read the first half of each conversation carefully. Cross out the wrong answers.

Example: Is her house the one with the green door?   ~~If you prefer~~. / **I think so.**

1   I love going to the beach!   *Me too! / I do!*
2   What a great pizza!   *Is it there? / It is, isn't it?*
3   Whose is this pencil?   *It's mine. / That's right.*
4   I can swim 500 metres.   *So do I. / That's great.*
5   Will it stop raining later?   *I hope so. / Yes, a bit.*
6   Why don't we go on Saturday?   *Not now. / I'd rather not.*

◉ Some *Key* candidates make mistakes in Part 3a because they don't look carefully at the tense in the first part of the conversation.

3 Read the first half of the conversation carefully. If the answer is right, put a tick (✔). If it is wrong, put a (✗).

Example: Where did you buy those jeans?

   a   I'll get them next week.   ☐

   b   From the shop on the corner .   ☑

1   I've never been to Canada.

   a   Oh, I have.   ☐

   b   Didn't you like it?   ☐

2   That picture you drew is so good!

   a   I'm sure it is.   ☐

   b   I'm glad you like it.   ☐

3   Are you going to play tennis later?

   a   Yes, I had to stay later at school.   ☐

   b   Yes, if it doesn't rain!   ☐

Questions 11–15

Complete the five conversations.
For questions **11–15**, mark **A**, **B** or **C** on your answer sheet.

Example:

0

Here's a drink for you!

A Of course not!

B Thanks a lot!

C I'm afraid I can't.

Answer: | 0 | A B C

---

11 Which of these cakes do you want?

    A Shall I make them?

    B I don't mind.

    C I won't do that.

12 Why are you wearing Jane's coat?

    A Of course I don't!

    B Doesn't she want it?

    C It isn't hers!

13 I think you're better at maths than Carl.

    A Why did he say that?

    B Do you think so?

    C He's not, is he?

14 Go straight ahead – you'll see the café on your left.

    A It's all right.

    B I think I will.

    C Thanks for your help.

15 Let's get the bus home now.

    A I'd like to stay a bit longer.

    B I'm sure it is.

    C That doesn't matter.

Advice

11 A This is an offer to help, or to do something. Does it fit here?

14 The speaker is giving information. How should you answer if someone gives you this type of information?

15 If you don't agree with a suggestion, you usually give a reason.

- How many people are speaking in Part 3b?
- How many answers must you find?
- How many answers must you choose from?

Time and place

1 **Look at the sentences. Decide if each person is talking about a time or a place. Cross out the wrong answers.**

Tip! The people in Part 3b often talk about times and places.

Example: Are you free this afternoon?   **time / ~~place~~**

1   We're not doing that until next term.   *time / place*
2   Would you like to come to my house?   *time / place*
3   We went to London.   *time / place*
4   That's too early. Let's go at half past.   *time / place*
5   I've never been there before.   *time / place*
6   I'm afraid I'm busy then.   *time / place*
7   How about at the bus stop?   *time / place*
8   Do you know when it starts?   *time / place*

2 **Choose two correct answers for each sentence. Cross out one wrong answer.**

Tip! Think about the type of information you need to answer a question or sentence.

Example: Are you free later?   ***No. I have to study. / ~~No, but it wasn't expensive.~~ / No, but tomorrow is OK.***

1   We should go cycling together.   *I'd like that. / Great idea! / I think so.*
2   Which shoes did you buy?   *The blue ones. / They were in my room! / I'm wearing them!*
3   My mum will give us a lift.   *That's nice of her. / Will she mind? / Yes, she's too busy.*
4   Do you mind helping me?   *Of course not. / Not at all. / No I'm not.*
5   Will there be many of us?   *We're not going. / Not really, no. / About ten, altogether.*
6   Why are we going so early?   *It's a long way. / At 7 o'clock. / I'm not sure. I'll ask Dad.*

3 **Complete the conversation. Choose a reply A–H from the box.**

Tip! Remember that your answer must make sense with the sentence before the space and the one after it!

Example: Chris: We're going on a school trip next week!   Alex: ...G...   Chris: I know.

1   Chris: We haven't been on one for ages!   Alex: ....   Chris: To an art museum.
2   Chris: I love art – especially painting.   Alex: ....   Chris: Really?
3   Chris: Can you teach me?   Alex: ....   Chris: Thanks!
4   Chris: Are you free at the weekend?   Alex: ....   Chris: Great.
5   Chris: How about Saturday?   Alex: ....   Chris: Fantastic!
6   Chris: Is 10 a.m. too early?   Alex: ....   Chris: See you then!

> **A** I prefer photography.
> **B** I'd love to.
> **C** Where are you going?
> **D** OK. In the morning.
> **E** No. That's fine.
> **F** Is it good?
> **G** ~~Lucky you!~~
> **H** Yes. I've got nothing planned.

Questions 16–20

Complete the conversation between two friends.
What does Lola say to Kim?
For questions **16–20**, mark the correct letter **A–H** on your answer sheet.

Example:

Kim: Hi Lola! Do you know anything   about the school art trip?

Lola: **0** ....**E**.........

Answer:

Kim: Oh, I didn't know that!

Lola: **16** ....

Kim: Me too. I've never been on an art trip before.

Lola: **17** ....

Kim: What was that like? What did you do?

Lola: **18** ....

Kim: That sounds difficult! I'm better at photography than painting or drawing.

Lola: **19** ....

Kim: I'd love to. Come to my house this Saturday. We'll take some pictures together.

Lola: **20** ....

Kim: No, that's fine. See you then.

A   We copied some famous pictures in a museum.

B   It's a shame, isn't it? But I'm still excited about going!

C   When did you start work on your art project?

D   Really? Can you teach me? I've just got a new camera.

E   Yes, we're not going until next term I'm afraid.

F   These are excellent pictures.

G   Great thanks! Is 10 o'clock too early?

H   I went on the last one. We went to London.

Advice

16 *Lola understands that Kim isn't happy. Which answer has an expression which shows this?*

18 *Which answer mentions something which answers the question* **What did you do**?

19 *What kind of answer do you need here? It could be agreement, disagreement, or maybe surprise.*

- How many questions are there in Part 4?

- Are you given answers to choose from in Part 4?

 Tip! There are two types of Part 4. This Part 4 is a three-option multiple choice.

1 Read the text and the questions. For each question, write the number of the line in the text where you found the information you needed.

Tip! In Part 4, you need to find the part of the text which will help you to answer each question. The order of the questions is the same as the order of the information in the text.

> ¹Giant pandas are members of the bear family and can be found in western China. Their ²bodies are mostly white, with black areas around their eyes and mouths, and on their ears, ³legs and shoulders. When a panda is born, it only weighs about 100 grams. It takes about ⁴four years for a panda to grow to its adult size, of between 125 and 160 kilos. There are ⁵between 1,000 and 2,000 wild pandas in China, and about another 300 live in zoos around ⁶the world. Pandas eat mostly bamboo, which is a plant, but they can also eat meat.

Example: Which animal family do giant pandas belong to? line ....1..........

1 How much does an adult giant panda weigh?   line ....

2 What colour are giant pandas' bodies?   line ....

3 What colour are giant pandas' ears?   line ....

4 What part of China do giant pandas live in?   line ....

5 How many wild giant pandas are there?   line ....

6 What do giant pandas usually eat?   line ....

2 Read the short texts? Choose the correct answer A, B or C.

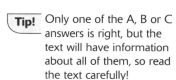 **Tip!** Only one of the A, B or C answers is right, but the text will have information about all of them, so read the text carefully!

Text: *Tom got a guitar for his birthday last year, and now he has lessons every week. At the end of last term, he decided to buy his teacher a present because she was getting married.*

1 The present is for

   A the teacher's birthday.   **B** the end of term.   **C** the teacher's wedding.

Text: *Tom thought about getting a lamp. His sister suggested a plant, but Tom wasn't sure. Their mum said a clock might be good, and Tom agreed that was better than a lamp or a plant.*

2 Tom decided to buy

   A a plant.   **B** a clock.   **C** a lamp.

Text: *Tom has guitar lessons on Wednesday afternoon, so on Monday he went to the shops, and on Tuesday he wrapped the present in coloured paper.*

3 Which day did Tom buy the present?

   A Monday   **B** Tuesday   **C** Wednesday

Text: *Tom's teacher was really pleased with the present. 'It's just the right size for my house,' she said. 'Best of all, it's my favourite colour!' Tom said he hoped it was something she needed.*

4 What did the teacher like most about her present?

   A she needed one   **B** the colour   **C** the size

Questions 21–27

Read the article about a giant panda and answer the questions.
Are sentences **21–27** 'Right' **(A)** or 'Wrong' **(B)**?
If there is not enough information to answer 'Right' **(A)** or 'Wrong' **(B)**, choose 'Doesn't say' **(C)**.
For questions **21–27**, mark **A**, **B** or **C** on your answer sheet.

Qizai the panda

Most giant pandas are black and white, but not all. In the last 25 years, seven brown pandas have been seen in China, and Qizai is one of them. Qizai was born in the wild, but now he lives in a nature reserve – an area where animals are looked after, but have more space than in a zoo.

When Qizai was only two months old, his mother, who was black and white, left him alone in the mountains, and he became thin and sick. Luckily, someone found him. At first, he was put with other pandas, but they always stole his food, probably because he looked different. Now Qizai has his own space to live in. Qizai doesn't move or eat as fast as the other pandas, but he eats the same plants. Like the other pandas, when someone calls his name he goes to them.

Qizai is from the Qinling Mountains. Most of the pandas there are black and white, but even some of the black and white pandas have areas of brown hair. Brown pandas have the same size teeth as other pandas, but because their heads and bodies are not as big, their teeth look bigger.

Qizai is now old enough to be a father. Scientists think his babies will help them to understand more about why some pandas are born with his unusual colour.

Example:

0   What colour are giant pandas?

    A   always black and white   **B**   usually black and white   **C**   often brown   *Answer:*

0	A	B	C
	_	▬	_

---

21   How many brown pandas have been seen?

    A   1   **B**   7   **C**   25

22   Where does Qizai live?

    A   in a zoo   **B**   in the wild   **C**   in a nature reserve

23   Qizai's mother

    A   stopped looking after him.   **B**   was also brown.   **C**   became ill.

24   Qizai lives alone because

    A   other pandas take his food.   **B**   he needs more space.   **C**   he looks different.

25   How is Qizai different from other pandas?

    A   He knows his name.   **B**   He eats special food.   **C**   He moves more slowly.

26   Brown pandas

    A   are smaller.   **B**   have bigger teeth.   **C**   have some black and white hair.

27   Who do scientists want to study?

    A   Qizai   **B**   Qizai's babies   **C**   Qizai's father

Advice

22 The article mentions three places. Where does he live now?

24 The article talks about what happened when he lived with other pandas. Do the keepers really know why his happened?

26 Read carefully. Which part of the pandas is smaller or larger than other pandas?

- How many missing words are there in Part 5?
- How many possible answers must you choose from?

Grammar Determiners

1 Complete the sentences using *a, an, the, one, other, both* and *several*. You can use the same word more than once.

Example: People all over ~~the~~ *the* world have heard of his music.

1 Rainforests can be tropical or temperate. .... types receive a lot of rain.
2 I've got .... books about rainforests at home.
3 In .... 19th century, people didn't use mobile phones.
4 .... of my friends gave me this scarf for my birthday.
5 .... lot of people have pets such as cats or birds.
6 Our teacher told us .... interesting story about the rainforest in India.

Remember!

A and **an** are singular.
The can be singular or plural. It's for something we already know about.
We use **one** to talk about a particular person or thing in a group.
Both is for two things.
Several is for more than two things, but not lots of things.

Grammar Modals

2 **Cross out the two wrong modals in each sentence.**

Example: There **need** / **may** / **shall** be hundreds of spiders in 1m² of forest.

1 My cousin *can / must / could* already ride a bike when he was only three.
2 I *must / can / would* still remember the first time I ever saw the sea.
3 I can go to the cinema on the bus. You don't *must / need / should* to drive me there.
4 You *will / can / would* choose any colour sweet you like, but leave one for me!
5 My guitar teacher said that I *may / will / should* practise more.
6 You *will / may / must* be careful when you are cutting something with a knife.

Tip! Modal verbs are often tested in Part 5.

Grammar Prepositions and adverbs

3 **Complete the sentences using words from the box.**

| of | between | a | ~~over~~ | than | under | about |

Example: You have to be ......over...... 18 years old to watch that film.

1 25% .... the world's medicines come from rainforest plants.
2 Some plants can grow more than 20cm .... day.
3 There's a sale on today. Everything is .... £20.
4 More .... 500,000 people live in that town now.
5 It took .... ten years to build the castle.
6 The race is only for people ....12 and 16 years old.

Remember!

over means more than
under means less than
50% **of** the money
use **than** with more or less
use **between** when something is in the middle of two numbers.

Questions 28–35

Read the article about rainforest plants.
Choose the best word (**A, B** or **C**) for each space.
For questions **28–35**, mark **A, B** or **C** on your answer sheet.

Rainforests

There are two types of rainforest: tropical rainforests and temperate rainforests. Tropical rainforests **(0)** .... found in South America, Africa and Asia, and temperate ones mainly in North America, Chile and New Zealand. **(28)** .... types of rainforest receive **(29)** .... 200cm of rain every year.

There **(30)** .... be as many as 8,000 different types of plants
(31) .... in a single rainforest. It is very dark on the forest floor
(32) .... some smaller plants climb up trees to get to the sun. Many
(33) .... them can do this very quickly. For example, some plants
can grow up to 22.5cm **(34)** .... day.

About 25% of the world's medicines now come from rainforest plants.
That's why these places are very important **(35)** .... humans.

Example:

0	**A** been	**B** are	**C** was	*Answer:*	

28 **A** Both   **B** Any   **C** Another

29 **A** between   **B** over   **C** past

30 **A** shall   **B** need   **C** may

31 **A** grew   **B** growing   **C** grows

32 **A** so   **B** that   **C** for

33 **A** from   **B** of   **C** between

34 **A** one   **B** the   **C** a

35 **A** for   **B** with   **C** by

Advice

28 Which word do we use about two things that are the same in some ways.

29 Which word can mean **more than**?

32 Which of these words do we use to talk about the reason why something happens?

34 Which of these words is another way of saying **each**?

- How many words must you write in Part 6?
- What kind of help are you given?

Vocabulary Camping and weather

1 Read the sentences about things you take when you go camping. If the information is right, put a tick (✔). If it is wrong, put a cross (✗).

Example: *You need to wear **boots** on a hot, sunny day.* ☒

1 When you go camping, you sleep in a **tent**. ☐
2 You might take a **pillow** so you don't get cold at night. ☐
3 You take **a blanket** to cook your food on. ☐
4 You will need a **plate** to put your food on. ☐
5 Some people take **raincoats** if they think the weather will be hot. ☐
6 You could take a **football** so you can play with friends. ☐

> **Tip!** In the instructions for Part 6, you will be told what the words are about, e.g. animals, or things you can find on a beach.

2 Read the descriptions of types of weather and complete the words.

Example: You need to carry an umbrella for this type of weather. r a i n

1 The trees move a lot in this type of weather. w _ _ _ y
2 In very cold places, you can see this on the top of water in winter. i _ _
3 This is white, and falls from the sky in cold places in winter. s _ _ w
4 People often go to the beach in this type of weather. s _ _ _ y
5 This word means quite hot. w _ _ m
6 You won't see very much sun on this sort of day. c _ _ _ d y

3 Match the words and descriptions below with words from the box.

> **Tip!** In Part 6, there are often words or phrases which have a similar meaning to the word you need for the answer.

umbrella   barbecue   beach   knife   ~~lamp~~   chair   field   fire

Example: *a light* ....lamp......

1 a meal cooked outside over fire ....
2 an open area in the countyside ....
3 something you use for cutting ....
4 something to keep you dry in the rain ....
5 a place near the sea where you might camp ....
6 a seat ....
7 you make this to keep warm ....

Vocabulary Times of day

4 Look at the descriptions below and underline the part in each one which talks about a time of day. Then complete the answers.

Example: *You might do this when you sleep <u>at night</u>.* dream

1   This is a meal you usually eat in the middle of the day.   l _ _ c _
2   Most people do this in the morning, after they get up.   dr _ _ _
3   This is round and you can see it in the sky at night.   m _ _ _
4   You turn this on in your house when it gets dark.   l _ g _ t
5   People usually eat this meal in the evening.   d _ n _ _ _
6   You can see these in the sky at night if there are no clouds.   s _ _ r _

Tip! In Part 6, sometimes there are words in the description that tell you what time of the day you see, do, or use something. This information will help you with the answer.

5 Read this story about Sunita's camping trip. Underline eight more words about things to wear.

Sunita and her family decided to go on a camping trip. It was summer, so the day before they left, Sunita packed her <u>shorts</u> and lots of different T-shirts. She also put a hat in her bag, because she doesn't like the sun on her face. 'It gets cold in the evenings when you're camping,' said her mum, 'you'll need to take some sweaters too.' So Sunita put three jumpers in her bag.

On the first day of the trip, the family went for a walk in the countryside. Sunita wore her trainers. She also wore sunglasses, because it was very sunny. However, the next day it rained. 'I've got nothing to wear,'said Sunita. 'Don't worry,' her mum said, 'I brought your jeans and boots. It always rains when we go camping!'

Vocabulary Silent letters

6 Correct the spelling of the underlined words by adding a silent letter to each one.

Example: *We need to go this way. There's a ~~sin~~ for the campsite*
            .....sign......

1   It starts to get cold in the <u>autum</u>, but I love the   ....
    colours of the trees.
2   <u>Lisen!</u> Can you hear those insects?   ....
3   Did you bring your <u>gitar</u>? We could sing some songs.   ....
4   Who's going to <u>bild</u> the fire tonight? I did it yesterday. ....
5   Is there going to be a <u>gide</u> on our walk tomorrow?   ....
6   My <u>stomac</u> hurts. I think I ate too much last night.   ....
7   Look at my hair! I forgot to bring my <u>com</u>!   ....
8   I'm hungry. Do we have any <u>biscits</u>?   ....
9   Who's got the <u>sissors</u>? I need to cut something.   ....

Tip! English is difficult to spell sometimes because some words have silent letters. These are letters which you see, but don't hear.

Vocabulary Homonyms

7 Look at the words below and find words in the box which rhyme (sound similar) with them.

Tip! Another reason why English words can be difficult to spell is that the same sound can be spelt in different ways.

| foot | shoe | white | they | break | go | bought | ~~eat~~ | free |

Example: meet ....**eat**....

1 take ....
2 snow ....
3 night ....
4 we ....

5 day ....
6 sort ....
7 put ....
8 do ....

8 Now complete the following sentences with some of the words from Exercise 7.

Example: High mountains often have ....**snow**.... at the top.

1 What .... of books do you like reading?
2 When my mum went shopping yesterday she .... me a new jacket.
3 Are you .... tomorrow? Shall we go to the cinema?
4 I don't want .... gloves. Do you have any other colours?
5 I've got one .... on, but I can't find the other one.
6 Do you have a long .... for lunch at school?
7 Where are .... ? Did you tell them where to meet?
8 I hurt my .... yesterday, and it's really hard to walk now.

Vocabulary Jobs

9 Look at the descriptions below and match them to the words in the box.

Tip! Sometimes in Part 6, the answer will be a person's job, and the description will often tell you what they do in their job.

| guide | cleaner | pilot | ~~farmer~~ |
| mechanic | teacher | doctor | |

Example: This person works outside, and may grow vegetables to sell. ....**farmer**....

1 This is the person you go to see if you are ill. ....
2 Students learn a lot from this person. ....
3 This person can repair your car if there is a problem with it. ....
4 Part of this person's job is to wash floors. ....
5 This person's job is to fly aeroplanes. ....
6 If you are on holiday in a city, this person can show you around. ....

Test 2 Exam practice   Reading and Writing • Part 6

Questions 36–40

Read the descriptions of some words about camping.
What is the word for each one?
The first letter is already there. There is one space for each other letter in the word.
For questions **36–40**, write the words on your answer sheet.

Example:

0 You usually sleep in one of these when camping.   s _ _ _ _ _ _ _ _ _ _

Answer: | **0** | sleeping bag |

---

36 If the weather is like this, your tent might fall down!   w _ _ _ _

37 You put wood on this and sit around it to keep warm in the evening.   f _ _ _

38 If it rains, you can wear these to keep your feet dry.   b _ _ _ _

39 You use this light to help you see at night.   l _ _ _

40 Some people like to play this instrument and sing.   g _ _ _ _ _

Advice

*38 The sentence says **these**. Do you need a singular or plural word?*

40 Watch out for the silent letter in this word.

- How many missing words are there in Part 7?
- Are you given words to choose from for your answers in Part 7?

Grammar Connecting words

1   Cross out the wrong words in each sentence.

*Example: I have two brothers **and** / ~~or~~ a sister.*

1   I'm learning to play the piano, *so / but* I'm not very good yet.
2   I really like living here *because / except* it's near the sea. I love the beach!
3   I was ill on Monday, *but / so* I didn't go to school.
4   Mum's taking me to the park later *when / if* it doesn't rain.
5   Shall I phone you, *or / and* would you prefer a text message?
6   I usually walk to school, *as / or* it's not far from my house.

> **Tip!** If the missing word is in the middle of a longer sentence, it may be a connecting word such as **because**, **and** or **but**.

Grammar Prepositions

2   Complete the sentences below using prepositions in Remember!

*Example: In the morning I meet my friend and we walk ......**to**....... school together.*

1   I always meet my friend .... the shop near my house.
2   What about you? Do you live .... a city?
3   Can you tell me .... your family? Do you have brothers and sisters?
4   I'll send you a picture .... my house next time I write.
5   I love art, and my teacher says I'm good .... it.
6   I'll give my phone number .... you, so you can call me.

> **Tip!** If the missing word comes before a noun (or an adjective + noun), a pronoun or an *-ing* word, it might be a preposition such as **about**, **to**, **at**, **of** or **in**.

Grammar Question words

3   Complete the text below with question words from the box. Use each word only once.

> **Tip!** If the missing word is the first word in a question, it might be a question word.

| who | what | why | which | when | where | ~~how~~ |

| From: | Hana |
| To: | Lena |

Hi Lena.

(0) .....**How**...... did your violin exam go on Friday? We always do our music exams at a hall near our school. **(1)** .... did you go for yours? **(2)** .... went with you – your teacher, or your mum? I've just done my level 3 exam in piano. **(3)** .... level did you do on the violin? We usually have to wait about 6 weeks to find out if we passed. **(4)** .... will you know about your exam?

Now that we've sent each other a few emails, maybe we could speak on the phone. **(5)** .... don't I call you this weekend? **(6)** .... time are you usually at home?

From Hana

> **Remember!**
> to find out / read / talk / know **about** something
> to be glad / sad / angry / sure / pleased **about** something
> to send / give **something** to someone
> to go/walk **to** a place
> to live / be **in** a place
> to be interested **in** something
> to take / have a photo **of** someone or something
> to be at the end / start **of** something
> to be / meet someone **at** a place
> to be good **at** something

Questions 41–50

Complete the email to a new friend.
Write ONE word for each space.
For questions **41–50**, write the words on your answer sheet.

Example: | **0** | m y |

From: Sali
To: Bea

Hi Bea,

I'm really pleased you're going to be **(0)** .... new

penfriend. I've never had a penfriend **(41)** .... Africa

before. I want to know all **(42)** .... you when you write to

me! **(43)** .... is your school like? **(44)** .... you got any

brothers or sisters?

I live near the centre of a small seaside town. At home there

(45) .... my parents, my two brothers and me. My school

is not **(46)** .... from my home, so I usually walk there.

I enjoy most of my subjects, **(47)** .... I don't like maths

very **(48)** .... I started learning the drums a year

(49) .... and I've played in the school jazz band

(50) .... the last three months.

Please write soon!

Sali

Advice

43 The missing word is the first word in a question. Which question word do you need?

46 If he usually walks, then the school is near. What is the opposite of **near**?

50 Which word do we use with the present perfect to say how long we've done something?

- How many texts must you read in Part 8?
- How many pieces of information must you write in the notes?

Vocabulary Focus on meaning

1   Read the short texts below. Cross out the wrong answers.

Example: *Let's do the shorter run, as it's our first time.*   **5 km** / ~~10 km~~

1	I think we should do the middle date.	*10th July / 12th July / 14th July*
2	Let's do the more expensive course – it should be better.	*£25 / £40*
3	I have a tennis lesson that afternoon, so we'll take the later train.	*5 p.m. / 5.30.p.m.*
4	We're too young for the adults course, so we'll do the other one.	*12–17s / over 18s*
5	I think the lower level lessons will be right for us.	*Beginners / Advanced*
6	There are two castles – we'll visit the older one.	**BUILT IN 1420 / BUILT IN 1645**

2   Read the texts and answer the questions.
Did you find the answers in Text 1 or Text 2?

 Tip! Some of the answers for Part 8 will come from the first text, and some will come from the second text.

Text 1

GREENFIELD SPORTS CENTRE
New Activities
Climbing:
Wednesdays, 4 p.m. and 6.p.m.
Badminton:
Wednesdays, 5 p.m. and 6 p.m.
£3 per class, £2 for under 18s

Call 077 5345 7867 for more information.

Text 2

From:	Ben
To:	Edwin

Can you call the sports centre and book one of their new classes? My new phone hasn't arrived yet. The classes aren't expensive, especially as we're only 14! Ferdy wants to come too, so there'll be three of us. We're all free on Wednesdays, so let's try climbing – badminton sounds boring! Let's meet in the playground after school. We can go on foot. It's not far, and the bus is slow. I don't think we'll get there by 4 p.m., so we'll go to the later class. By the way, my new number will be 077 4754 2280.

Example: *Name of sports centre*   <u>Greenfield</u>   <u>Text 1</u>

1	Sports centre phone number	....	....
2	Activity they'll do	....	....
3	Time of our class	....	....
4	Number of people	....	....
5	Price they'll pay	....	....
6	Where they'll meet	....	....
7	How they'll get there	....	....

Questions 51–55

Read the advertisement and the email.
Fill in the information in Alex's notes.
For questions **51–55**, write the information on your answer sheet.

Riverside Club
One-day water sports courses
Sailing / Windsurfing
AUGUST 10, 14, 18
£25 PER COURSE OR £40 FOR TWO COURSES
We can lend you sailing shoes, but don't forget a warm jacket!

| From: | Jon |
| To: | Alex |

Mum says I can do a watersports course with you! Let's do the middle date – I'm not free on 10 or 18 August. I want to try sailing; windsurfing sounds hard! There are buses to the club, but it's close enough to go by bike, so let's do that.

Alex's Notes
Water sports course with Jon

Place:	Riverside Club
Date:	**51**
Cost for me:	**52** £
What to take:	**53**
Which water sport:	**54**
How will we travel there:	**55**

Advice

51 There are three possible dates in the advertisement. Which one is in the middle?

53 What do you need to take, and what can you borrow from the club?

55 Jon talks about two ways of travelling. Which does he say they'll use?

● How many pieces of information must you write in Part 9?

1 **Match the words in bold with sentences and questions about a sports centre.**

Example:	ask ...	Would you like to play tennis with me tomorrow?
1	suggest	We need to be at the sports centre by about five.
2	thank ...	I'm sorry I lost your football. I'll buy you another one.
3	invite ...	*Do you know what time the sports centre opens?*
4	say what time ...	Thanks for booking the tennis court.
5	tell ...	I can't come swimming because I have to visit my grandad.
6	explain why ...	The new sports centre opened last weekend.
7	say sorry ...	Why don't we play badminton on Tuesday?

Tip! In Part 9, you may be asked to **invite** someone, or **thank** someone for something. These words will be written in **bold**, and it's important to read them carefully and to follow the instructions correctly.

2 **Read each sentence and decide if the writer is suggesting, inviting, or thanking someone.**

Example: Thank you for inviting me to your party.   thanking.

1 Maybe we could go to the beach tomorrow.   ....

2 Do you want to come to my house later?   ....

3 Shall we see if Lola wants to come with us?   ....

4 It was really nice of you to take me shopping.   ....

5 How about playing football in the park after school?   ....

6 Why don't we go by bus?   ....

Remember!

Making suggestions:
Shall we (go … ?)
How about (going … ?)
Let's (go …)
We could (go …)
Inviting:
Would you like (to go …?)
Do you want (to go …?)
Thanking:
Thanks / Thank you for invit**ing** me.
It was very / really nice / kind of you to (take / give, etc.)

3 **Underline the mistake in each sentence and correct it.**

Example: I can't go on Friday <u>so</u> it's my brother's birthday.   <u>because</u>

1 Rafa asked me call you because his phone isn't working.   ....

2 We need to leave early in the morning while it's a long journey.   ....

3 I'm really sorry than I arrived so late!   ....

4 I'm sorry and I won't be able to come out with you on Sunday.   ....

5 My mum says the concert finishes too late except I can't come.   ....

6 I don't free then because I'm playing in a school football match.   ....

7 I'm afraid but I can't come swimming with you this afternoon. I'm ill.   ....

8 It was really nice of you to invite me if I can't come.   ....

4 Use the correct form of *play*, *go* or *do* to complete the following sentences about sport. Use **Remember!** to help you.

Example: I love ..playing.. table tennis with my sister.

1 Dad's taking me to the lake at the weekend. I can .... fishing!

2 We .... aerobics at school yesterday. It was fun.

3 My brother .... climbing in the mountains every week.

4 I'm learning to .... chess in a club at school.

5 I love horses! I .... riding most weekends.

6 Can you .... badminton? My dad is teaching me.

> **Remember!**
>
> Use **play** to talk about ball sports or games and activities which are a competition.
> Use **go** to talk about activities which end in *-ing*.
> Use **do** to talk about sports or activities which don't use a ball and are not a competition.

Key candidates often make mistakes with *at*, *by* and *on*.

5 Complete the messages with *at*, *by* or *on*.

> **Remember!**
>
> **by** bus / train / bike / taxi,
> **on** foot / the bus / the train / my / bike
> **at** six o'clock, on Tuesday, **by** 10.30

Dear Gemma,
Let's go into town (**0**) *by* bus tomorrow – it's too far to walk. There's a bus (**1**) .... ten past two, so we need to be at the bus stop (**2**) .... two o'clock, or we'll miss it.
Bye,
Sandi

Hi Monica.
The match starts (**3**) .... 3 p.m. this afternoon. We're going (**4**) .... car – Dad's going to drive us. We'll have to park a long way from the stadium, so we'll have to do the last part (**5**) .... foot.
Bye,
Alex

Peter,
Sara told me that you're coming here (**6**) .... the train. I thought you were coming (**7**) .... bus! We want to be (**8**) .... the station when you arrive, so let us know what time your train arrives.
Bye,
Louis

Grammar Irregular verbs

Key candidates often make mistakes with irregular verbs when they write about something they did in the past.

6 Read the sentences below and write the verb in brackets ( ) in the correct form.

> **Tip!** Make sure you learn the irregular verb forms.

Example:

When I was shopping yesterday I (buy) a present for my sister. ..bought..

1 About twenty people (come) to the party last Saturday. ....

2 How much did your new bike (cost)? ....

3 We (fly) to France because the car journey from Poland was too long. ....

4 I (leave) my phone on the bus this morning! Mum's going to be really angry! ....

5 I don't know where I (put) my keys? I can't find them anywhere. ....

6 I've (bring) some money with me so we can buy something to eat. ....

7   Underline nine more spelling mistakes in the message.

Dear Jo,
Thank you for invitting me to your house on Saterday. It's very kind if you. Wuld you like me to bring someting? Maybee some fud or drinks? I dont mind. Culd you send me your adress, please?
Thanks,
Max

0   invitting   *inviting*
1   ....
2   ....
3   ....
4   ....
5   ....
6   ....
7   ....
8   ....
9   ....

8   Read the phrases below and decide if we use each one to start or end a message.

Example: *Dear Ingrid*   *start*

1   Love, Cristina   ....
2   from Bobbi   ....
3   Hi Inka, ...
4   See you soon!   ....
5   Bye for now   ....
6   Best wishes, Pamela   ....
7   Dan xx   ....
8   Hello Aden   ....
9   To Maria   ....

9 Read this Part 9 task and the messages to Sami written by three *Key* candidates, Alfredo, Brad and Christophe. Then answer questions 1–6 below.
Read the email from your English friend, Sami.

Tip! Read the instructions carefully! Remember you must write all three parts of the message to get a good mark.

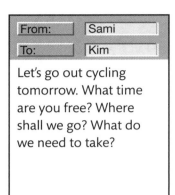

From: Sami
To: Kim

Let's go out cycling tomorrow. What time are you free? Where shall we go? What do we need to take?

From: Alfredo
To: Sami

Hi Sami.
That's a great idea! I'm free all day tomorrow. I think we need to take jackets, because it might be rain, and maybe a drink.

From: Brad
To: Sami

Dear Sami,
That sounds good. Tomorow are you free at 10 a.m.? We need taking our bicicles and a picnick.
Brad

From: Christophe
To: Sami

Hello Sami,
11 o'clock is fine for me. Why don't we cycle on the path near the beach?
We will need some water and maybe a snack.
Christophe.

Which writer (Alfredo, Brad or Christophe):
1 has included all three parts of the message?
2 forgot to put their name at the end?
3 has written fewer than 25 words?
4 should check their spellings and grammar?
5 has not made any grammatical mistakes?
6 might get the best mark?

Test 2 Exam practice Reading and Writing • Part 9

Question 56

Read the email from your English friend, Frankie.

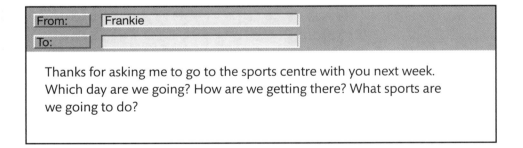

From: Frankie
To:

Thanks for asking me to go to the sports centre with you next week. Which day are we going? How are we getting there? What sports are we going to do?

Advice
which day – *check that you spell the name of the day correctly.*

how – *will you need to use* ***with****, or* ***by*** *to talk about transport?*

what sports – *remember that for some sports we use* ***play****, but for others we use* ***do*** *or* ***go****.*

Write an email to Frankie and answer the questions.
Write **25–35** words.
Write the email on your answer sheet.

- How many questions are there in Part 1?
- How many picture answers must you choose from?

Vocabulary Appearance and clothes

1 🎧 35 **Which of the girls in the picture is Eva's cousin? Listen and decide.**

Tip! In Part 1, you might have to listen to someone describing a person, and choose the right picture.

2 🎧 36 **Which man is the girl's father? Listen and choose the right answer (A, B or C).**

    A   B   C

3 🎧 37 **What is each person going to buy? Listen and choose the right answer (A, B or C).**

Tip! Sometimes the descriptions will include the clothes.

1

   A   B   C

3
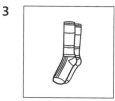   

   A   B   C

2

   A   B   C

4
      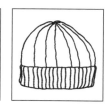

   A   B   C

4 🎧 38 What will Jessica wear for the party? Listen and choose the right answer (A, B or C).

   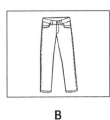   

    A   B   C

5 🎧 39 Look at the picture. Where is each person's book? Listen and put a number in the box next to each book.

1	Alfie's book.	**3**	Harry's book
2	Rania's book.	**4**	Lucy's book

Tip! In Part 1, you often have to answer questions about where something is.

Vocabulary Weather and time

6 🎧 40 What was the weather like for the tennis match? Listen and choose the right answer (A, B or C).

Tip! You often have to answer questions about the weather in Part 1.

    A   B   C

7 Match the clocks below with the times in the box. There are two you don't need.

Tip! Times are often tested in Part 1 too.

> quarter past four   twenty to twelve   five past eight
> nine thirty   ten o'clock   quarter to five

1    **2**    **3**    **4**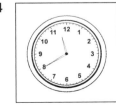

....

Questions 1–5

You will hear five short conversations.
You will hear each conversation twice.
There is one question for each conversation.
For each question, choose the right answer (**A**, **B** or **C**).

Example: What did the teacher forget to bring to school?   *Answer:*

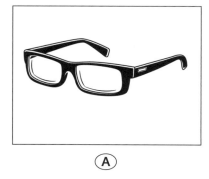

A

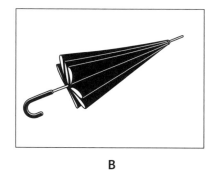

B

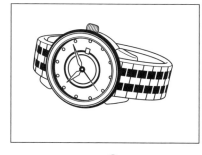

C

1 What did Hanna do on Sunday?

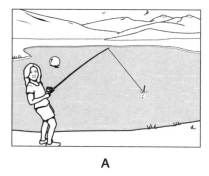

A

B

C

2 What time must John get on the train?

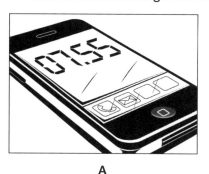

A

B

C

3 Where is the girl's magazine?

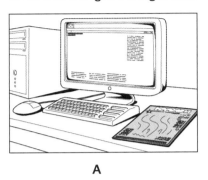

A

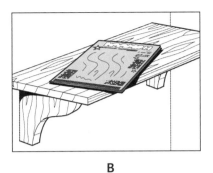

B

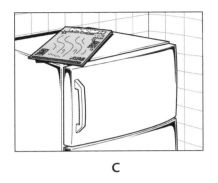

C

4 Which photo is Sam talking about?

A

B

C

5 What was the weather like at the beginning of the concert?

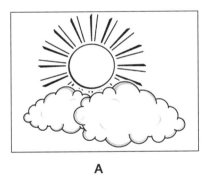

A

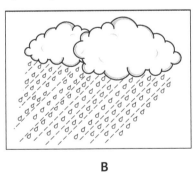

B

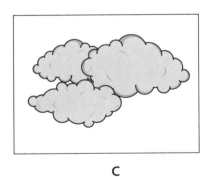

C

Advice

2 John talks about all of these times, but at what time will he **get on** the train?

4 Sam talks about his Dad. What does he say about him?

5 Which word means the same as '**beginning**'?

- Do you have to listen to one long conversation or five short conversations?
- Do you have to write words or match two lists?

Vocabulary Focus on meaning

1 🎧 42 Listen and match each person with what their friend says about them.

Tip! In the second list, the words you hear are often different from the words you read.

Example: Britt ——— brave

1 Ada   clever

2 Nicole   funny

3 Sara   kind

4 Katy   *musical*

5 Serena   quiet

6 Esther   tidy

2 🎧 43 Listen. Why do the people like the activities? Listen and cross out the wrong answer.

Tip! The words you hear and read in the first list will always be the same. You'll hear the first list in the same order as you read it. In the second list, the words may be the same or different from what you hear.

Example: going to school   **~~learning~~ / being with other people**

1   running   being outside / keeping fit
2   travelling   seeing new places / meeting new people
3   winter   skiing / snowboarding
4   the film   the music / the story
5   birthday   the party / the presents

3 🎧 44 You will hear Peter talking to his aunt. Where are each of Peter's family members at the moment? Listen and write a letter A – G next to each person.

Tip! Remember, you can only use each answer once, and you won't need two of the answers.

FAMILY   PLACES

Example: Peter's mother ——— A   library

1   Peter's father   B   airport
2   Peter's brother   C   bank
3   Peter's sister   D   café
4   Peter's grandmother   E   post office
                            F   *sports centre*
                            G   supermarket

🎧 45 **Questions 6–10**

Listen to Maria telling her teacher about why she likes some people in a story.
What reason does Maria give for liking each person?
For questions **6–10**, write a letter **A–H** next to each person.
You will hear the conversation twice.

Example:

0   Miss Stevens | D | *Answer:* | **0** | A B C D E F G H |

PEOPLE

6   Olga   [ ]

7   Trudy   [ ]

8   Mrs Jenson   [ ]

9   Ursula   [ ]

10   Alice   [ ]

REASONS

A   She's brave.

B   She's clever

C   She's funny.

D   She's interesting.

E   She's kind.

F   She's polite.

G   She's pretty.

H   She's quiet.

Advice

A What is another way of saying **she's brave**?

C What does a funny person do?

E What does someone who is kind do?

- How many questions do you have to answer?
- Do you have to write words or circle the answer?

Tip! Sometimes there are questions about school subjects or homework.

Vocabulary School

1 Match the school subjects with the descriptions.

Example: In this subject you might learn about electricity. ⎯⎯⎯⎯⎯⎯

art

1   This subject is popular with people who enjoy drawing and painting.

geography

2   In this subject you learn how to use numbers.

chemistry

3   In this subject you learn about things that happened in the past.

biology

4   You might learn about the different parts of a flower in this subject.

physics

5   In this subject you can learn about different places around the world.

maths

6   In this subject you often mix things together to see what happens.

history

Understanding conversations

Tip! In Part 3, one of the speakers gives all of the information you need to answer the questions.

2 46 **Listen to a girl called Elsa telling a friend about her holiday. Look at the answers. If the answer is right, put a tick (✔). If it is wrong, put a cross (✗).**

Example: Which country did Elsa go to?   *Spain* ✗

1   Which family member missed the trip?   Elsa's brother

2   How long did Elsa stay?   ten days

3   What was the temperature when Elsa was there?   29 degrees

4   What was Elsa's favourite activity?   sightseeing

5   Who can speak Spanish?   Elsa's father

6   What did Elsa bring back from her holiday?   jewellery

Tip! The answers you hear will usually be the same as the words you read, but not always. If you're not sure about an answer, you should still choose one of the options.

Vocabulary Focus on meaning

3 47 **Listen to a conversation in a tourist information office. Cross out the wrong words.**

Example: Where should the girl get the bus from?   ~~*Castle Street*~~ / *River Gardens*

1   How long can you use the bus tickets for?   *12 hours / 24 hours*

2   How much will the girl pay for her ticket?   *£20 / £25*

3   What time does the Castle Museum open at the moment?   *9.30 a.m. / 10 a.m.*

4   When was the cathedral finished?   *13th century / 15th century*

5   When is the tower closed?   *when it is windy / in the winter*

6   What can you buy in the market today?   *food / clothes*

🎧 48 **Questions 11–15**

Listen to Jim talking to his sister about a school trip.
For each question, choose the right answer (**A**, **B** or **C**).
You will hear the conversation twice.

Example:

0 They went on the trip

    A   by train.

    (B)   by coach.

    C   on foot.

Answer:

---

11 The group went on the trip to about learn about

    A   art.

    B   geography.

    C   biology.

12 The castle has been there since the

    A   10th century.

    B   13th century.

    C   17th century.

13 How much did it cost to visit the castle?

    A   £5

    B   £7

    C   £8

14 Where did they have their picnic?

    A   by a river

    B   in the village

    C   on a hill

15 What was the weather like on Jim's trip?

    A   sunny

    B   rainy

    C   foggy

Advice

11 You won't hear the same words as you read here, so listen carefully.

13 Be careful. One of these is the answer to the question **How many…?** (not **How much…?**)

15 What does Jim say they had to use? What does this tell you about the weather?

- Do you listen to one or two people talking in this part?
- How many questions do you have to answer?
- Do you have to write words or tick answers?

Vocabulary Numbers

1 🎧49 Listen to people talking about the prices of different things. If the answer is right, put a tick (✔). If it is wrong, put a cross (✘).

Tip! You often have to answer questions about prices in this part of the test.

Example:	A child's ticket for the show costs:	£5	✘
1	Price of a return ticket on the river trip.	£3.50	☐
2	One drink costs:	75 cents	☐
3	The book costs:	£7.99	☐
4	Tickets for the concert cost:	£12.50 each	☐

Remember! You will probably hear more than one price. Listen carefully and choose the right one.

2 🎧50 Listen and complete the notes.

Example: Student price for ice-skating   ~~£3.30~~

1 Parents need to pay: £ ....
2 Entry to the museum costs: $ ....
3 The watch costs: £ ....

4 The bag costs: $ ....
5 A sweet costs: .... pence
6 Price of a bus ticket: $ ....

3 🎧51 Listen and write the ages.

Example: Sarah started guitar lessons at   ...**8**... years old.

1 The film is for people aged .... or older.
2 To do the course you have to be at least .... years old.
3 The play is for children from .... to 8 years old.
4 The bicycle is for children under .... years old.
5 Entry is free for children under .... years old.

Tip! You sometimes have to write someone's age on the form.

Tip! Write numbers such as ages in numbers, not in words.

4 🎧52 Read the form, and think about what kind of information you will have to write in each space. Write your guesses in column A. Then listen and complete the information in column B.

Tip! Look carefully at the form before you listen. Try to predict what kind of information you will need to write for each question.

Trip to farm	A	B	
Example: Date of trip:	a date, with the month	March 25th	
1 Name of farm:	....	.... farm	
2 How we'll travel:	....	....	
3 Time we'll leave school:	....	.... p.m.	
4 What to take:	....	....	
5 Entry price for students:	....	£	

🎧 53 **Questions 16–20**

You will hear a boy asking for information about a zoo.
Listen and complete questions **16–20**.
You will hear the conversation twice.

Trip to Zoo

Name of zoo: Garden Zoo

Price of child's ticket: **(16)** £ ....

Saturday opening time: **(17)** .... a.m.

Subject of talk: **(18)** ....

Place of talk: **(19)** .... Centre

Photography exhibition: **(20)** Animals in the ....

Advice

16 You will hear more than one price. Which is the correct one for a child?

18 Think before you listen. At the zoo, what could the subject of a talk be?

19 This is a word you have to spell. Listen carefully, and don't forget the capital letter at the beginning.

- What is the only difference between Listening Part 4 and Part 5?

Vocabulary Numbers

1 🎧 **54** Are these numbers correct? Listen. If the answer is right, put a tick (✔). If it is wrong, put a cross (✗).

Example: *Channel to watch:*   *2*   ✗

1	Number of people on the trip:	10	☐
2	House number:	16	☐
3	Sports centre phone number:	0163 296 0683	☐
4	Page to read:	68	☐
5	Number of pages to write:	4	☐

> **Tip!** You often have to write numbers in this part of the test.

2 🎧 **55** Listen and write the numbers.

Example: *Flat number:* ....**15**.........

1 Number of teams in the competition: ....
2 Number of football game for sale: ....
3 Length of running race: .... metres.
4 How many can travel on school bus: ....
5 Callie's phone number: ....
6 Screen number for our film: ....

> **Tip!** You sometimes have to write longer numbers such as telephone numbers. In telephone numbers we say each number.

> **Remember!**
> You will hear more than one number. Listen carefully and choose the correct number to write down.

3 Correct the mistakes.

Example: **mats** ...maths...

1	histry	....	4	kemistry	....
2	sience	....	5	fysics	....
3	biology	....	6	giografy	....

> **Tip!** You will sometimes need to write the names of school subjects in this part of the text. Make sure you can spell them.

4 🎧 **56** Listen and write the words for each category.

Sports
1 ....   2 ....   3 ....

Hobbies
1 ....   2 ....   3 ....

Ways to travel
1 ....   2 ....   3 ....

Places in a town
1 ....   2 ....   3 ....

Animals
1 ....   2 ....   3 ....

Possessions
1 ....   2 ....   3 ....

> **Tip!** You might have to write the names of sports, hobbies, places in a town, possessions, ways to travel or animals.

 **Questions 21–25**

You will hear a teacher talking to her students about a television programme.
Listen and complete questions **21–25**.
You will hear the information twice.

New TV programme

Day programme will be on: Wednesday

Name of programme: **(21)** Exploring ....

Channel: **(22)** ....

Time programme begins: **(23)** .... p.m.

First programme

Date: **(24)** ....

About: **(25)** ....

Advice

22 *TV channels usually have numbers.*

23 *What is another word for* **begins***?*

24 *Remember to write the name of the month with a capital letter at the beginning.*

- How many students will be in the room when you do your Speaking test? How many examiners will there be?
- Who do you have to speak to in Part 1?

1   **Match the questions and answers. Which answer isn't used?**

1	How do you spell your surname?	a	Yes, I am. I go to school.
2	Where do you come from?	b	He's called George. He's fun!
3	Are you a student?	c	Rome. It's the capital of Italy.
4	What is your favourite subject at school?	d	It's K-R-A-U-Z-E-R.
5	Tell me about your best friend.	e	I haven't got any brothers or sisters.
		f	Geography. I like English too.

Tip! Make sure you know how to spell your surname in English.

2   🎧 **58** **Listen to students spelling their surnames. Choose the correct answer (a or b) for each student.**

Student 1:   a   Noaliz   b   Morales   **Student 3:**   a   Hayashida   b   Heyeshita

Student 2:   a   Jacobsson   b   Yakovson   **Student 4:**   a   Cheung   b   Cheong

3   🎧 **59** **Read the questions and listen to Adil's answers. If the information is right, put a tick (✔). If it is wrong put a (✘).**

1	What's your surname?	Yilmaz	☐
2	Where do you come from?	Istanbul	☐
3	Do you study English at school?	Yes	☐
4	What's your favourite subject at school?	Science	☐
5	How many English classes do you have each week?	2	☐

Tip! Get ready for your Speaking test. Practise talking about yourself. Don't worry if the other student knows more English than you do.

4   **Now ask and answer the questions with a partner.**

5   🎧 **60** **Listen to a student and an examiner. How many questions does student ask the examiner to repeat?**

Tip! If you don't understand what the examiner says, ask him/her to repeat the question.

6   **Listen again and tick (✔) the phrases the student uses.**

Can you say that again, please? ☐

Could you repeat that? ☐

Sorry? ☐

What? ☐

I'm sorry, what did you say? ☐

I don't understand. ☐

Sorry, I didn't hear what you said. ☐

Which words or phrases didn't you hear? Which of them is not a polite way to ask someone to repeat something?

7 🎧 61 Listen to the examiner talking to another student.
Read the sentences and correct the mistakes. Write the correct information.

1 Evgeni's surname is Petrovsky.   ....
2 He's from the west of Russia.   ....
3 He goes to school in England.   ....
4 His favourite subjects are maths and science.   ....
5 He has three English classes at school.   ....
6 He has a small family.   ....
7 His sister is studying at school.   ....
8 She likes sport.   ....

> **Remember!**
> At the end of Part 1, the examiner will ask you a question which begins *Tell me about* ... . He/She might ask you about your hobbies, everyday life or friends and family.

8 Read the *Tell me about* ... questions. Practise asking and answering them with a friend.

> Tell me about where you live.

> Tell me about a teacher you like.

> Tell me about what you did last weekend.

> Tell me about what your favourite food.

> Tell me about your best friend at school.

> Tell me about your hobbies.

Test 2 Exam practice   Speaking • Part 1

🎧 62 Listen to the examiner and answer the questions.

- Who do you ask and answer questions with in Part 2?
- How many questions and answers do you ask and give?

Asking and answering questions

1 Read the questions and answers about a school party. Complete the conversation with words from the box.

> food   Where   on   How   per   What   for
> evening   time   in   eat   ~~When~~

A: ....When.... is the school party?
B: It's **(1)** .... 12th August.
A: **(2)** .... is the party?
B: It's **(3)** .... Grey Rock Park.
A: Do I need to take anything to **(4)** .... or drink?
B: There is **(5)** .... but you should bring something to drink.
A: What **(6)** .... does the party start?
B: It starts at six o'clock in the **(7)** .... and finishes at 10 p.m.
A: **(8)** .... much does it cost?
B: It's £3.50 **(9)** .... person.

2 Look at the information about a play. Complete the questions.

Student play:	Danny and Black Socks
Monday 3rd May	1 When ....?
starts at 7 p.m.	2 What ....?
Canton Theatre	3 Where ....?
Tickets £4 for students	4 How ....?
a boy and his horse	5 What .... about?

> **Tip!** Make your answers short and clear. Don't add any new information.

3 Now answer the questions in Exercise 2.

1 It's on ....
2 It starts ....
3 It's ....
4 They are ....
5 It's ....

4 Use the prompts to make questions about the quiz nights.

> **Quiz nights!**
> where / quiz night?   1 Where are the quiz nights?
> what day?   2 ....
> time / start?   3 ....
> prize?   4 ....
> need / book place?   5 ....

5 🎧 63 Listen to two students asking and answering the questions about a skiing competition. Do they ask and answer the questions in the correct order?

Skiing competition

on Snowy Mountain

Saturday 5th December

Races for all ages

WIN A PAIR OF SKI BOOTS

10 a.m.– 3 p.m.

Skiing competition

♦ what time / start ?

♦ prizes ?

♦ who / enter ?

♦ where ?

♦ date / competition ?

Remember!

You must ask all five questions. Don't worry if you forget to ask one. You can ask it at the end and you won't lose marks. Try to say thank you to your partner for the information they give you. You could add words like Great! and Oh! as well.

6 Listen again. What does the girl say when she forgets a question?

Test 2 Exam practice Speaking • Part 2

Listen and follow your teacher's instructions.

Candidate B Go to page 223

CANDIDATE A – your answers

CANDIDATE A – your questions

School camping trip for ages 11–16

18-20 May
at Green Leaves Forest
Coach leaves 9 a.m.
School tents for everyone
Bring warm clothes!
Only £30
Interested? See Mr Smith

School barbecue

♦ barbecue start?
♦ where / get tickets?
♦ what / eat?
♦ play games?
♦ invite other people?

🎧 64 Listen to a model conversation for the School camping trip task.

🎧 65 Listen to a model conversation for the School barbecue task.

Questions 1–5

Which notice **(A–H)** says this **(1–5)**?
For questions **1–5**, mark the correct letter **A–H** on your answer sheet.

Example:

0   You have to buy lunch to sit here.

Answer:

0	A	B	C	D	E	F	G	H
	▢	▢	▢	▢	▢	▢	▢	▬

---

1   Don't throw this away, as it may save you money.

2   You can go and watch this in the afternoon.

3   There are several different places where you can buy food.

4   You will not be able to visit this building today.

5   You can sit here and eat your own sandwiches.

A
> **These tables are for people with picnics**

B

> **Keep this ticket and get £10 off your next visit!**

C

> **Welcome to Funland!**
> Rides, cafes, restaurants snack-bars and zoo!

D

> **JUNGLE CAFÉ** →
> Stand this side to buy hot food

E
> **TIPTON ZOO**
> Monkey house closed all week

F
> ADVENTURE LAND
> SPECIAL PRICE FOR GROUPS OF TEN
> OR MORE £15 PER PERSON

G
> *Green Park*
> Outdoor show, 2 p.m. daily
> Tickets £5.00

H
> **Tables for people buying drinks only are in the garden.**

Questions 6–10

Read the sentences about a boy who goes to see his grandmother.
Choose the best word (**A**, **B** or **C**) for each space.
For questions **6–10**, mark **A**, **B** or **C** on your answer sheet.

Example:

0   Tom doesn't see his grandmother ....

   A sometimes   **B** often   **C** rarely

Answer: | 0 | A B C |

---

6   Tom lives in London, but his grandmother lives a .... way from there.

   A large   **B** wide   **C** long

7   Tom's father drove him to his grandmother's house and it .... four hours to get there.

   A got   **B** took   **C** went

8   Tom's grandmother cooked an evening .... for them.

   A food   **B** course   **C** meal

9   Tom's father .... him with his grandmother and drove back to London.

   A gave   **B** left   **C** sent

10   Tom loves .... sailing with his grandmother on the lake behind her house.

   A going   **B** making   **C** having

Questions 11–15

Complete the five conversations.
For questions **11–15**, mark **A**, **B** or **C** on your answer sheet.

Example:

0

Do you want something to drink?

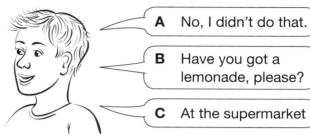

A   No, I didn't do that.

B   Have you got a lemonade, please?

C   At the supermarket

Answer:

---

11   Shall I buy this CD for Jane's birthday?

    A   That's a good idea.

    B   It doesn't look like it.

    C   That's all right.

12   I'm very hungry.

    A   You can do it.

    B   Let's have a snack.

    C   Do you really?

13   Do you mind if I use your phone?

    A   It doesn't matter.

    B   No, that's fine.

    C   I hope not.

14   I need some help with my class project.

    A   Would you like to help me?

    B   Do you have to?

    C   What's the problem?

15   What time should we go shopping?

    A   How about after lunch?

    B   I'll be ready then.

    C   Try not to be late.

Questions 16–20

Complete the conversation between friends.
What does Kate say to Tony?
For questions **16–20**, mark the correct letter **A–H** on your answer sheet.

Example:

Tony: Hi, Kate. Where are you going?

Kate: **0** ....**G**.........

Answer:

Tony: Are you meeting anyone there?

Kate: **16** ....

Tony: Yes, they live near me. There good friends of mine.

Kate: **17** ....

Tony: That's a great idea. But I'll have to go home and get some money first.

Kate: **18** ....

Tony: Thanks, Kate. Are you sure? Have you got enough?

Kate: **19** ....

Tony: Brilliant! And look – here comes our bus!

Kate: **20** ....

Tony: You're right. We mustn't get on that one.

A   Well, I brought £10.00 with me today

B   Really? Well, why don't you come with me to meet them?

C   It'll take about half an hour.

D   Stephen and Matt Brown. Do you know them?

E   Try not to spend all of it.

F   You don't need to. I can lend you some.

G   I'm on my way to the park.

H   No, that's the 445 to the hospital.

Questions 21–27

Read the article in which three teenagers talk about their love of photography.
For questions **21–27**, mark **A**, **B** or **C** on your answer sheet.

Young photographers

A Farah

My love of taking photos started when a friend showed me some fantastic pictures on a photo-sharing website. Now I take photos all the time, especially of my friends. I take pictures of them in different clothes, shoes, and hats. That's the type of photography I'd like to do as a job. These days we all have great cameras on our phones, so getting work taking pictures is much easier than it was years ago.

B Dora

I love photography, and people say I'm good. I came first in a competition for young photographers – I got some money and a fantastic new camera! But for me, taking photos is only for fun – they aren't for sale! All my friends take photos and put them online. People our age have a different way of looking at things, and you can see that from our photos – they're different from the ones adults take.

C Isabel

Last year I joined the photography club at school. I want to be a photographer when I'm older. At the moment I print my pictures and only show them to people in the club. In the future I might start a website and put them on that. There are lots of photographers that I like, but the best is Michelle Rainer. She's fantastic! I asked my parents to buy me the type of camera she has, and they did!

Example:

0 Who has won a prize with one of her photographs?

    A Farah   **B** Dora   **C** Isabel   *Answer:*   0   A B C

---

21 Who chose the same camera as her favourite photographer?

    A Farah   **B** Dora   **C** Isabel

22 Who thinks that it was more difficult to become a photographer in the past?

    A Farah   **B** Dora   **C** Isabel

23 Who thinks teenagers take more unusual pictures than older photographers?

    A Farah   **B** Dora   **C** Isabel

24 Who wants to be a fashion photographer when she's older?

    A Farah   **B** Dora   **C** Isabel

25 Who became interested in photography after seeing photos online?

    A Farah   **B** Dora   **C** Isabel

26 Who does not put her photographs online?

    A Farah   **B** Dora   **C** Isabel

27 Who is not interested in earning money from her photographs?

    A Farah   **B** Dora   **C** Isabel

Questions 28–35

Read the article about telling the time.
Choose the best word (**A**, **B** or **C**) for each space.
For questions **28–35**, mark **A**, **B** or **C** on your answer sheet.

Using the sun to tell the time

Today when people want to know the time they usually look at **(0)** .... watch. But what did people do **(28)** .... they had watches or mobile phones?

The first way **(29)** .... people could tell the time was by **(30)** ....at the sun. When it was directly **(31)** .... their heads, it meant it was midday. When it was very low in the sky, it was early morning or early evening.

(32) .... have been many different types of clock over the years. One early clock is called a sundial. These were first used about 5,500 years **(33)** .... The problem with sundials is that you can only use them **(34)** .... the day. It also **(35)** .... to be a sunny day, of course.

Example:

0	**A** the	**B** their	**C** there	*Answer:* 

---

28 **A** when   **B** if   **C** before

29 **A** how   **B** that   **C** where

30 **A** look   **B** looked   **C** looking

31 **A** on   **B** above   **C** through

32 **A** There   **B** It   **C** These

33 **A** after   **B** already   **C** ago

34 **A** across   **B** during   **C** among

35 **A** has   **B** must   **C** can

Questions 36–40

Read the descriptions of some things you can get as a birthday present.
What is the word for each one?
The first letter is already there. There is one space for each other letter in the word.
For questions **36–40**, write the words on your answer sheet.

Example:

0   You can listen to music with this present.   M _ _ _ _ _ _ _

Answer:	**0**	MP3 player

---

36   You can take photographs with this present.   c _ _ _ _ _

37   You put this on your wall and it may be a picture of a sports star.   p _ _ _ _ _

38   If you get this as a present, you may want to ride it around the park.   b _ _ _

39   If you are given this, you can choose what to buy.   m _ _ _ _

40   This is very sweet and you shouldn't eat too much of it.   c _ _ _ _ _ _ _ _

Questions 41–50

Complete the email.
Write ONE word for each space.
For questions **41–50**, write the words on your answer sheet.

Example:

0	*to*

From: Ben
To: Ivan

Hi Ivan,

I'm writing **(0)** .... say we have moved house! We now

(41) .... in a flat in the city. It's better **(42)** .... our

village house. It's got a **(43)** .... of rooms. We're near a

sports centre **(44)** .... a cinema.

I miss my friends from the village, but I'm glad we moved

because I love city life. Now, I don't have **(45)** .... get a

bus to school. I walk there **(46)** ....day with a new friend

who **(47)** .... called Kwame.

Write to **(48)** .... very soon! I **(49)** .... love to hear

your news.

This is **(50)** .... new address:

15b, Newfield House,

Mandleside

Ben

Questions 51–55

Read the advertisement and the note.
Complete the information in Helen's notes.
For questions **51–55**, write the information on your answer sheet.

Quiz Evenings

Manor School
6–8 people per team
Age 10–12: 24 November
Age 13–15: 31 November
7 p.m. – 10 p.m.
Tickets: £3 per person
Drinks and snacks from 50p
Prizes:
1st: Cinema tickets
2nd: T-shirts

Hi Helen

Thanks for joining our quiz team – there will be seven of us now. We're all over 13 years old, so we'll go on 31st November instead of the 24th. Bring £5.00 to pay for your ticket and some food!

See you,
Sue

Helen's Notes

Quiz Evening

Place:	Manor School
Date I will go:	51
Number of people in my team:	52
Cost to do quiz:	53 £
Time quiz finishes:	54 p.m.
Prize for best team:	55

Question 56

Your friend did not come to your English class yesterday. He wants to know about the homework.
Write a note to your friend.
Say:

- **what** you did in class

- **what** you have to do for homework

- **when** you have to give the homework to the teacher.

Write **25–35** words.
Write the note on your answer sheet.

Questions 1–5

You will hear five short conversations.
You will hear each conversation twice.
There is one question for each conversation.
For each question, choose the right answer (**A**, **B** or **C**).

Example: How much is a large cup of hot chocolate?

Answer:

A

B

C

---

1 Where was the grey bird that Adam saw?

A

B

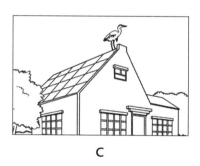

C

2 What are cheaper than usual at the moment?

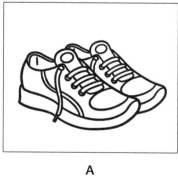

A

B

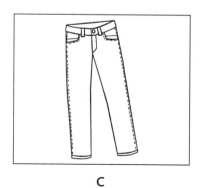

C

3 How will Francine let her friend know about the guitar?

A

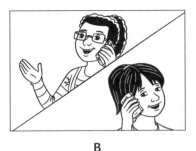

B

C

4 What did Andreas watch on TV last night?

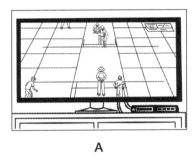

A

B

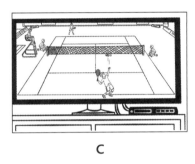

C

5 Where is the girl's phone?

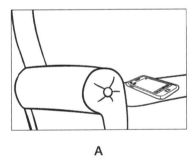

A

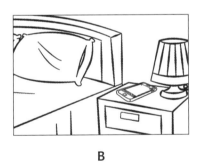

B

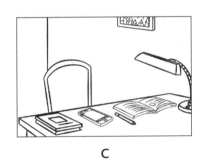

C

🎧 67 **Questions 6–10**

Listen to Julia talking to her friend about the school holidays.
What did she do on each day?
For questions **6–10**, write a letter **A–H** next to each day.
You will hear the conversation twice.

Example:

0 Sunday [G]

Answer:

0	A	B	C	D	E	F	G	H
	▭	▭	▭	▭	▭	▭	▬	▭

DAYS		ACTIVITIES	
6	Monday [ ]	A	climbing
7	Tuesday [ ]	B	cycling
8	Wednesday [ ]	C	went to a museum
9	Thursday [ ]	D	painting
10	Friday [ ]	E	swimming
		F	studying
		G	went to a café
		H	watched a film

🎧 68 **Questions 11–15**

Listen to Katerina talking to her friend, Seth, about an art club.
For questions **11–15**, choose the right answer (**A**, **B** or **C**).
You will hear the conversation twice.

Example:

0 How long has Katerina been going to the art club?

   A a year

   B nine months

   C two months

   Answer: | **0** | **A** **B** **C** |

---

11 What will Katerina do at the art club this term?

   A photography

   B painting

   C drawing

12 Where is the art club?

   A in a college

   B in a library

   C in a school

13 What time does the art club start?

   A 09:30

   B 10.00

   C 10.15

14 What will Seth need to take?

   A some money

   B some paper

   C a book

15 Where will Katerina and Seth meet?

   A near the shop

   B at Seth's house

   C at the end of Seth's road

🎧69 **Questions 16–20**

You will hear a phone conversation about a school project.
Listen and complete questions **16–20**.
You will hear the conversation twice.

School project

School subject: geography

Which teacher: **(16)** Mr ....

What Ryan should write about: **(17)** the ....

How much to write: **(18)** .... pages

Where to find information: **(19)** ....

When to give it to the teacher: **(20)** on ....

🎧 70 **Questions 21–25**

You will hear a man talking about a radio competition.
Listen and complete each question.
You will hear the information twice.

Radio competition

Name of radio station: Real Radio

Send in a photo of your: **(21)** ....

How many prizes there will be: **(22)** ....

First prize: **(23)** a .... with the radio station's name

To enter you must be no more than: **(24)** .... years old

Send your answer by: **(25)** .... March

You now have 8 minutes to write your answers on the answer sheet.

Questions 1–5

Which notice (**A–H**) says this (**1–5**)?
For questions **1–5**, mark the correct answer **A–H** on your answer sheet.

Example:

0   You can't leave early by this gate.

Answer:

0	A	B	C	D	E	F	G	H
	▢	▢	▢	▢	▢	▬	▢	▢

1   You can buy things more cheaply here if you let staff see this.

2   Go here for more information about a competition.

3   If you go out, it's not possible to come back.

4   You have to show what you are carrying with you.

5   There are some of these left for people to buy.

A

STADIUM ENTRANCE
Please have bags ready
for staff to check

B

**PLEASE DO NOT STAND
DURING THE MATCH**

C

Photography competition
for teenagers
First prize – sportsbag!

D

**Stadium Ticket Office 100
seats still available for
tonight's game**

E

WIN TICKETS TO NEXT WEEK'S GAME.
FULL DETAILS AT STADIUM SHOP!

F

**EXIT CLOSED UNTIL
THE END OF THE
MATCH**

G

Stadium GiftShop

*Show your ticket to get a
10% discount*

H

EXIT GATE
You cannot return after leaving
the stadium

Questions 6–10

Read the sentences about a girl who likes art.
Choose the best word **(A, B** or **C)** for each space.
For questions **6–10**, mark **A, B** or **C** on your answer sheet.

Example:

0　Grace .... how to paint when she was very young.

　　A　learned　　　**B**　began　　　**C**　taught

Answer:

6　Grace .... a lot of time on the internet looking for ideas for her art.

　　A　makes　　　**B**　spends　　　**C**　keeps

7　Grace's bedroom is .... of her pictures.

　　A　crowded　　　**B**　busy　　　**C**　full

8　Grace often .... her art with friends online.

　　A　joins　　　**B**　shares　　　**C**　offers

9　Last month, Grace .... an art competition and did very well.

　　A　went　　　**B**　showed　　　**C**　entered

10　Grace .... to study art at college when she leaves school.

　　A　hopes　　　**B**　believes　　　**C**　understand

Questions 11–15

Complete the five conversations.
For questions **11–15**, mark **A, B** or **C** on your answer sheet.

Example:

0

Did you borrow
my dictionary?

A Yes, I'll bring it back tomorrow.

B No, not yet.

C No, is that all right?

Answer:

---

11 Don't forget we're going to Sam's
barbecue on Sunday.

A How about Wednesday then?

B What time does it start?

C Would you like some?

12 Did Sara lend you her books?

A Actually, I didn't need them.

B They're fine, thanks very much.

C No, she mustn't go there today.

13 I've just downloaded a really great film.

A Which one?

B Let's go later.

C Why not?

14 Can you help me with the history homework?

A I can't remember who it is.

B I didn't know we had any.

C I'm not sure you can.

15 My mum says she'll take us to the
new water park tomorrow.

A When was that?

B I've finished it already.

C That sounds fun!

Questions 16–20

Complete the conversation between two friends.
What does Billy say to Zac?
For questions **16–20**, mark the correct letter **A–H** on your answer sheet.

Example:

Zac: Hello Billy. Let's go to the cinema this weekend.

Billy: **0** ....**F**........

Answer: | **0** | A | B | C | D | E | F | G | H |

Zac: That new film about football.
        Have you heard about it?

Billy: **16** ....

Zac: That's right. Everyone says it's brilliant.

Billy: **17** ....

Zac: Sure. No problem. I'm free all day.

Billy: **18** ....

Zac: You don't need to. My dad says he'll pay.

Billy: **19** ....

Zac: We'll need to check the film times online.

Billy: **20** ....

Zac: Thanks Billy, but can you text me?
        I'm at band practice this evening.

A   I think the tickets are £10.

B   I think so. Is it the Brazilian one?

C   That's really kind! I'll just bring enough for
       sweets, then.

D   I don't mind doing that. I'll call you later.

E   What about going on Saturday?

F   Good idea. What do you want to see?

G   I'm busy then. Can we go later?

H   Great! I'll ask Mum for money for the tickets.

Questions 21–27

Read the article about a thirteen-year-old girl who tried an activity called wing-walking.
Are sentences **21–27** 'Right' **(A)** or 'Wrong' **(B)**?
If there is not enough information to answer 'Right' **(A)** or 'Wrong' **(B)**, choose 'Doesn't say' **(C)**.
For questions **21–27**, mark **A**, **B** or **C** on your answer sheet.

A young wing-walker

Wing-walking is an activity that's exciting to watch, but it's not one that most people will ever try. To do it you stand on the wing of a plane while it is flying. Thirteen-year-old Olivia Brook first saw someone wing-walking when she was five years old. The pilot of that plane was her uncle, Henry. Henry flies planes in shows all over the world, and has a team of wing-walkers who work with him.

Olivia has wanted to try wing-walking since she was eight years old, but Henry always said no. Finally, last month, he agreed, but only after asking her parents if it was OK first. On the day of the flight, they had to wait for a few hours for good weather. Then Henry checked the plane carefully before they took off.

Olivia spent about 20 minutes in the air. Afterwards, she said, 'It was fun, but very cold! I couldn't get warm again for hours. I know I'm not the youngest person ever to do wing-walking, but that's okay. There was a story about me in the local newspaper, and a picture of me, and everyone at school tells me I'm famous. That's enough for me!'

Example:

Olivia likes watching wing-walkers.

   A Right   **B** Wrong   **C** Doesn't say   *Answer:*

---

21 Olivia's uncle Henry travels to different countries because of his job.

   A Right   **B** Wrong   **C** Doesn't say

22 When Olivia was eight, Henry said she should try wing-walking.

   A Right   **B** Wrong   **C** Doesn't say

23 The weather was perfect all day when Olivia went wing-walking.

   A Right   **B** Wrong   **C** Doesn't say

24 Henry made sure everything on the plane was working well before the flight.

   A Right   **B** Wrong   **C** Doesn't say

25 Olivia was a little afraid before she started the wing-walk.

   A Right   **B** Wrong   **C** Doesn't say

26 Olivia felt cold for along time after her wing-walk.

   A Right   **B** Wrong   **C** Doesn't say

27 A journalist wrote about Olivia and took her photograph.

   A Right   **B** Wrong   **C** Doesn't say

Questions 28–35

Read the article about the River Thames in London.
Choose the best word **(A, B or C)** for each space.
For questions **28–35**, mark **A**, **B** or **C** on your answer sheet.

Cleaning the Thames

Fifty years **(0)** .... , London's River Thames was very dirty.

In fact, it was one of the **(28)** .... rivers in the whole of

Britain. At that time, all the dirty water from the city's houses

and factories **(29)** .... into the Thames. Nothing could live

in it, so scientists described it as 'dead'.

Then, things began to improve. There were new instructions **(30)** .... said that businesses should

not put **(31)** .... dirty water into the river, and water from houses had to be cleaned before it was

returned to the river. It took **(32)** .... long time for things to get better, but now 125 types of fish,

as well as **(33)** .... birds, and larger animals **(34)** .... as dolphins, live in the Thames.

(35) .... can call the river dead now.

Example:

0   **A** past   **B** ago   **C** before   *Answer:*   0   A   B   C

---

28 **A** bad   **B** worse   **C** worst

29 **A** going   **B** went   **C** been

30 **A** which   **B** where   **C** who

31 **A** its   **B** their   **C** his

32 **A** the   **B** this   **C** a

33 **A** lots   **B** much   **C** many

34 **A** both   **B** such   **C** each

35 **A** Nobody   **B** Anybody   **C** Everybody

Questions 36–40

Read the descriptions of some things you can find in a hotel.
What is the word for each one?
The first letter is already shown. There is one space for each other letter in the word.
For questions **36–40**, write the words on your answer sheet.

Example:

0   This is the place where you have your meals.   r _ _ _ _ _ _ _ _ _

Answer: | **0** | restaurant |

36   Hotels often have one of these for guests to swim in.   p _ _ _

37   This light is near your bed and will help you read at night.   l _ _ _

38   You can look at yourself in this when you do your hair.   m _ _ _ _ _

39   This machine takes you to the different floors of the hotel.   l _ _ _

40   You can sit at this and use your computer.   d _ _ _

Questions 41–50

Complete the emails.
Write ONE word for each space.
For questions **41–50**, write the words on your answer sheet.

Example:

0	*on*

From:	Penny
To:	Melanie

You're going to Raquel's party **(0)** .... Saturday, aren't you?

(41) .... you know what you're going to wear? I **(42)** .... got

a problem because all my clothes are too small for me **(43)** .... the

moment! **(44)** .... I borrow one of your dresses? I think we're

(45) .... same size. I'll be very careful and I'll look after it!

from
Penny

From:	Melanie
To:	Penny

(46) .... course I'll lend you something to wear! **(47)** .... don't you

come here on Saturday afternoon, and I'll help you choose a dress? Then

(48) .... can go to the party together. It'll **(49)** .... fun! I'll ask Mum to

drive us there. I'm sure **(50)** .... won't mind.

from
Melanie

Questions 51–55

Read the advertisement and the email.
Complete the information in Lily's notes.
For questions **51–55**, write the information on your answer sheet.

POP CONCERTS AT THE WINDMILL

The Paintings
Friday 2 June / Saturday 3 June

Red Fox
Friday 9 June / Saturday 10 June
Doors open 6 p.m.
Concert starts at 7 p.m.

Tickets £10 from our website
£15 on the door
www.windmill.com

From:	Anna
To:	Lily

I'm really excited about the concert at the Windmill. Dad went on line last night and got three tickets – two for us and one for him. He wanted to see The Paintings but I told him we like Red Fox, so we chose that. He can only do Saturday – he's busy on Friday.

Lily's notes

Concert with Ana

Place: The Windmill

Name of band: **51** _____

Date: **52** _____

Time music begins: **53** _____ p.m.

Number of tickets needed: **54** _____

Price per person: **55** £ _____

Question 56

Read the email from your English friend, Kathryn.

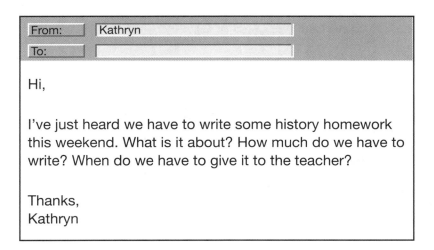

From: Kathryn

To:

Hi,

I've just heard we have to write some history homework this weekend. What is it about? How much do we have to write? When do we have to give it to the teacher?

Thanks,
Kathryn

Write an email to Kathryn and answer the questions.
Write **25–35** words.
Write the email on your answer sheet.

Questions 1–5

You will hear five short conversations.
You will hear each conversation twice.
There is one question for each conversation.
For each question, choose the correct answer (**A**, **B** or **C**).

Example: Which is the girl's first lesson this morning?

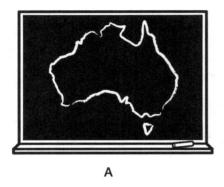

A

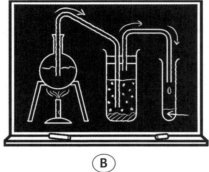

B

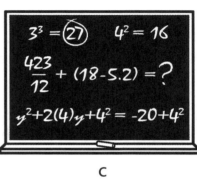

C

1   What will Billy clean first?

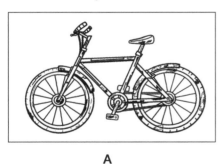

A

B

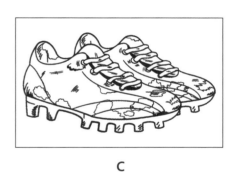

C

2   What was the weather like on the school trip to the sea?

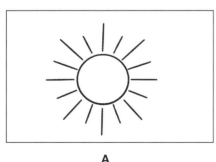

A

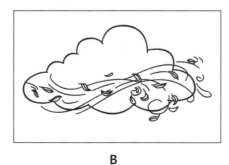

B

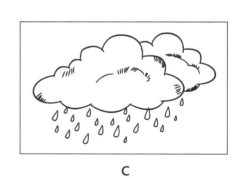

C

3 Where did Georgia go on Saturday afternoon?

A

B

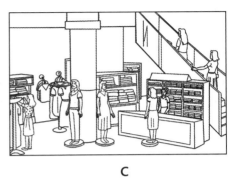

C

4 What time does the school's computer club end?

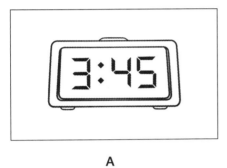

A

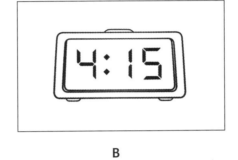

B

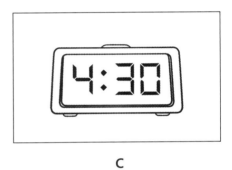

C

5 How will the girl get home?

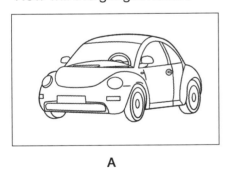

A

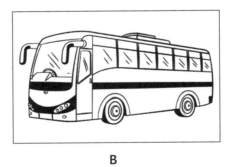

B

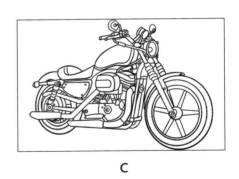

C

🎧 72 **Questions 6–10**

You will hear Diana telling her mother about what her friends are doing today.
What is each friend doing?
For questions **6–10**, write a letter **A–H** next to each person.
You will hear the conversation twice.

Example:

0   Fiona | E | *Answer:* | **0** | **A** **B** **C** **D** **E** **F** **G** **H** |

| **FRIENDS** | | **ACTIVITIES** |

6   David | |

7   Ella | |

8   Thomas | |

9   Vicky | |

10 Simon | |

A   cooking

B   doing homework

C   playing a game

D   doing sport

E   travelling

F   repairing something

G   visiting family

H   watching a match

73 **Questions 11–15**

Listen to Tom telling his friend Andy about a pop concert.
For each question, choose the right answer (**A**, **B** or **C**).
You will hear the conversation twice.

Example:

0   Tom's mum found tickets for

    A   Black Fox.

    B   Moonstar.

    C   Crowd 5.

Answer:

11   Tom's family found out about the concert by

    A   reading a poster.

    B   looking at a website.

    C   listening to the radio.

12   What's the date of the concert?

    A   19 June

    B   23 June

    C   25 June

13   Tom's tickets are for seats at the

    A   back.

    B   front.

    C   side.

14   What does Tom say is good to buy at the concert?

    A   CDs

    B   T-shirts

    C   photos

15   Where will the boys meet tomorrow?

    A   in the playground

    B   in the sports hall

    C   in the library

🎧 74 **Questions 16–20**

You will hear a student asking a supermarket customer some questions for a school project.
Listen and complete questions **16–20**.
You will hear the conversation twice.

Supermarket project

Name of supermarket: .... Costright ....

Where customer lives: **(16)** ....

Customer's age: **(17)** ....

Travels to supermarket: **(18)** by ....

Usually spends: **(19)** £ ....

Always buys: **(20)** vegetables, milk and ....

🎧 75 **Questions 21–25**

You will hear a sports coach leaving a message about a hockey match.
Listen and complete questions **21–25**.
You will hear the information twice.

Next hockey match

Day of match: Saturday

Place: **(21)** .... Sports Centre

Travel there by: **(22)** ....

Time to meet: **(23)** .... a.m.

Colour of kit to take: **(24)** ....

Coach's new phone number: **(25)** ....

You now have 8 minutes to write your answers on the answer sheet.

Questions 1–5

Which notice (**A–H**) says this (**1–5**)?
For questions **1–5**, mark the correct letter **A–H** on your answer sheet.

Example:

0   You mustn't take one of these on the bus.

Answer:

0	A	B	C	D	E	F	G	H
	▭	▭	▭	▬	▭	▭	▭	▭

---

1   You can't use these at the moment.

2   You shouldn't ride bikes on the green areas.

3   There is a special place for passengers' bags.

4   Car drivers should not use these.

5   Make sure you have everything before you get off.

A
> **No cycling**
> ON THE GRASS. PLEASE USE THE PATH.

B
> *Bus drivers don't sell tickets – please use the machines.*

C
> Please leave luggage in the space near the train doors.

D
> **NO BIKES ON THE BUSES, PLEASE.**

E
> Don't forget your bags when you leave the train!

F
> STATION TICKET MACHINES AREN'T WORKING TODAY.

G
> **PARKING SPACES FOR BICYCLES AND MOTORBIKES ONLY!**

H
> **PLEASE DRIVE CAREFULLY – BUSES STOP HERE.**

Questions 6–10

Read the sentences about Vera's day at the beach with her family.
Choose the best word (**A, B** or **C**) for each space.
For questions **6–10**, mark **A, B** or **C** on your answer sheet.

Example:

0   Yesterday morning, Vera and her family .... up early to
     drive to the beach.

  A put   **B** took   **C** got

Answer: | 0 | A B C |

---

6   Vera .... her swimming costume and towel into a bag.

  A collected   **B** packed   **C** entered

7   Vera's mother .... a picnic for their lunch.

  A did   **B** cooked   **C** made

8   The journey to the beach was quite .... , so Vera listened to music.

  A long   **B** far   **C** wide

9   At the beach, Vera .... most of the day playing with her brother.

  A spent   **B** filled   **C** kept

10 At the end of the day, Vera felt .... but happy.

  A busy   **B** tired   **C** slow

Questions 11–15

Complete the five conversations.
For questions **11–15**, mark **A**, **B** or **C** on your answer sheet.

Example:

0

I saw Abby at the shopping centre.

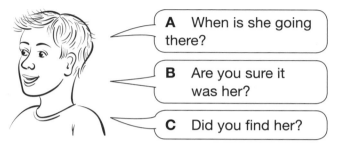

A   When is she going there?

B   Are you sure it was her?

C   Did you find her?

Answer: 0   A B C

---

11   Sorry for calling you so late.

    A   Oh, I wasn't asleep.

    B   Sure, I can wait.

    C   Yes, let's hurry.

12   Is your sister feeling better today?

    A   Yes, you're right.

    B   Yes, thanks for asking.

    C   Yes, she often does that.

13   Someone left a jacket in the classroom.

    A   Shall we look for it in the hall?

    B   Maybe it'll be there later.

    C   I think it's Rob's.

14   Shall I meet you after school?

    A   I have to be home early today.

    B   Yes, that's a good place.

    C   I don't think we do.

15   Thanks for coming with me.

    A   Sorry I can't help you.

    B   Would you like me to come?

    C   It's no problem at all.

Questions 16–20

Complete the conversation.
What does Nina say to Alana?
For questions **16–20**, mark the correct letter **A–H** on your answer sheet.

Example:

Nina: Hi, Alana. How was your weekend?

Alana: **0** .... **E** ....   *Answer:*   

Nina: So you didn't get the shoes you wanted?

Alana: **16** ....

Nina: I'd like that. Are you free on Saturday?

Alana: **17** ....

Nina: That one near the castle. My friends go there quite often.

Alana: **18** ....

Nina: Lots. And they're really good.

Alana: **19** ....

Nina: After lunch is better for me. Shall we walk?

Alana: **20** ....

Nina: Yes, that's fine. See you then.

A   OK. Does it have shoe shops?

B   There wasn't time. Shall we go shopping together soon?

C   No. What about you?

D   The bus is much quicker. Shall we meet at your house at two?

E   Really busy. I had to help Mum at home a lot.

F   Great. What time do you want to go?

G   I know. Is that a good time?

H   If I don't get homework! Which shopping centre do you prefer?

Questions 21 – 27

Read the article about a boy called Jack.
Are sentences **21 – 27** 'Right' **(A)** or 'Wrong' **(B)**?
If there is not enough information to answer 'Right' **(A)** or 'Wrong' **(B)**, choose 'Doesn't say' **(C)**.
For questions **21 – 27**, mark **A**, **B** or **C** on your answer sheet.

A Young Cook

Sixteen-year-old school boy Jack Houghton started cooking when his mother asked for help preparing the family meals. She was amazed at how quickly he became the best cook in the family.

Then, during one of his school holidays, he got a job at a restaurant. He practised many new dishes, which the customers loved. The chef there told him about a cooking competition for teenagers, and Jack decided to enter. Two months later, he and 20 other young people from all over Britain travelled to the Young Chef competition in London. Each teenager had to cook a cheap, healthy meal. They only had 30 minutes to do this, which was the hardest part for Jack.

Three famous British chefs chose the winner. As well as watching the teenagers in the kitchen, they tried the dishes, and asked them questions about food and cooking. Finally, they decided that Jack was the winner. Afterwards he said, 'I always knew I wanted to be a chef and winning the competition will help me to do that.'

Jack's plan for next summer is to go to a cooking school in Italy. 'The best way to learn about a country's food is to go there,' he said.

Example:

0   All Jack's family have to help in the kitchen.

    A Right   **B** Wrong   **C** Doesn't say   *Answer:*

---

21   Jack soon became better than his mother at cooking.

    A Right   **B** Wrong   **C** Doesn't say

22   Jack left school to work as a cook in a restaurant.

    A Right   **B** Wrong   **C** Doesn't say

23   Jack found out about the competition from a customer at the restaurant.

    A Right   **B** Wrong   **C** Doesn't say

24   Jack and the other 20 young cooks travelled to the competition by train.

    A Right   **B** Wrong   **C** Doesn't say

25   It was difficult for Jack to cook the competition meal in the available time.

    A Right   **B** Wrong   **C** Doesn't say

26   The famous chefs did several things before choosing the winner.

    A Right   **B** Wrong   **C** Doesn't say

27   Jack thinks Italian food is the best in the world.

    A Right   **B** Wrong   **C** Doesn't say

Questions 28–35

Read the article about horses.
Choose the best word (**A, B** or **C**) for each space.
For questions **28–35**, mark **A**, **B** or **C** on your answer sheet.

Horses and people

Thousands of years **(0)** ...., horses were wild animals,
like zebras are today. Then, in **(28)** .... 3,500 BCE, people
began **(29)** .... horses to carry things. Later, they started
to ride horses too. People **(30)** .... travel much further
by horse than on foot, because horses run much faster.

(31) .... a long time, horses helped people do their work,

(32) .... on farms. Now, we have machines to do most of these jobs and we have **(33)** ....

ways to travel, such as bicycles, trains and cars. **(34)** ...., people still enjoy riding and racing

horses, and in some places the police ride horses, **(35)** .... they can move through a crowd more

easily than a car or motorbike.

Example:

| 0 | **A** before | **B** ago | **C** still | *Answer:* | 0 | A B C |

---

28 **A** round **B** over **C** about

29 **A** use **B** using **C** used

30 **A** could **B** might **C** should

31 **A** Since **B** For **C** During

32 **A** exactly **B** actually **C** especially

33 **A** other **B** enough **C** some

34 **A** Instead **B** Anymore **C** However

35 **A** as **B** but **C** or

Questions 36–40

Read the descriptions of some things you can find in a kitchen.
What is the word for each one?
The first letter is already shown. There is one space for each other letter in the word.
For questions **36–40**, write the words on your answer sheet.

Example:

0   You sit at this to eat your meals.   **t** _ _ _ _

Answer:	**0**	table

---

36   This is where you wash the plates.   **s** _ _ _

37   You put food in here to keep it cold.   **f** _ _ _ _ _

38   You can keep plates or glasses inside this.   **c** _ _ _ _ _ _ _

39   This is the type of plate you use for soup.   **b** _ _ _

40   You put food on this or inside to make it hot.   **c** _ _ _ _ _

Questions 41–50

Complete the post on a school website.
Write ONE word for each space.
For questions **41–50**, write the words on your answer sheet.

Example:

0	My

Hi, everyone. **(0)** .... name is Janine, and I'm **(41)** ....
Class 7. I really like music, and I want to start a school band. I
(42) .... spoken to Mr Wells, the music teacher, and **(43)**
.... thinks it's a good idea. Now, we just need musicians!
So, **(44)** .... you play an instrument, and you'd like to be
in a band, come to the music room on Friday **(45)** ....
lunchtime. We **(46)** .... going to meet there **(47)** ....
week, and maybe do a concert before the end **(48)** ....
term. Please show this message **(49)** .... any other
students you know **(50)** .... play instruments too. Thanks!

Questions 51–55

Read the notice and the text message.
Complete the information in Bethany's notes.
For questions **51–55**, write the information on your answer sheet.

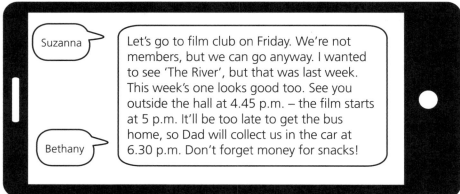

Bethany's Notes

Where to see the film:	Room 4
Film we'll see:	**51**
Time to meet:	**52**
Price I'll pay:	**53** £
What to take:	**54**
How we'll get home:	**55**

Test 5 Reading and Writing • Part 9

Question 56

You are on a beach holiday. Write a postcard to your English friend, Kim.

Say:

- where you are
- what you have done
- what the weather is like.

Write **25–35** words.
Write the postcard on your answer sheet.

76 **Questions 1–5**

You will hear five short conversations.
You will hear each conversation twice.
There is one question for each conversation.
For each question, choose the right answer (**A**, **B** or **C**).

Example: When is Michael's birthday?

Answer: 0 | A B C

A   B   C

---

1 What will Marina wear tomorrow?

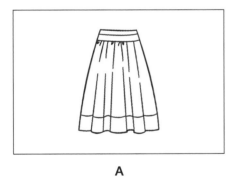

A   B   C
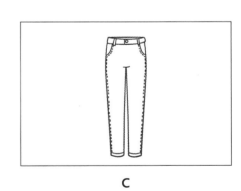

2 Which is Jim's grandmother?

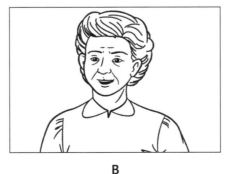

A   B   C

3 What will Annie do at art club this week?

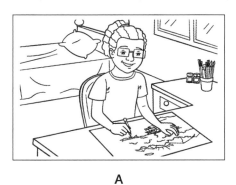

A

B

C

4 What has Ben lost?

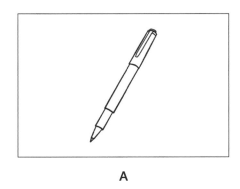

A

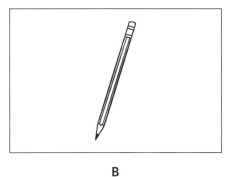

B

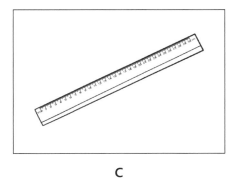

C

5 How long will it take to walk to the cinema from Ali's house?

5 minutes	10 minutes	20 minutes
A	B	C

 **Questions 6–10**

Listen to Alicia and her friend talking about her collection of postcards.
Where is each postcard from?
For questions **6–10**, write a letter **A–H** next to each place.
You will hear the conversation twice.

Example:

0	castle	F

Answer:

0	A	B	C	D	E	F	G	H

POSTCARDS

6   mountain

7   lake

8   beach

9   city

10   forest

COUNTRIES

A   Argentina

B   Australia

C   China

D   Italy

E   Kenya

F   Spain

G   Switzerland

H   United States

🎧 78 **Questions 11–15**

Listen to to Daisy telling her friend Adam about a play.
For each questions, choose the right answer **(A, B** or **C)**.
You will hear the conversation twice.

Example:

0 When is the play on?

   A today

   B tomorrow

   C next week

Answer:

---

11 Who is going to be in the play?

   A Naomi

   B Linda

   C Gina

12 The play is about

   A a storm.

   B a king.

   C a house.

13 When will they see the play?

   A Wednesday

   B Thursday

   C Friday

14 The theatre is near

   A the station.

   B the school.

   C the library.

15 How much will Adam pay?

   A £3

   B £8

   C £10

🎧 79 **Questions 16–20**

You will hear a boy, David, telling his friend, Eva, about a competition.
Listen and complete questions **16–20**.
You will hear the conversation twice.

Photography competition

What to take a photograph of: .... *food* ....

Age to enter: **(16)** less than .... years old

Who chooses the winner: **(17)** Pat ....

How to send photograph by: **(18)** ....

When to send photograph: **(19)** to arrive by ....

First prize: **(20)** ....

🎧 80 **Questions 21–25**

You will hear a teacher giving his class some information about a quiz.
Listen and complete questions **21–25**.
You will hear the information twice.

Year 5 quiz

Date of quiz:	2nd April
Number of people in each team:	(21) ....
Where quiz will be:	(22) ....
Questions about:	geography, history, maths and
	(23) ....
Prize for winners:	(24) ....
Write team names on list by:	(25) ....

Questions 1-5

Which notice **(A-H)** says this **(1-5)**?
For questions **1-5**, mark the correct letter **A-H** on your answer sheet.

Example:

0 This has changed to a different day.

Answer:

0	A	B	C	D	E	F	G	H
	☐	▬	☐	☐	☐	☐	☐	☐

1 See this person if you've lost something.

2 These are for people who haven't played the sport before.

3 You must only play football in one area.

4 Be careful about which shoes you wear here.

5 You can watch this sport without paying.

A
Trainers for sale.
Call Julia on 453 566.

B
Cricket team: we're playing our match on Friday this week, not Wednesday.

C
BADMINTON LESSONS FOR BEGINNERS STARTING MONDAY AFTER SCHOOL

D
TRAINERS ONLY IN THE SPORTS HALL
No football boots!

E
*Sports shop: **free socks** with every pair of football boots*

F
Ball games in the playground only – NOT on the paths

G
Two free tickets for a basketball game. Interested? Speak to Mr Greene

H
Rugby shirt left in sports hall. Speak to school secretary.

Questions 6–10

Read the sentences about a boy called Leo who plays the drums. Choose the best word (**A**, **B** or **C**) for each space. For questions **6–10**, mark **A**, **B** or **C** on your answer sheet.

Example:

0   Leo .... some drums as a birthday present.

A earned   **B** preferred   **C** received

Answer:
0	A	B	C
	▭	▭	▬

6   Leo is very .... with his drums because he knows they were expensive.

A careful   **B** safe   **C** correct

7   Leo's brother .... him a book on learning to play the drums.

A kept   **B** lent   **C** set

8   Leo .... the drums every day because he wants to get better.

A prepares   **B** improves   **C** practises

9   Leo's cousin plays the drums well and has .... to give Leo lessons.

A discussed   **B** offered   **C** invited

10   When he can play well, Leo would like to be a .... of the school band.

A member   **B** partner   **C** colleague

Questions 11–15

Complete the five conversations.
For questions **11–15**, mark **A**, **B** or **C** on your answer sheet.

Example:

0

When are you going out?

A It's two o'clock

B I'm not sure yet.

C Yes, later this afternoon.

Answer:

| 0 | A | B | C |

---

11 I love that song!

    A Where is it now?

    B Do you know it?

    C Who's it by?

12 Shall we choose a film to watch?

    A Isn't there anything else to do?

    B Is it the one about a horse?

    C Haven't you done it yet?

13 Let me know if you can come.

    A Yes, I will.

    B Yes, I am.

    C Yes, I do.

14 Have you ever met Anna?

    A She didn't come.

    B I don't think so.

    C Yes, she has.

15 Here's the book I borrowed from you.

    A I've already given it back to you!

    B When do you need it?

    C Did you enjoy it?

Questions 16–20

Complete the conversation between two friends.
What does Clara say to Daniel?
For questions **16–20**, mark the correct letter **A–H** on your answer sheet.

Example:

Clara: Hi Daniel. What's that book you're carrying?

Alice: **0**   ....**F**........   *Answer:*

Clara: Not yet, but everyone says the story's really good.

Daniel: **16** ....

Clara: It's my favourite way to spend my free time.

Daniel: **17** ....

Clara: I didn't know there was one. When do you meet?

Daniel: **18** ....

Clara: What do I need to do to join?

Daniel: **19** ....

Clara: OK. Do you read a different book every week?

Daniel: **20** ....

Clara: Of course! Well thanks. I'll see you on Thursday.

A   Well, you should join the school book club!

B   That's true. What are your hobbies?

C   It is! Do you like reading?

D   Nothing. Just come along. We meet in the library.

E   Me too. But not very often.

F   It's called *The Photograph*. Have you read it?

G   On Thursdays. After school.

H   Usually, but it depends how long it is.

Questions 21–27

Read the article in which three people talk about a museum they have visited.
For questions **21–27**, mark **A**, **B** or **C** on your answer sheet.

A visit to a museum

A

Klaus

I went to this museum because my cousin said it's very good. It's quite far from where I live, but I'm glad I went. There's lots to see, and also some things you can pick up, like bears' teeth – they're really big and heavy! They're amazing! There's a restaurant on the top floor, but I didn't go in. I did go in the shop, though. I collect stamps, and they had some interesting ones for good prices, so I got five.

B

Luiz

This museum isn't far from my house, but I didn't know it was there. I was really surprised when my aunt told me about it. She and I did a tour with a member of the museum staff, which was very interesting. Afterwards we stayed for hours, just looking at things by ourselves. We only went home because we wanted something to eat, I'd like to go back one day. Lots of tourists were buying things at the shop, but I didn't see anything I liked.

C

Andre

I saw an advertisement for this museum on a website. I don't usually like museums, but actually this one's really good! There's lots to see, and it's fun for little children because they can get near to the things, and even hold some of them. I might take my little brother next time, and maybe do a tour with a guide. The café's good too – I had a great cake!

Example:

0   Who found out about the museum online?

   A Klaus   **B** Luiz   **C** Andre

Answer: 

---

21 Who bought something at the museum?

                                               A Klaus

                                             B Luiz

                                             C Andre

22 Who went around the museum with a guide?

                                             A Klaus

                                             B Luiz

                                             C Andre

23 Who held something at the museum?

                                             A Klaus

                                             B Luiz

                                             C Andre

24 Who ate something at the museum?

                                             A Klaus

                                             B Luiz

                                             C Andre

25 Who went to the museum with someone from their family?

                                             A Klaus

                                             B Luiz

                                             C Andre

26 Who was surprised that he enjoyed the museum?

                                             A Klaus

                                             B Luiz

                                             C Andre

27 Who lives near the museum he visited?

                                             A Klaus

                                             B Luiz

                                             C Andre

Questions 28–35

Read the article about the history of sunglasses.
Choose the best word (**A**, **B** or **C**) for each space.
For questions **28–35**, mark **A**, **B** or **C** on your answer sheet.

The history of sunglasses

Lots of us wear sunglasses **(0)** .... it's sunny outside. However,

sunglasses were not always **(28)** .... to stop the sun hurting people's

eyes. In the 12th century, people in China sometimes wore dark glasses

so other people **(29)** .... not see how they felt. In the 18th century, an

Englishman called James Ayscough tried using blue or green glasses to help

people **(30)** .... had eye problems or illnesses, **(31)** .... he didn't

design the glasses to keep the sun out of **(32)** .... eyes. Sunglasses

didn't become really popular **(33)** .... about 1929, in Hollywood, USA. In **(34)** .... early days

of film, very bright lights were used. **(35)** .... these made people's eyes become red, many actors

wore sunglasses when they weren't working. Fans saw actors wearing sunglasses, and wanted to look

like them.

Example:

0 **A** when   **B** as   **C** than   *Answer:*

---

28 **A** use   **B** using   **C** used

29 **A** could   **B** may   **C** shall

30 **A** which   **B** who   **C** what

31 **A** and   **B** if   **C** but

32 **A** their   **B** her   **C** your

33 **A** since   **B** by   **C** until

34 **A** the   **B** some   **C** this

35 **A** While   **B** Because   **C** So

Questions 36–40

Read the descriptions of some words about travelling by plane.
What is the word for each one?
The first letter is already there. There is one space for each other letter in the word.
For questions **36–40**, write the words on your answer sheet.

Example:

0   This is what we call people who are travelling.   p _ _ _ _ _ _ _ _ _

Answer:	**0**	*passengers*

---

36   This person's job is to fly the plane.   p _ _ _ _

37   You need this document to fly to a different country.   p _ _ _ _ _ _ _

38   If you've forgotten something for your trip you can buy it here.   s _ _ _

39   This is what you put your clothes in for your journey.   s _ _ _ _ _ _ _

40   If your flight is late, you can go here to eat something.   r _ _ _ _ _ _ _ _

Questions 41–50

Complete the emails.
Write ONE word for each space.
For questions **41–50**, write the words on your answer sheet.

Example: | **0** | Have |
|---|---|

From:	David
To:	Abe

Hi Abe,

(0) .... you done your maths homework? I understood the first question, **(41)** .... I'm having a few problems **(42)** .... the second question. **(43)** .... you've done yours already, maybe you could explain it to **(44)** .... I'm free after school tomorrow – **(45)** .... you?

from

David

From:	Abe
To:	David

Hi David,

Yes, of course I **(46)** .... help you. I did that homework yesterday, and I found **(47)** .... quite difficult too. **(48)** .... don't you come to **(49)** .... house after school? Let's meet in the playground **(50)** .... four o'clock.

from

Abe

Reading and Writing • Part 8

Questions 51–55

Read the advertisement and the email.
Fill in the information in the notes.
For questions **51–55**, write the information on your answer sheet.

Perfume Concerts

Greenfield Stadium

July 22nd and 23rd

For tickets call: 0121 496 0691

Adults £15

Students £10

Let's go to a 'Perfume' concert! We get cheaper tickets because we're still at school. I'm busy on the first date, so we'll go on the second. Mum says she'll take us by train because the stadium car park is too small. Let's go to the concert in our 'Perfume' T-shirts! And we can buy one of their sweaters at the concert! Call me when you've got your ticket. My new number is 07700 900847.

Gemma's notes – Perfume concert

Where:	Greenfield Stadium
Date we'll go:	51
Price I'll pay:	52
Phone number for tickets:	53
How we'll travel:	54
What to wear:	55

Question 56

Read the email from your English friend, Sandy.

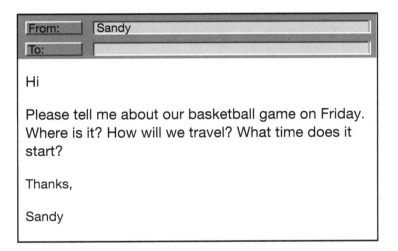

| From: | Sandy |
| To: | |

Hi

Please tell me about our basketball game on Friday. Where is it? How will we travel? What time does it start?

Thanks,

Sandy

Write an email from Sandy and answer his questions.
Write **25–35** words.
Write the email on your answer sheet.

🎧 81 **Questions 1–5**

You will hear five short conversations.
You will hear each conversation twice.
There is one question for each conversation.
For each question, choose the correct answer (**A**, **B** or **C**).

Example: Which kind of ice cream does the girl buy?

Answer: | 0 | A B C |

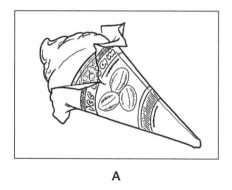

A

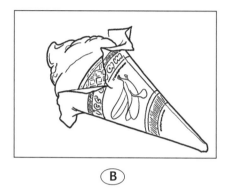

B

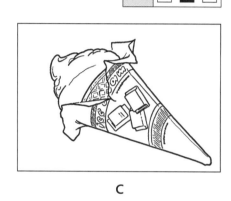

C

---

1 Where is the bank?

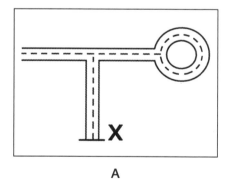

A

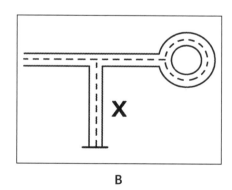

B

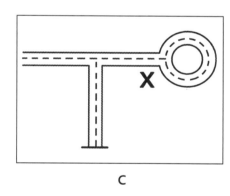

C

2 What will the weather be like today?

A

B

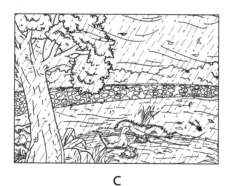

C

3 How much will the girl have to pay to swim?

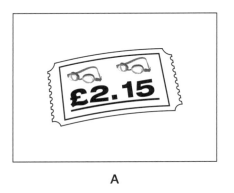

A

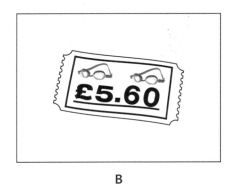

B

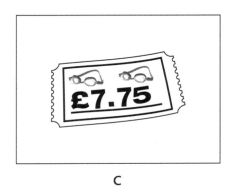

C

4 Where is Luc's father?

A

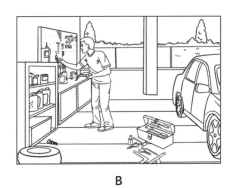

B

C

5 What did Sara do last weekend?

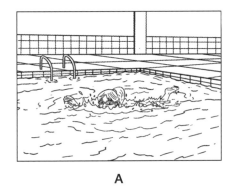

A

B

C

82 Questions 6–10

Listen to Andres and his grandmother talking about the activities his friends do.
Who does each activity?
For questions **6–10**, write a letter **A–H** next to each person.
You will hear the conversation twice.

Example:

0   Marcus | H | *Answer:* | 0 | A B C D E F G H
                                                          ▭ ▭ ▭ ▭ ▭ ▭ ▭ ▬

FRIENDS		**ACTIVITIES**
6 Tanya		**A** cycling
7 Steven		**B** jewellery making
8 Lina		**C** photography
9 Paolo		**D** playing football
10 Jenny		**E** playing tennis
		F running
		G shopping
		H swimming

🎧 83 Questions 11–15

Listen to Tamsin telling her friend Ryan about a video game.
For each question, choose the right answer (**A**, **B** or **C**).
You will hear the conversation twice.

Example:

0   What time is Tamsin going to Ryan's house?

   A   3.00 p.m.

   B   3.15 p.m.

   C   4.00 p.m.

Answer:

---

11   What is the game called?

   A   Journey

   B   Visitor

   C   City

12   In the game, players have to

   A   race other people.

   B   answer questions.

   C   collect something.

13   Who gave Tamsin the game?

   A   her cousin

   B   her friend

   C   her mum

14   How many levels does the game have?

   A   four

   B   six

   C   twelve

15   How much does the game cost?

   A   £15

   B   £20

   C   £25

You will hear a girl, Laura, telling her friend Jon about a guitar that her brother wants to sell.
Listen and complete questions **16–20**.
You will hear the conversation twice.

Guitar for sale

Type of guitar:	Kosman
Price of guitar:	(16)
Colour of guitar:	(17)
Laura's brother's phone number:	(18)
Laura's address:	(19) 16 .... Road
Can see the guitar on:	(20)

85 **Questions 21–25**

You will hear a girl called Rosa telling her class about a race she did.
Listen and complete questions **21–25**.
You will hear the information twice.

<u>**Triathlon**</u>

Day of the race: Saturday

Where Rosa swam: **(21)** in a ....

How far Rosa cycled: **(22)** .... km

Rosa completed the race in: **(23)** .... minutes

Everyone received a free: **(24)** ....

Date of next race: **(25)** ....

LISTENING PART 1
Training

 1

Dad: Are you walking to your grandmother's house, Stella?

Girl: I was thinking about taking the bus.

Dad: The traffic's really bad this morning. I think you should take the train. There's one in ten minutes.

Girl: Thanks, Dad. I'll do that.

 2

When are Mia and her family flying to Australia?

Boy: Hi Mia. Are you free on December 17th? It's my birthday, and I'm having a party.

Girl: Sorry, Nico, but I'll be on holiday. We're going to Australia.

Boy: Of course – I forgot! When do you go?

Girl: On the 10th. And we don't fly back until 5th January!

 3

Which day will Leo and Tiana practise their song?

Girl: Leo, we have to practise our song! The show is on Friday!

Boy: I know! How about Thursday? Are you free then?

Girl: I've got a dance class. What about Wednesday? It's the only day I'm free this week.

Boy: Then that's the day we'll have to practise! I'll meet you in the playground after school.

 4

What is Luc doing now?

Jess: Hi Luc! Wow – what a lot of noise! Are you in a shopping centre?

Luc: It's this film on TV. It's too loud, isn't it?

Jess: Yeah, a bit. Are you free tomorrow? There's a concert in the park. Shall we go?

Luc: That sounds great.

 5

What is Sofia going to do this afternoon?

Dad: Sofia, I'm going to the supermarket. Can you come with me?

Girl: But I want to play on my computer!

Dad: You can do that after lunch. I need your help now. And what about your homework? Are you going to that this afternoon too?

Girl: I've already finished it!

 6

What has James lost?

Girl: James, can I borrow your ruler?

Boy: Yeah – here it is. Have you seen my rubber? I can't find it.

Girl: No. Is it in your school bag?

Boy: I've already looked. Can I use yours?

 7

Girl: Dad, have you seen Jasmine? I thought she was still in her bedroom, but the bed is empty.

Dad: I can hear the shower, so that must be her in the bathroom. Have you tidied your bedroom?

Girl: Not yet. I was helping Mum in the living room.

Dad: Good. Thanks. I'll ask Jasmine to do her room once she's dressed.

 8

One

Boy: Wow, Barbara,! What a lot of earrings! How many pairs are there here? Forty? What do you need 40 pairs for?

Girl: I don't! There are fourteen there. I counted them last week!

Two

Dad: Anna, I think you've spoken to your friend enough today! You've called five times!

Girl: Well, I haven't seen her for ages. She's been off school for four days!

Dad: I don't understand why once isn't enough – or at most twice!

Three

Girl: How was your party, Billy? Did everyone come? You invited twenty people, didn't you?

Boy: Twenty two, actually. Only 12 came, but it was still good fun.

Four

Girl: Yes sir, can I help you?

Man: Thank you. Two strawberry ice creams, and one chocolate, please. So that's three altogether. How much is that?

 9

How much are the shoes which Jonathan and his mother decide to buy?

Mum: What about these, Jonathan?

Boy: They're really nice, but isn't £35.70 quite expensive? We usually only spend about £25.95.

Mum: But they're very good ones. Look at these others – they're £14.50, but they're not as good.

Boy: Yeah, I see what you mean. OK, we'll get the ones you suggest.

Exam practice

Example

How many new T-shirts did Ellen get?

Girl: I went shopping with Dad yesterday. He bought me lots of different T-shirts in the market.

Boy: How many did you get, then, Ellen? Five?

Girl: I got two more than that. But they were really cheap.

Boy: So you got seven! Wow, you're lucky!

One

Why didn't the boy buy an ice cream?

Mum: I'm surprised you didn't get an ice cream, John. Didn't you have enough money?

Boy: That wasn't the problem, Mum. They only cost £1.50.

Mum: So was the shop closed when you got there?

Boy: It was still open, but they didn't have any chocolate ice cream and that's the only kind I really like at the moment.

Two

Who will Bella call on her phone next?

Grandma: Are you still talking to your friend, Bella? Dinner's nearly ready!

Bella: OK, Grandma! I won't be long. I'm talking to Mr Robins now, my piano teacher. I've got to change the time of my next lesson.

Grandma: All right. You'll need to phone your Mum afterwards. Say she should come and collect you at about 8 o'clock.

Bella: OK, I'll do that in a minute.

Three

How will friends travel to school tomorrow morning?

Girl: How are you getting to school tomorrow morning?

Boy: On the school bus, as usual.

Girl: Didn't you hear? It broke down yesterday and won't be back on the road for a few days. I'm going to have to walk. Dad won't let me ride my bike.

Boy: My mum'll give us a lift. She works near here and always parks by the school anyway.

Four

What day will Matt get his new tennis racket?

Boy: I phoned the sports shop, Mum. The tennis racket that I want won't be there until Friday.

Mum: Well, if we buy one online today instead, it might arrive on Wednesday.

Boy: That's true. But the post is often delayed, isn't it? I want to be sure I'll have it for my match on Saturday.

Mum: OK! Best to get it from the shop then!

Five

What's on TV this evening?

Boy: Are you going to watch that singing competition on TV later tonight?

Girl: I'd like to, but Dad might want to watch the other channel! When does that programme about street dancing start?

Boy: Not until next week. And did you see the skiing last night?

Girl: No, I missed it, but I might watch it on my computer later.

LISTENING PART 2
Training

 2

Example

Which activity did each person enjoy?

Girl: We went for a walk. I wasn't that interested in the birds, but climbing trees was fun.

One

Boy: We had maths at school this morning. It was much better than history, which we did later.

Two

Girl: I spent the day with my grandad. He showed me some really interesting old photos. Then we had to go shopping, which was a bit boring.

Three

Boy: My family and I went to the cinema yesterday evening. The movie wasn't great, but the food we ate afterwards was fantastic!

Four

Boy: I went to the park with my friend at the weekend. We tried playing tennis, but my racket broke. But then we had a really fun football game with some other boys.

Five

Girl: We spent a lot of time on the beach on holiday. I didn't really like lying in the sun. Swimming in the sea was a lot better.

Six

Boy: I made some biscuits with my mum this morning. They were really easy. Making a big cake was more difficult, so that was less fun!

 3

How did each person in Karina's family help on the day of the party?

Boy: I saw your mum on Saturday, Karina. She said you were all really busy!

Girl: Yeah, she was buying a present for my brother when you saw her – it was his birthday. She also wanted a break from the party preparations.

Boy: And what did you have to do?

Girl: We divided the work up. My sister made the cake and put the snacks out. She spent last week looking for cake recipes on the internet.

Boy: So you got the house ready – moving tables and chairs around?

Girl: We did that the night before. I was downloading all my brother's favourite songs. I did it on the laptop I bought last week.

Boy: It takes a long time to do that, doesn't it? How about your dad?

Girl: Well, he spent most of the morning trying to find his camera. It was in a cupboard in the kitchen that we don't usually open. I don't know who put it there!

13 Exam practice

Girl: How was the first week of your school holiday, George?

George: It was great! On Monday, I went to the cinema.

Girl: What about Tuesday?

George: Well, my brother went shopping, but I went to the beach with four friends. I had my first windsurfing lesson. It was amazing!

Girl: Wow! Did you do anything exciting on Wednesday?

George: Mum took us to a farm that's just opened near our home. The weather wasn't great, but we had a good time anyway.

Girl: Did you go out on Thursday too?

George: No. Mum was out shopping all day, so my brother taught me to use some photography software. I spent the day doing that.

Girl: Interesting!

George: It was! Then on Friday, I went to my tennis club with Carl. We've known each other since we were three and we always have so much fun together.

Girl: Sounds good.

George: And on Saturday, Dad took us out on his boat. It made me feel a bit ill, actually, but I liked lying in the sun afterwards.

LISTENING PART 3
Training

 1

Example

Which room are you staying in at the hotel? I'd like to phone you there.

One

How long did the film last? Was it long?

Two

How many people will there be at your house on Sunday?

Three

How much was that T-shirt?

Four

How big is your new bedroom?

Five

How often do you usually see your grandmother?

Six

What time does the sports centre open?

 2

Mum: So, how was your first day, Raquel?

Raquel: It was fine, Mum, thanks; except I went to the wrong room! I went to room 6B, and someone had to take me to 8B, which is my room.

Mum: And is your teacher nice?

Raquel: Yes, he's called Mr Walters. He's not as nice as Mrs Taylor in my old school, but I like him.

Mum: Who did you sit next to?

Raquel: A girl with long red hair like Jane has. Her name is Emma.

Mum: Do you have a long break for lunch?

Raquel: I think it was about an hour. No – it was actually 45 minutes, I remember now.

Mum: And what did you eat?

Raquel: The food was good! I had soup and bread. The salads looked good too. I think I'll have one tomorrow.

Mum: What about the bus home? What time does it stop at the school?

Raquel: It comes at quarter to four. We finish school at 3.30 so it's perfect.

Mum: Is that the time you finish every day?

Raquel: Every day except Thursdays. We finish early then so we can do sports. I want to join the football team – they also practise at lunchtime on Tuesdays.

 3

Girl: Eddie, I missed geography today. What were you learning about?

Boy: Well, remember we learnt about rivers last week? We've started looking at the sea now. It's interesting!

Girl: Is the information in our textbooks?

Boy: Well, today we just watched a short film from the internet, so there's not really anything in the textbook that you can look at.

Girl: Oh. And did you learn about fish?

Boy: We were actually learning about where the water comes from, and where it goes.

Girl: Interesting. What about homework?

Boy: We have to write down ten things you can find on the beach.

Girl: Oh, that's a lot easier than the picture we had to draw last week! Anything else?

Boy: Yes. We need to take in a bottle for next week's class. With no drink in it!

Girl: OK. Thanks.

 4

Girl: There's a great programme on TV tonight. I'm sure you'd love it!

Boy: Oh, what's it about? China?

Girl: Well, I know you're really interested in China. And India. But this one is about Japan. That's where my grandparents are from.

Boy: What time is it on? There's a football match on tonight that I want to see.

Girl: It's on at 7 o'clock. And it finishes at 8 o'clock. The football doesn't start until 9 o'clock.

Boy: Great. Then I'll watch it. Which channel is it on?

Girl: It's strange. Travel programmes are usually on Channel 4, but this one is on Channel 5. Then you'll need to turn to Channel 2 for the football!

Boy: OK. Thanks, Kira.

 Exam practice

Carla: Hi Vincent. I wasn't in school this morning. Did we get any homework for science or English?

Vincent: Hi Carla. No, just for geography.

Carla: Oh, OK. What do we have to do?

Vincent: Well, you know we're learning about rivers? We have to go online and get information about a river in Africa. We're doing South America next week and then Indian rivers after that.

Carla: Sounds difficult ...

Vincent: Don't worry. We saw some great photos and maps in class. I'll text you to say where to find them online.

Carla: Thanks. Do we have to write lots?

Vincent: No more than 500 words. I've written 300 already and it won't be difficult to do 200 more.

Carla: When must we finish this? Our next geography lesson's on Thursday, isn't it?

Vincent: Yes, but the teacher's away that day, so we've got until Friday. She'll give it back to us next Tuesday.

Carla: That's not much time. Can you help me with this?

Vincent: OK – after gym club tomorrow? That finishes at a quarter to five, but I'll need a shower, so how about a quarter past? I can stay about 45 minutes.

Carla: That's fine. Thanks, Vincent.

LISTENING PART 4
Training

 1

Girl: Mum, there's a show on at the theatre that I'd like to see. It's called 'Sleep'.

Mum: And which theatre is it at? The Royal?

Girl: It's at the Wylcott Theatre. That's W-Y-L-C-O-double T.

Mum: Oh yes, I know it. So is this show on now?

Girl: No, it starts on 2nd April. But we'll have to book tickets quickly, because it's only on until 30th April.

Mum: I haven't said we can go yet! How much are the tickets?

Girl: For adults it's £10, but as I'm a student you'll only have to pay £8 for me. Can we go?

Mum 2: Yes, all right then. I'll book it now.

 2

Example

Boy: The show is at the Lyceum Theatre. That's L-Y-C-E-U-M.

One

Girl: My new teacher is called Mr Alsopp.

Boy: How do you spell his name?

Girl: A-L-S-O-double P.

Two

Boy: I live at number 23 Ryedale Road. That's R-Y-E-D-A-L-E.

Three

Boy: The talk is at the Telus Centre

Girl: How do you spell that?

Boy: T-E-L-U-S

Four

Girl: What's the name of the town we're going to?

Boy: Churmount. You spell it C-H-U-R-M-O-U-N-T.

Five

Woman: The person coming to speak to us today is called Tom Aqinto. His surname is spelt A-Q-I-N-T-O.

Six

Man: Our website is www.japes.com. I'll spell that for you. It's www dot J-A-P-E-S dot com.

 3

Example

Man: I was born in a town called Relwick. You spell it R-E-L-W-I-C-K.

One

Woman: What's the name of the hotel we're going to?

Man: The Draycott Hotel.

Woman: How do you spell that?

Man: D-R-A-Y-C-O-double T

Two

Mum: Who teaches you piano?

Boy: Mrs Radisson.

Mum: Is that R-A-D-I-double S-O-N?

Boy: That's right.

Three

Boy: Where do we get the train from?

Girl: Johnston Green.

Boy: Johnson?

Girl: No, Johnston. J-O-H-N-S-T-O-N.

Four

Boy: If you're interested in buying the bike, call Maria Constantinou. That's spelt C-O-N-S-T-A-N-T-I-N-O-U.

Five

Boy: What's that video game you're playing?

Girl: It's called Dialhex.

Boy: What?

Girl: Dialhex. You spell it D-I-A-L-H-E-X.

Six

Girl: What do we have to do for geography homework?

Boy: Get information about the Ubangi River. I think it's in Africa.

Girl: How do you spell it?

Boy U-B-A-N-G-I.

 4

Example

Boy: I'm coming to hockey practice today, for the first time. What time does it start?

Girl: At quarter to four. Don't be late!

One

Girl: What time is the bus leaving from school for the museum tomorrow, sir?

Man: At quarter past nine, but we want everyone here by 9 a.m. Is that clear?

Girl: Yes, sir.

Two

Girl: Excuse me. What time is the talk on snakes?

Man: It starts at ten o'clock. It only lasts about half an hour, so it'll be over by 10:30.

Three

Boy Excuse me. What time is the next train to Manchester?

Woman: You've just missed one – the 5:08. The next one is at 5:28, so you'll have to wait a little while.

Boy OK. Thanks.

Four

Boy: You favourite band are going to be on TV tonight!

Girl: Thanks for telling me! What time?

Boy: The programme starts at five past seven. It finishes at 8 o'clock.

Five

Girl: What time do you think the concert will finish? I need to be home by 9.30!

Boy: Oh, you'll be fine, then. It says on the website that it's from 7.45 to 9 p.m.

Six

Girl: Do you think the shop on the corner will be open yet? I want to get a magazine before I go to school.

Boy: What's the time now?

Girl: Half past eight.

Boy: Oh, it's been open for an hour – since half past seven!

 5

Example

Boy: What time is your party starting on Friday, Nina?

Nina: Well, Mum says everyone has to leave by ten o'clock, so I'm telling everyone to come at 7.30 to give us long enough.

Boy: OK. See you then.

One

Girl: I want to go shopping early tomorrow. What time does the shopping centre open?

Man: Well, some of the shops don't open until ten, but the centre is open from 9:30, so we can go then.

Two

Woman: Hello. I'd like some information about the museum. Is it right that you open at quarter past nine today?

Man: That's only during the week. On Saturdays, we open at quarter to ten.

Woman: OK. Thanks.

Three

Boy: Your house is a long way from school, Penny. What time do you get home?

Penny: Well, there's a bus at 3:30, but I often miss that, so usually I walk. I get to my house by about ten past four.

Boy: Oh, that's a lot later than me. I'm usually home by 3:45.

Four

Girl: Did you find out about that art course?

Boy: Yes, it starts at ten o'clock and finishes at twenty to twelve.

Girl: Oh, so a bit less than two hours. That's OK.

Five

Boy: What time does the pool open in the afternoons? Is it still 2:15?

Girl: No, they've changed it. You can go at any time after 1 o'clock.

Boy: Great. Let's go this afternoon.

Six

Girl: What time does the film begin?

Boy: Eight twenty. Shall I meet you outside the cinema at 8 o'clock?

Girl: Let's say quarter to eight. It's a popular film!

 5 Exam practice

Boy: Belinda, you're English, but you were born in Canada. Right?

Belinda: Yes!

Boy: When did you start dancing? I read you were just five years old.

Belinda: I was three actually! And I was in my first show six years later.

Boy: Wow! So tell me about the show you're in at the moment.

Belinda: Well it's called 'Winter'. It's very beautiful. We have snow on the stage and everything!

Boy: And where's the show?

Belinda: It's on at the Aldhurst Theatre. You spell that A-L-D-H-U-R-S-T. You must come and see it.

Boy: I will! Do you practise there each day too?

Belinda: Oh yes. I'm usually there from 8:30 until about 3:30. But sometimes I need to be there at 6:30. There's so much to learn.

Boy: I don't suppose you have time for any hobbies ... ?

Belinda: I do! I love painting. I'm going to have an exhibition of my pictures soon, in fact.

Boy: Wow! Good luck with that. And thanks very much for talking to me.

Belinda: You're welcome.

LISTENING PART 5
Training

 2

Example

Woman: Listen now everyone. I've had to change the day of your dance class just for next week. It'll be on Thursday. Then, the week after that, we go back to our normal day – Monday.

One

Man: The TV programme I'd like you to watch for your science lesson is on Tuesday evening. We'll talk about it in your lesson on Thursday, so don't forget to watch it.

Two

Girl: I'm going to start in the next level at swimming, so I won't have my class on Saturday anymore. I start going every Sunday from next week.

Three

Boy: My birthday is next Wednesday, but I'm going to have my party on Saturday because we won't be at school then.

Four

Woman: Don't forget that we're going to the Science Museum next Monday. Please bring in the form from your parents by Friday. If you don't, you can't come to the museum!

Five

Man: We've got our first hockey match next Thursday, so please make sure you all come to practice on Wednesday. It's very important!

26 3

Example

Man: There's a great new book shop going to open in the High Street soon. It opens on September 20th, and there will be discounts on all books until 30th September, so don't miss that!

One

Woman: The school concert is on 30th May, and please tell your parents that we will be selling tickets from 13th May. They'll be £4 each.

Two

Man: There's a chess competition next month – that's in April. Please let me know by the 6th if you would like to enter – the competition is on the 16th, so make sure you keep playing!

Three

Woman: The pop group 'Shine' are going to play just one concert in this city. It's on 2nd November, and tickets go on sale on October 5th. You can buy them from any music shop.

Four

Man: OK, I think I've given you all the information about the photography competition, except the closing date! Please get your photos to us by 12th August. We'll be telling you who the competition winners are on 26th August. Good luck!

Five

Woman: Hello, I'm just leaving a message to confirm your hair appointment. It's on the 4th... . Oh, no, sorry, that's the time – four o'clock. It's actually on the 7th. That's this month, May, obviously. Please let us know if you can't come. Thank you.

Six

Man: Could you please let your parents know that there will be a parents' meeting – that's when your parents can talk to your teachers about your studies – on 5th February. I know that on the school website it says 6th February, but that's a mistake, and we're going to change it today.

 5

Example

Man: Listen, everyone. I've got the date of your art exam. I told you it might be any time after 15th May, remember? Well, it's going to be on 28th May, so you've got quite a long time.

One

Woman: The boat trip for club members will be on July 4th. Please make sure you pay by 30th June. It's just £4 each – we get a special price because there are lots of us going.

Two

Man: Now, I want to tell you about this year's festival in the park! It starts on 19th August, and finishes on 22nd – four days to enjoy ourselves!

Three

Girl: There's a new café opening near my house. My sister's going to work there. It'll be ready for customers on 18th March, but my sister has to start on 15th March to help get it ready.

Four

Man: Please remember, everyone that we have our geography trip just after the school holidays, on 10th September. We come back to school on 5th September, so it's very soon after the start of term.

Five

Girl: We have to give in our science project soon. Today's 2nd February, and it has to be in by the 6th! I haven't even started yet!

Six

Man: I have a new event to tell you about – our first School Quiz. It'll be after school on 15th November. Think about who you want in your team – no more than six of you – and let me know the team names by 12th November. It's just for fun!

 Exam practice

Mrs Pullar: Hello everyone. My name's Mrs Pullar and I'm from Park Hill College. I want to tell you about a one-day computer course you can do at our college next Tuesday. I need to know by Friday how many of you are coming, so please ask your teacher for the form. The college is for students between 16 and 18, but to do this course you can be as young as 12, so if any of you would like to go, that's fine.

It's going to be a very interesting course. In the morning, you'll learn how to make your own website and in the afternoon, we'll teach you how to make a game. Your friends and family will love playing it! The college opens every day at 8.30, and the course will begin at 9.15. There's an hour's break for lunch and we'll finish at 4.30. The course usually costs £35, but for students of this school there is a special price of just £27.50. I hope lots of you will come

TEST 1 SPEAKING PART 1

 1

Pablo: Hi, I'm Pablo.

Marianne: Hi, Pablo. I'm Marianne Dubois.

Pablo: That's an interesting surname. How do you spell it?

Marianne: It's D-U-B-O-I-S.

Pablo: Oh, you're French!

Marianne: Yes, I am. I came to England last year, with my brother and sister and my parents. I was 13 – but I'm 14 now.

Pablo: So am I. Do you like this school?

Marianne: Yes, I do. I like our sports lessons because we play football. I like that more than other sports.

Pablo: Is sport your favourite school subject?

Marianne: No. I love science most. I like studying English too.

 3

Woman: Hello! What's your name?

Boy: It's Juan Perez.

Woman: Can you spell your surname for me?

Boy: Yes, it's P-E-R-E-Z.

Woman: Thank you. How old are you, Juan?

Boy: I'm 13.

Woman: Where do you come from?

Boy: I'm Spanish. I come from Spain.

Woman: Are you a student?

Boy: Yes, I am.

Woman: Do you like your school?

Boy: Yes, I do. Everyone's very friendly.

Woman: Great! What's your favourite subject?

Boy: I really like geography.

Woman: Do you study any languages?

Boy: Yes, I do. I study French and English.

Woman: How many English classes do you have each week?

Boy: We have two English classes – on Mondays and Thursdays.

Woman: Thank you.

 7

Girl: I live in an apartment with my parents and my sister. It's a small apartment but it's in the centre of town. It's near the shops. I like it.

Examiner: What's your name?

Student: My name's Andrei.

Examiner: Thank you. And what's your name?

Examiner: Can you spell your surname for me, Andrei?

Student: Yes. You spell it P-E-T-R-A-N.

Examiner: Thank you. And how do you spell your surname?

Examiner: Where do you come from, Andrei?

Student: I come from Romania.

Examiner: And where do you come from?

Examiner: What's your favourite subject, Andrei?

Student: I like history best.

Examiner: And what's your favourite subject?

Examiner: Do you like playing or watching sport, Andrei?

Student: Yes, I do. I like playing and watching football.

Examiner: Do you like playing or watching sport?

Examiner: Tell me something about your family, Andrei.

Student: I've got a big family. I've got five brothers and sisters.

Examiner: Thank you. Now tell me something about your family.

SPEAKING PART 2
Training

 1

Which activity is the boy asking about?

Boy: Can you tell me about the classes?

Girl: Yes, I can!

Boy: When are the classes?

Girl: They're in the afternoons.

Boy: Are the classes at the weekend?

Girl: No, they aren't. They're during the week.

Boy: How long are the classes?

Girl: They're two hours.

Boy: What should I wear?

Girl: You should wear trainers.

Boy: What do you do at the classes?

Girl: We play sports.

 5

Boy: Where are the swimming classes, Julia?

Girl: They're at Hall Bank Swimming Pool.

Boy: Oh, right. When are they?

Girl: They're on Tuesday evenings.

Boy: OK. How long are the classes?

Girl: They're one hour long, from 5 until 6 p.m.

Boy: What can you do at the classes?

Girl: You can do races every week.

Boy: Great! Who can I call to book a place?

Girl: You can call Daniel. His number is 0118 496 0523.

Boy: Thanks, Julia!

LISTENING PART 1
Training

 1

Boy: Who are the people in this photograph, Eva?

Eva: That's my cousin and two of her friends.

Boy: Is this your cousin – the one with short dark hair and glasses? She looks a bit like you.

Eva: Yeah, we do both wear glasses but that's not her. She's the one with long dark hair.

 2

Girl: Andres – my Dad's going to pick you up on his way home from work and bring you to my house.

Andres: Great. I think I know what he looks like. He has a beard, doesn't he?

Girl: Not anymore! He's changed since you last saw him. He's really slim now too!

Andres: Oh, that's good that you told me. But he must still be tall!

 3

One

Woman: Can I help you?

Boy: Yes, I need something to wear at weekends.

Woman: What kind of shoes are you looking for? Or do you need a pair of boots?

Boy: Trainers, actually. I only wear shoes for school, and I already have a pair of those!

Two

Mum: Danny, I think you need some new clothes. You've only got one sweater!

Danny: I hardly ever wear them, Mum. And I've got lots of T-shirts!

Mum: Well, you need a shirt for your cousin's wedding. You can't wear a T-shirt for that!

Danny: OK. As long as you let me choose it!

Three

Dad: Are you going shopping with your mother later, Molly?

Molly: Yes, Dad. Do you need something? New socks?

Dad: Thanks – I have enough of those! I need some gloves, for driving.

Molly: OK. Mum says I need tights, but I never wear them!

Four

Girl: I like your new belt, Beth. It's really nice!

Beth: Thanks. It's new. I want a scarf in the same colour. Mum's going to take me shopping later to get one.

Girl: Good idea. It's a lovely colour – almost the same as my hat!

Beth: Not quite; your hat is red not orange.

 4

Mum: Do you want your jeans for the party, Jessica? I've washed them.

Jessica: Thanks, Mum, but I think I'll wear my red dress.

Mum: You don't usually wear dresses.

Jessica: No, but Alicia said that she's going to wear a skirt, and I think most of the other girls will too.

 5

Teacher: OK class, it's time to tidy up now – there are books all over the place. Alfie, is this yours, next to my bag?

Alfie: Yes, Miss, thanks. And I think this is Rania's, on the floor.

Teacher: The one between the two chairs?

Rania: Yes, Miss, that's mine.

Teacher: And what about yours, Harry?

Harry: Mine's on the table, Miss. With that glass on top of it.

Teacher: Oh, yes. I see. And what about yours, Lucy?

Lucy: It's there on the floor, Miss. Under your table.

 6

Girl: How did your tennis practice go this morning, Ted? It was very dark and cloudy.

Ted: Yeah, I thought it might rain, but we were lucky. Actually it was better than when it's really sunny, because we could see the ball more easily.

Girl: Yes, that's true.

 Exam practice

Example

What did the teacher forget to bring to school?

Woman: Hello, Stephen. What's the matter? You look worried

Stephen: I forgot my watch, Miss. What time is it?

Woman: Let me see . . . It's a quarter to ten, I think. I remembered to bring my umbrella to school today, but I left my glasses at home.

Stephen: Oh dear! Thanks.

One

What did Hanna do on Sunday?

Grandpa: Hello, Hanna! Did you have fun at the lake with Mum and Dad on Sunday?

Hanna: Yes, Grandpa! We went for a really long bike ride with a group of friends from our sailing club.

Grandpa: Did you do anything else?

Hanna: We didn't, but we saw some people fishing. I don't think they caught anything!

Two

What time must John get on the train?

Mum: There's no school bus next week, John. Are you going to catch the train instead?

John: Yes, Mum. I'll have to leave home at five to eight because it stops at our station at five past.

Mum: So what time will you get to school then?

John: I'll get there by twenty-five past eight. It'll be fun to go by train.

Three.

Where is the girl's magazine?

Girl: Have you seen my new magazine, Dad? I left it on the bookshelf.

Dad: I know. Look on top of the fridge. I had to take it away from your baby brother!

Girl: OK. It's got something in it about software for drawing on computers. You should read it! It's really interesting!

Dad: Right! Well, perhaps if I have time.

Four.

Which photo is Sam talking about?

Girl: Who are these two girls with you in the photo, Sam?

Sam: Oh, they're my cousins from Canada. They came and stayed with me and Dad last summer. On that day, the four of us went to the mountains to do some fishing.

Girl: So did your dad take the photo?

Sam: Yes, he prefers being behind the camera.

Five.

What was the weather like at the beginning of the concert?

Girl: Hi! Was the rock concert good? It was such a shame I couldn't go.

Boy: It was great. We were lucky not to get wet!

Girl: I know it was cloudy, but did it rain too?

Boy: On the way there, yes! Dad was quite worried! But then the sun came out just before the first band started playing!

PART 2
Training

 1

Girl 1: Britt can play at least three different instruments.

Girl 2: Ada is so nice – she always helps people and is never horrible to anyone.

Girl 3: Nicola never has any problems in lessons – she always understands everything first time!

Girl 4: Sara makes everyone laugh. It's never boring when she's around!

Girl 5: Katy doesn't say very much. And when she does speak, it's really hard to hear her!

Girl 6: Serena will do anything, and she's never, ever scared!

Girl 7: Esther likes to keep everything in the right place.

 2

Example

Girl: I know we go to school to study, and that's great, but for me, the best thing is spending time with friends.

One

Boy: My dad goes running a lot. He says he does it because it's the only time he's not indoors. Of course, he keeps fit too.

Two

Girl: Travelling's great – visiting all those countries and cities you've never been to before. My mum likes to talk to people and find out things from them, but I leave that to her!

Three

Boy: Where I live it's really cold in winter. All my family ski, and I can do it, but I've never really enjoyed it. Then last year I learnt to snowboard. It's brilliant!

Four

Girl: We watched a film on TV yesterday. The music was wonderful – much better than the story!

Five

Boy: It was my birthday last week. It's a shame not many people came to my party, but I really enjoyed playing with the things that people bought me.

 3

Aunt: Hello Peter. It's Auntie Lisa. Can I speak to your mum?

Peter: Sorry, she's gone for a swim. She's started going every Saturday.

Aunt: Oh, OK then. What about your dad? He usually goes shopping on Saturday morning, doesn't he?

Peter: Usually, but today he's gone to pick up a friend who's just flown in from China.

Aunt: Right. And is your brother out too?

Peter: Yes. Mum gave him some money to send an important letter for her, so he's doing that.

Aunt: And did your sister go with him?

Peter: She's meeting a friend for a coffee and a chat. After that she's going to the library.

Aunt: Oh well, perhaps I'll call your grandmother. She might be able to help me.

Peter: I saw her yesterday at the supermarket. She told me she had to go out this morning to talk to someone about getting a credit card.

Aunt: That's right, I remember she told me. Well, tell your mother I called, Peter.

Peter: I will. Bye.

 Exam practice

Mr Sharp: Hello, Maria.

Maria: Good morning Mr Sharp. I'm reading a fantastic story about a girls' school.

Mr Sharp: I'm pleased you're enjoying it. Tell me more.

Maria: Well, I really like all the people in it. For example, there's a teacher called Miss Stevens. She's such an interesting person. She's not like anyone I've ever met!

Mr Sharp: And what are the pupils like?

Maria: Well, Olga's the oldest girl in the class. I like her because she's not afraid of anything!

Mr Sharp: I see.

Maria: And another girl, Trudy, is just like my sister. She doesn't say much.

Mr Sharp: So she prefers listening to speaking?

Maria: That's right. And Mrs Jenson's the headteacher. She studied at a really famous university and knows the answer to any question the girls ask her!

Mr Sharp: Really?

Maria: Yes! And Ursula, another student, always tries to look good – she has lots of pretty clothes. But I like her because she's so nice to everyone. She loves helping people.

Mr Sharp: Well, you're like that too!

Maria: Thank you. And her friend's called Alice. She's great because she makes everyone laugh. But some people get angry with her because she's never quiet!

Mr Sharp: Sounds like a great book!

LISTENING PART 3
Training

 3

Boy: Hi Elsa. Have you been on holiday?

Elsa: Yes, we went to a city called Cartagena.

Boy: That's in Spain, isn't it?

Elsa: There *is* a city called Cartagena in Spain, but I went to the one in Colombia.

Boy: Oh, I see. Did your whole family go?

Elsa: Me, my parents and my sister. My brother couldn't go because he's away at university.

Boy: How long did you stay there?

Elsa: Well, it's a long flight – about ten hours, so we stayed for 18 days. It was great.

Boy: The weather's really hot there, isn't it?

Elsa: Yeah. I read that in August it's 29 degrees. It was about 27 when we were there, in January, but that's not really much cooler!

Boy: So what did you do there?

Elsa: Well, lots of people go there for the beaches, but it was too hot for me. I preferred looking around the streets. The city is so interesting.

Boy: What about the language? Did you have any problems?

Elsa: I do German at school, so that was not good! But my dad speaks really good Spanish, so he did all the talking.

Boy: And what did you bring back with you?

Elsa: Not much. I saw a really beautiful necklace, but Mum said it was too expensive. So I got a book, and Mum brought back some coffee for her and Dad.

 3

Girl: Hello. I want to take a bus tour around the city. Where can I get it from?

Man: Well, it stops at various places. The nearest to here is Castle Street, but I think the best place to start is River Gardens.

Girl: OK, thanks. And how long can you use the tickets for?

Man: For 24 hours. In other cities you can only use them for 12 hours, so it's good.

Girl: Great. And how much will I pay for a ticket?

Man: The adult price is £25, but for students like you it's only £20. You have to show your student card.

Girl: Thanks, I'll do that. Now – about places to see. What time does the Castle Museum open?

Man: They're on the summer timetable now, so you can get in from 9.30. In the winter it's ten o'clock.

Girl: The cathedral is really famous too, isn't it? When was it built?

Man: Well, it took a long time. It was started in the 13th century, but not completed until the 15th.

Girl: Oh, that *is* a long time. Can you go up the tower?

Man: Yes, but they do close it sometimes if it's windy. Obviously that happens more in the winter, but it can happen at this time of the year as well.

Girl: Right. And I want to buy something to eat. Is there a market?

Man: There's a market every day, but for different things. Today it's clothes. Food is tomorrow.

Girl: Oh, never mind. Thanks very much for the information.

 Exam practice

Girl: Hi Jim. How was your trip to Ashford?

Boy: Great!

Girl: Did you go by train?

Boy: Not this time. We went there by coach, then went around on foot.

Girl: Who took you?

Boy: Mr Anson. He wanted us to learn about forest flowers, and collect some plants to study at school.

Girl: Oh I see. And there's a really old castle there too, isn't there?

Boy: Yes. That was built in the 10th century. It's beautiful, but no-one's lived in it since the 17th century. We also saw some old wooden houses that were built there in the thirteenth century.

Girl: Was it expensive to visit the castle?

Boy: It's seven pounds usually. But it was five pounds for us because there were more than eight people in our group.

Girl: That's good! What about lunch?

Boy: There's a hill outside the village, so we climbed up and had it there. We could see the river from the top. Then later we went for a walk.

Girl: What about the weather?

Boy: Well, we had umbrellas, so we kept dry. It's a shame it wasn't sunny.

Girl: Oh no, it was foggy here.

PART FOUR
Training

49 **1**

Woman: How much are the tickets for the show?

Man: £5 per person. Are you bringing any children?

Woman: Yes, I'll be bringing two.

Man: They get in for just £3 each.

One

Woman: Excuse me. How much are the tickets for the river trip?

Man: £3.50 for a return trip.

Woman: And what about if we only want to go one way?

Man: That's two pounds per person.

Two

Boy: How much for all of these things?

Woman: That's two dollars and 25 cents.

Boy: Oh! How much are the drinks, then?

Woman: Those are 75 cents each.

Three

Girl: Excuse me. How much is this book?

Man: Well, it's usually £7.99, but we have a sale on this week, so it's only 5.99.

Girl: Thanks. I'll take it.

Four

Boy: Shall we go to the concert at the weekend?

Girl: Yeah, that sounds good.

Boy: Tickets are £6.25, so for the two of us it'll be £12.50.

Girl: That sounds fine.

50 2

Example

Boy: Excuse me. Do you have a special price for students?

Woman: Yes. The full adult price is £4.50, but if you have a student card, you only pay £3.30.

Boy: Thanks very much.

One

Girl: Sir, do we have to pay for this trip?

Man: Yes, Kelly. We'll be sending a letter to your parents, asking them for £2. The actual cost is £5 per student, but the school will pay the rest.

Girl: Thanks. I'll tell my mum.

Two

Man: Hello. Ashcroft Museum.

Girl: Hello. How much does it cost to get into the museum?

Man M: It's $4. We have a special photography exhibition on at the moment, but if you want to get into that you have to pay an extra $2.

Girl: Oh, OK. Thanks

Three

Man: Excuse me. I'd like to buy that watch in the window. The red one. The ticket says £25.

Woman: I'll just get it from the window. Actually, it's £28. Sorry, the writing wasn't very clear.

Man: Don't worry, it's not that much different!

Four

Woman1: I like your new bag. Where did you get it?

Woman 2: I bought it online. It was a great price. They cost fifty dollars in the shops!

Woman 1: So how much did you pay?

Woman 2: Only $35.50. That's $14.50 less!

Five

Boy: How much are those green sweets?

Woman: They're five pence each. How many would you like?

Boy: I'll have ten, please.

Six

Boy: I don't think I've got enough money for the bus. How much is it?

Woman: A dollar twenty. How much have you got?

Boy: 90 cents. Can you lend me 30 cents so I can buy a ticket?

Woman: Of course.

 51 3

Boy: How old were you when you started learning the guitar, Sarah?

Girl: I had my first lesson when I was eight. I'm 12 now, so that's four years ago.

One

Boy: Excuse me. I don't know if I'm old enough to see this film. I'm twelve.

Woman: Sorry, but no. You need to be at least 15 to see this one.

Two

Boy: Hello. I'm interested in the drama course that's starting soon.

Woman: Yes, it's for people aged 10 to 14. It starts on the 6th.

Boy: OK. Thanks.

Three

Man: I'm taking my little brother to see a play next month.

Woman: Oh. Maybe my cousin would like it. She's six.

Man: Yeah, bring her. It's for three to eight year olds.

Four

Woman: Hi. I saw your poster. I'd like to buy your bike.

Boy: OK. It's a children's bike. I've had it since I was six.

Woman: So it's no good for a five year old?

Boy: No, it's too big. I had it until I was about eight.

Five

Woman: Hi. Four tickets, please.

Man: How old is the little child?

Woman: She's two.

Man: Then you don't have to pay for her. Children under three go in free.

 52 4

Teacher: Quiet now, class. I want to tell you about our trip to the farm.

Girl1: When are we going, Mr Chandler?

Teacher: On March 25th. That's just before the end of term. Term finishes on March 30th.

Boy: Which farm is it, sir? Is it Wilton Farm? That's the nearest.

Teacher: We're going to Kendall Farm, Sam. It's bigger, so there are more animals to see.

Boy: How do you spell Kendall?

Teacher: K-E-N-D-A-LL. Right, any more questions?

Girl 2: How are we going to get there, sir?

Teacher: Good question. I was thinking about going by train, because it's quick, but the walk to the station is quite long, so we're going by coach. I think that's easiest.

Girl 2: So are we going for the whole day?

Teacher: No, just for the afternoon. We'll have lunch a little earlier than usual – at 12 o'clock. We'll leave here at quarter to one, and we should be at the farm by half past one.

Girl 3: Do we have to bring anything with us, sir?

Teacher: Well, we don't need a picnic – as I said, we'll have lunch here before we go. But do bring raincoats, as the weather isn't always good at this time of the year.

Girl 3: Mr Chandler, will our parents have to pay for this trip?

Teacher: Yes, Dani, but we get a special student price, which is £4.50. Usually it costs £7 to get in, so it's a good price. Right, I think that's everything. Let's do some maths now.

 53 Exam practice

Woman: Good afternoon. Garden Zoo. Can I help you?

Man: Oh hello. I want to bring my two little cousins to the zoo. How much are the tickets?

Woman: Adult tickets are £13.50, and it's £8.70 for children under 12.

Man: What time do you open?

Woman: On Saturdays and Sundays we open at 9:30 and on weekdays at nine. We close at 7:20 every day.

Man: OK. Is anything special happening this weekend?

Woman: Yes, there's a talk about lions. You'll learn a lot about these amazing animals if you go to that.

Man: Do I need to book?

Woman: No, just go to the Wilton Centre at 2 p.m.

Man: How do you spell that?

Woman: It's W I L T O N. It's easy to find – it's not far from the entrance.

Man: Thanks. Oh, and I heard about a photography exhibition, called Animals in the Forest. Is that still on?

Woman: That's finished – we've got another one now, called Animals in the Sea. There are lots of wonderful pictures of fish. Don't miss it!

Man: I won't, thanks.

PART 5
Training

 1

Example

Woman: There are two things I would like you to do this evening children. The first is to read page 6 of your books, and the second is to watch the programme about mountains on Channel 5. It's on at 6 o'clock this evening.

One

Man: It's quite a small group of us going on the trip tomorrow – 10 people in total, six adults and four children.

Two

Woman: My address is 4, Oakland Road. There are only 16 houses in the street, so it's not hard to find. If you walk from town, you'll come to number 16 first, so just keep walking down.

Three

Man: For more information, please call 0-1-6-3 2-9-6 0-6-8-3. If you call after 10, you'll get the answering machine. We'll be open again the next morning at 6, and we're open seven days a week.

Four

Woman: For your homework I'd like you to read a page from your history book. It's page 67. We looked at page 66 today, and we'll do page 68 next time. It's not much to read.

Five

Man: This project is only a short one – you don't have to write very much, only four pages. And because it's short, I'm going to give you only five days to write it. I'm sure you can all do that.

 2

Example

Man: I live at number 425, Station Road. It's not a house – they are flats, and we're number 15.

One

Girl: The maths competition is much bigger this year. Last year there were only eight teams, but this year there are 14, so we'll have to work really hard to win!

Two

Boy: I'm selling my football game. I want to get the new one, which is three-five-seven. It's the older one I'm selling: the three–five–three. I want £15 for it.

Three

Woman: For those of you who are doing the running AND the cycling race, listen carefully to this information; you have to run 500 metres, but for the cycling it's longer – 800 metres.

Four

Woman: We don't have much room on the school bus – only 20 places – so if you want to come and watch the team, let me know today. We need 12 places for the team, which means I can take eight people to watch.

Five

Boy: Callie's number has changed. She's not using 0163 254 6802 anymore. The new one is 0163 564 7885. She changed it last month.

Six

Woman: There are four screens at the cinema, and the film we're going to see is on at screen 3. It's the second on the left when you go through the doors.

 4

Sports

One

Man: I'm going to be showing you how to play cricket, today.

Two

Woman: I'm watching a fishing programme on TV. It's actually really interesting!

Three

Man: And after the news tonight, we'll be showing the golf. That's at ten past nine.

Hobbies

One

Girl: I love listening to music. It's what I spend all my free time doing.

Two

Boy: This is a great website for people who like watching films. It's got lots of information.

Three

Girl: There's a photography exhibition at the museum this week.

Places in a town

One

Man: The new theatre is nearly finished. It looks great!

Two

Woman: Can you tell me the way to the university, please?

Three

Man: I'll meet you at the café at half past four.

Possessions

One

Man: Please make sure that you bring a pen, as we'll be writing down information.

Two

Woman: Don't forget to bring a coat with you, as it may be cold.

Three

Man: Is that a new book? What's it about?

Ways to travel

One

Woman: What time does the plane leave?

Two

Man: We're going to travel by boat. It should be really good!

Three

Woman: Is this the way to the station?

Animals

One

Boy: There's a programme on TV about monkeys. Do you want to watch it with me?

Two

Girl: We saw elephants at the zoo. They're amazing!

Three

Girl: Do you have any pets? I've got a rabbit. He's two years old.

 57 Exam practice

Teacher: Now I'd like to tell you about a new television programme that I'm sure you'll find interesting. It's going to be on every Wednesday through the autumn and winter terms. It's about things you're going to learn about in your physics, biology and chemistry lessons and it's called Exploring Science. There'll be lots of useful information which will help with your studies. Now make a note of the channel please. You'll find it on 63. There'll be a total of 20 programmes. Try not to miss any of them! It starts at 5:40 and it's on for half an hour. That's immediately after the 5:30 'News for Schools' programme.

The first programme will be on 15th October, that's a week before the half term holiday on 22nd October. If you watch that one, you'll find out all about insects. These little animals are so important in our world, although some people don't like them.

SPEAKING PART 1
Training

 58 2

Girl: It's Morales. That's M-O-R-A-L-E-S.

Boy: My surname's spelt J-A-C-O-B-double S-O-N

Girl: You spell it H-A-Y-A-S-H-I-D-A.

Boy: It's C-H-E-O-N-G.

59 3

Woman: Hello! What's your name?

Boy: It's Adil Yilmaz.

Woman: How do you spell your surname?

Boy: It's Y-I-L-M-A-Z.

Woman: Where do you come from, Adil?

Boy: I come from Turkey. I'm from a town called Alanya in the south.

Woman: And do you study English at school?

Boy: No, I don't. I go to classes after school.

Woman: How many English classes do you have each week?

Boy: I have three. Three hours.

Woman: What's your favourite subject at school, Adil?

Boy: I like science. It's really interesting.

60 5

Man: Hello! What's your name?

Girl: It's Carla Rossi.

Man: How do you spell your surname?

Girl: I'm sorry, what did you say?

Man: Can you spell your surname for me?

Girl: Yes, it's R-O-SS-I.

Man: Thank you. Where do you come from, Carla?

Girl: I'm Italian.

Man: And how old are you?

Girl: Sorry?

Man: How old are you?

Girl: Oh ... I'm fourteen.

Man: And are you a student?

Girl: Yes, I am. I go to school.

Man: How do you travel to school?

Girl: Can you say that again, please?

Man: Yes. How do you travel to school?

Girl: I go by bus.

Man: Tell me something about your family.

Girl: I don't understand.

Man: Can you tell me about your family?

Girl: Erm ... I've got two sisters. They're both older than me.

Man: Thank you, Carla.

 61 7

Man: Hello. What's your name?

Boy: I'm Evgeni Petrov.

Man: And where are you from, Evgeni?

Boy: Sorry?

Man: Where do you come from?

Boy: Oh, I'm Russian. I come from the east of Russia.

Man: Thank you. Are you a student, Evgeni?

Boy: Yes, I am. I go to school here in Scotland.

Man: What's your favourite subject at school?

Boy: Erm ... I like studying maths and English.

Man: How many English classes do you have each week?

Boy: I have two classes of English every week at school and one class after school.

Man: Tell me about your family.

Boy: It's a big family. I have four brothers and a sister. There's just one girl in my family!

Man: Tell me about your sister.

Boy: I'm sorry, what did you say?

Man: Can you tell me something about your sister?

Boy: Yes. She's studying French at university. She likes dancing.

Man: Thank you.

62 Exam practice

Examiner: What's your name?

How do you spell your surname?

Are you a student?

How do you travel to school?

What time does your school start and finish?

What's your favourite subject?

Tell me something about your favourite hobby.

SPEAKING PART 2
Training

 5

Girl: I've got some questions about the skiing competition.

Boy: OK.

Girl: What time does the skiing competition start?

Boy: It starts at 10 a.m. and finishes at 3 p.m.

Girl: Are there prizes?

Boy: Yes – you can win a pair of ski boots.

Girl: Oh! Who can enter the competition?

Boy: There are races for all ages.

Girl: Great! What date is the competition?

Boy: It's on Saturday 5th of December.

Girl: Oh, I forgot a question! Where is the competition?

Boy: It's on Snowy Mountain.

Girl: OK. Thanks!

 Exam practice

School camping trip – model conversation

Girl: Can I ask you some questions about the school camping trip?

Boy: Yes, of course.

Girl: When is the camping trip?

Boy: It's between the 18th and 20th of May.

Girl: Oh. Is it expensive?

Boy: No. It's only £30.

Girl: Great! Where will we sleep?

Boy: In school tents at Green Leaves Forest.

Girl: Will we travel there by train?

Boy: No, there's a coach. It leaves at 9 a.m.

Girl: Oh! What do I need to take?

Boy: You need to bring warm clothes.

Girl: OK. Thanks a lot!

School barbecue – model conversation

A: I've got some questions about the school barbecue.

B: OK.

A: When does the barbecue start?

B: At 4 p.m. on Saturday. And it finishes at 7 p.m.

A: Oh. Where can I get tickets?

B: They're available from the school office. They're £2 each.

A: OK. What is there to eat?

B: There will be sausages, burgers and salads.

A: Great! Will we play games?

B: Yes. There will be football and basketball matches!

A: Oh, OK! Can we invite other people?

B: Yes, you can bring your friends and family.

A: Great! Thank you very much.

SPEAKING PART 1

 66 Questions 1–5

Example.

How much is a large cup of hot chocolate?

Girl: Can I have a cup of hot chocolate, please?

Man: Do you want a small one? That costs 95p. Or it's £1.55 for a large one. That comes with cream.

Girl: Great! I've got £2.85, so I'll have a large one, please.

Man: Here you are and here's your change.

One

Where was the grey bird that Adam saw?

Mum: Did you have a good walk with Grandad, Adam?

Boy: Yeah. We saw a big grey bird. Grandad said that type of bird usually lives near rivers.

Mum: And were you near a river when you saw it?

Boy: That's the strange thing. We were still in town. It was on top of a house. But there were some trees in a park nearby.

Two

What are cheaper than usual at the moment?

Boy: I like these jeans, Mum.

Mum: Mm. It's better to buy jeans when they're in a sale. What about these T-shirts. It says 'half-price' on the sign.

Boy: I've got lots already. What I really need are some trainers.

Mum: OK. They don't have discounts on those, but the prices are quite good here anyway.

Three

How will Francine let her friend know about the guitar?

Dad: Francine, are you emailing your friend to tell her that she left her guitar here yesterday?

Girl: Actually, I'm doing my homework, Dad. I tried calling her, but she didn't answer. I can just tell her at school tomorrow.

Dad: OK. Maybe she can come home with you and pick it up then.

Four

What did Andreas watch on TV last night?

Girl: Did you watch the tennis last night, Andreas? It was really exciting!

Boy: Yeah, that's what my brother said. He watched it. I didn't want to miss the football, so Dad let me borrow his computer.

Girl: Did he watch it with you?

Boy: No, my Dad prefers cricket. There wasn't any on last night, so he watched the tennis too.

Five

Where is the girl's phone?

Girl: Have you taken my phone again, Sam?

Boy: No! I saw it on the table next to your bed. You always leave it there.

Girl: Well it's not there now! Mum said she saw you put a phone on your desk!

Boy: Yes, I did – my phone! What's that over there on the sofa? Look – there's yours! I told you I didn't have it!

PART 2

67

Boy: Hi Julia. Did you enjoy your week off school? You went for a bike ride with my sister on Sunday, didn't you?

Julia: We wanted to go for a bike ride but it was raining, so we met up and had hot chocolate.

Boy: That's right. Did you go shopping with her on Monday?

Julia: No, we decided to go to the pool instead. It was really fun. Why didn't you come out with us?

Boy: I was at the sports centre on Monday. I did some climbing. What did you do on Tuesday?

Julia: I had some reading to do for school, about mountains. But Wednesday was better!

Boy: Why, what did you do then? Shopping for clothes?

Julia: No, I went to the cinema with some friends.

Boy: Great. And on Thursday? You planned to go to a museum, didn't you?

Julia: Yeah, with my mum. It was great. We saw some beautiful paintings. But my favourite day was Friday.

Boy: Oh, that's the day I had to help my dad paint our kitchen. What did you do?

Julia: I went out on my new bike with my brother. We went all the way to the shops.

Boy: Wow! You really did have a busy week!

PART 3

68 Questions 11–15

Seth: Hi Katerina. Do you have a moment? I'd like to ask you a few questions. I want to join the Saturday art club. You've been going to it for a long time now haven't you?

Katerina: I started going last summer, so about nine months, but it took me two months before I could draw anything well.

Seth: What do you do there?

Katerina: It's different each term. Last term we did painting, and now we're going to start drawing. The teacher said it'll be photography after that, which I love!

Seth: And where is the art club?

Katerina: Well, you know where I go to school? It's in the library just behind there. The teacher works at a college, but there are no rooms free there on Saturdays.

Seth: OK. What time does it start?

Katerina: I usually get there at 9:30, when they open the doors. Most people arrive by ten, ready for the beginning of the class at ten fifteen. We finish at 12:30.

Seth: That's fine. Do I need to take anything?

Katerina: They give us everything we need for the art, such as paper. And the teacher brings in books on art to give us ideas. There's a café, so money for a snack in the break would be good.

Seth: All right. Can we go together?

Katerina: Sure. I go by bus. It stops near the shop at the end of your road. I have to go past your house, so I can just come there.

Seth: Thanks. That's great. See you on Saturday.

PART 4

 **69 Questions 16–20**

Ryan: Hi Lin – I wasn't at school yesterday. Did we get any homework?

Lin: Hi Ryan. Yes, a project. For geography.

Ryan: Oh, for Mr Haslop.

Lin: No, we had a new teacher. Mr Bauckham. You spell it B-A-U-C-K-H-A-M. He's going to be teaching us for the next few weeks.

Ryan: OK. What's the project about?

Lin: He put us in groups. My group is doing the desert and yours is doing the sea. There's another group doing the sky.

Ryan: And do we have to write a lot?

Lin: Not really – just six pages. And out of those, two pages can be pictures, so it's not that much.

Ryan: Where do I get the information from?

Lin: He said he doesn't want us to use the information in our textbooks. He wants something different, so we should look at websites. He checked that everyone can do that.

Ryan: All right. And when do we have to give it to him?

Lin: Not Monday, because that's not enough time, and we have a school trip on Wednesday, so Friday. That's when we have our next lesson.

PART 5

 **70 Questions 21–25**

Man: Good morning, you're listening to Real Radio! I have a competition to tell you about. Lots of you send in photos of yourselves and of your friends, which is just great. But not many people send photos of their pets, and I want to see them! I'll then choose the ones I like the most. We'll have more than one prize – three in total. The two people who come second and third will get a pen, and the winner will be sent a T- shirt. All of the prizes will have the name of the radio station on.

As this is a station for younger listeners, not adults, you can only enter if you're 16 or under. It doesn't matter how young you are – even if you're less than eight years old, you can still enter the competition!

We'll give you a few weeks to send in your photos. Today is 13th March, so I think the 24th should be okay. Make sure we get your photos by then. Have fun!

LISTENING PART ONE

 Questions 1–5

Example.

Which is the girl's first lesson this morning?

Girl: Have you seen my maths textbook, Dad?

Dad: Is that for your first lesson this morning?

Girl: No. That's our first lesson after lunch. We've got science first today, then double geography before lunch.

One

What will Billy clean first?

Woman: Can you clean the garden table for me, Billy? Then we can have lunch outside later?

Billy: OK, Grandma, but I want to clean my football boots before I do that.

Woman: All right. Perhaps you could do your bike later too. It's really dirty after your ride yesterday morning.

Billy: I know! I always enjoy cleaning my bike … I'll do that after lunch!

Two.

What was the weather like on the school trip to the sea?

Dad: Oh hello! You're back! Did you enjoy your school trip to the beach? I hope it wasn't too windy.

Girl: That wasn't a problem, but it rained all day, which was a shame.

Dad: Oh, not like your last trip to the castle when you were all too hot.

Girl: I know! Maybe next time we'll get sunny weather.

Three.

Where did Georgia go on Saturday afternoon?

Boy: Did you have time to go to the new sports centre on Saturday afternoon, Georgia?

Georgia: Actually, it was my aunt's birthday so we went out for lunch instead.

Boy: Oh, she's got a fashion shop in the town centre, hasn't she?

Georgia: That's right, but she took the day off on Saturday. Why don't we try and go to the sports centre together next weekend?

Four.

What time does the school's computer club end?

Girl: Excuse me, Mr Lea. When does the computer club finish this afternoon? Dad wants to know what time I'll be home.

Mr Lea: At a quarter past four, Kim, so you'll be able to get the four thirty bus.

Girl: And we must all be in the computer room by a quarter to four. Is that right?

Mr Lea: Yes. I'm sure everyone will enjoy it.

Five.

How will Lucy get home?

Lucy: Are you coming to get the bus home with me, Ben?

Ben: Not today, my brother will be here soon. He's giving me a lift home.

Lucy: On his motorbike? You lucky thing! I'd love to have one of those!

Ben: Oh, he had to sell his motorbike, unfortunately. He's got a car now, so he's picking me up in that. Look! Here he is!

PART TWO

 Questions 6–10

Diana: I'm so bored, Mum. All my friends are busy!

Mum: Really? What's Fiona doing?

Diana: She's just texted me from the airport. She's going away on holiday.

Mum: Why don't you call David, then?

Diana: I did. His uncle's staying with them, and they're putting a new wheel on his bike. The old one broke last week when he was cycling back from school.

Mum: Well spend some time with Ella. She's nice!

Diana: She's finishing her history project today. It's all about the village where her grandparents live.

Mum: Interesting! What's Thomas doing?

Diana: There's rugby on TV today, so he's watching the game. He loves sport!

Mum: Is Vicky free? Why don't you two go and play basketball together?

Diana: I'd like to, but her aunt's just had a baby boy so she's gone to see them. She's taken a cake with her! She made it yesterday.

Mum: Who else is there? Simon ….?

Diana: There's no football practice today, so he's at home trying a computer game he's just bought. Yes. Maybe I'll go and see him.

Mum: Good idea!

PART THREE

73 Questions 11–15

Tom: Andy, there are no tickets for the Black Fox or Moonstar concerts, but my parents have got some for Crowd 5. Do you want to come?

Andy: Yeah!

Tom: Mum found out about it online. There are posters in town now and adverts on the radio too.

Andy: Sounds great. When's the concert?

Tom: We wanted tickets for 19th June, but there weren't any, so we're going on the 23rd instead. The tour ends on the 25th.

Andy: Brilliant! Where are we sitting?

Tom: The seats at the front were really expensive, so Dad got ones on the side. You can't see much from the back.

Andy: All right. Shall I take some money for a T-shirt?

Tom: Yeah, they're the best things to get. The photos are never great and we don't need any more CDs.

Andy: I can't wait! Let's talk more after school tomorrow.

Tom: OK, shall I see you in the playground?

Andy: Fine, I'll be there at 4. I need to go to the library before that and I've got sports club later, so we can't talk for long.

Tom: No problem.

PART FOUR

 **74** **Questions 16–20**

Girl: Excuse me! I'm collecting information for my school geography project. Do you often shop here at Costright supermarket?

Man: Yes, I do.

Girl: Great! Can I ask you some questions?

Man: Yes, sure.

Girl: Thanks. My first question is, where do you live?

Man: I live in Oberleigh. It's a village not far from here. You spell it O-B-E-R-L-E-I-G-H.

Girl: Thanks – got that. And can I ask how old you are? I need to speak to people in their 20s, 30s and 40s.

Man: I'm 33.

Girl: That's great. And, how do you travel to the supermarket?

Man: Well, I don't have a car yet, so I come on the bus. If I buy a lot of shopping, I get a taxi home.

Girl: And, how much do you usually spend here?

Man: These days it's about £65. I remember a few months ago it was only £45.

Girl: And my last question – what sort of things do you always buy when you shop here?

Man: Let's see, bread, milk, vegetables. But not meat. I get that from the butcher in my village.

Girl: That's great. Thanks very much for your time.

Man: You're welcome.

PART FIVE

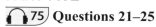 **75** **Questions 21–25**

Martin: Hi Pat. It's your hockey coach, Martin. I'm calling about the match next Saturday morning. We're playing at the Reynolds Sports Centre. You spell that R-E-Y-N-O-L D-S. It's not far from here.

Three of the players' parents want to come to watch the game so instead of using the bus, we're each driving a car. I'm taking Jim and Harry, and you can come with us too. The match begins at 10 but we to be there an hour before that, at 9, so I'll see you at 8:30, at the gates of the hockey club. Please don't be late. You'll probably be home around one thirty.

The other team have chosen to wear their blue and white kit so please bring your purple shorts and top. You should also bring some money so you can get a snack afterwards.

Call me if you can't play for any reason. I've just changed phones, so my number's 0 5 6 7 double zero 1 4 7 8 3. See you on Saturday!

LISTENING PART ONE

 76 **Questions 1–5**

Example.

When's Michael's birthday?

Girl: I'm 13 in January. When's Michael's birthday?

Boy: I'm not sure but I know it's in February. The 23rd perhaps ...?

Girl: I think it's earlier than that?

Boy: Oh yes! That's right. It's the 16th, just before mine.

One

What will Marina wear tomorrow?

Dad: Marina, I'm going to wash some clothes. Do you need your jeans for tomorrow?

Marina: It's going to be warm tomorrow, so I'll be too hot in jeans. Can you wash my blue skirt, please?

Dad: But you're going to the park on your bike! Don't you think you should wear shorts for that?

Marina: Oh yeah, you're right, Dad. They'll be much better.

Two

Which is Jim's grandmother?

Girl: Is your grandmother coming to watch the concert, Jim? I just saw an older woman who looks a bit like your mum.

Jim: Yeah, she is. Was she wearing glasses?

Girl: She was. And she had short dark hair.

Jim: Oh, my grandma's hair is blonde. Maybe she's not here yet.

Three

What will Annie do at art club this week?

Annie: Mr Taylor, are we going to do any photography at art club this term?

Mr Taylor: In a few weeks, Annie. I'd like you all to finish your paintings first.

Annie: So that's what we're going to do this week. What about our drawings?

Mr Taylor: I've already put those on the wall, and they look fantastic!

Four

What has Ben lost?

Girl: Ben, can I borrow your ruler? I can't find mine.

Ben: OK. Have you seen my pencil? I'm sure you borrowed it yesterday.

Girl: I did, but I gave it back to you. Isn't that it, next to your rubber?

Ben: No, that's my pen. I'll have a look in my bag.

Five

How long will it take to walk to the cinema from Ali's house?

Girl: How far away is the new cinema, Ali? Can we walk?

Ali: Yes, easily. The film starts at 4, and we should be there ten minutes earlier to buy tickets. Let's leave my house at 3:30 – 20 minutes will be enough.

Girl: OK. It'll take me five minutes to get to your house, so I'll leave home at 3:25.

Ali: Fine. See you later then.

PART TWO

 77 **Questions 6–10**

Boy: Wow, you have so many postcards, Alicia.

Alicia: Yeah. People send them to me because I collect them.

Boy: I love this one of a castle. Is that in Italy?

Alicia: Spain, actually. It's beautiful, isn't it?

Boy: Mm, and I like this one of a mountain.

Alicia: My cousin sent me that. She lives in the United States, but that's in Argentina – she was there on holiday.

Boy: Oh! I sent you this one of the lake! That's in Switzerland. Oh! it says Italy on the back! I'm wrong!

Alicia: Look – this beach looks like Spain, but my dad sent it from Kenya.

Boy: Oh yes, he travels a lot for business, doesn't he?

Alicia: Yeah. This city view is from him. It's a place in Australia. He's there again now, and from there he's flying to China.

Boy: So which is your favourite?

Alicia: This one of a forest, because I've actually been there! It's in the United States. I went with my older sister before she moved to Switzerland.

Boy: Well, I'll send you a postcard when I next go on holiday!

Alicia: Thanks!

PART THREE

78 **Questions 11–15**

Daisy: Hi Adam. Did you see my email? I couldn't find you yesterday afternoon, so I sent it in the evening. Then I was going to text you this morning, but I forgot.

Adam: No, I don't look at my emails very often. What was it about?

Daisy: Would you like to come to see a play with me next week? Someone I know is going to be in it.

Adam: Oh, who's that?

Daisy: Do you remember my cousin Linda? Well it's her neighbour, Gina. Come and see it with me – Naomi's coming too.

Adam: Yeah, OK. Do you know what the play is about?

Daisy: Yes. There's a poster in the street near my house – it's about a storm. It sounds exciting – better than something from history like a story about a king.

Adam: When shall we see it?

Daisy: Well, the first night of the play is Wednesday, and they're doing three nights. Let's go on the last night – Friday. I'm busy on Thursday anyway.

Adam: OK. And where's the theatre?

Daisy: Just opposite the school. I have to go to the library that day – the one near the station, so I'll meet you at the theatre.

Adam: Great. Do you know the price of the tickets?

Daisy: Yes. Adult tickets are £10 each. We're students, so for us it's £8 each. I'll get the three tickets and you can pay me later.

Adam: OK. Thanks, Daisy.

PART FOUR

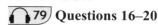 **Questions 16–20**

Eva: David, for the photography competition, can we take pictures of anything we like? Such as animals?

David: This year you have to take a photograph of food. It was animals last year.

Eva: Oh. And you how old do you need to be? Can my brother enter?

David: He's 12, isn't he? Then yes. You have to be under 14 to enter.

Eva: OK. Do you know who's going to choose the winner?

David: A photographer called Pat Hagerstown. You spell that H-A-G-E-R-S-T-O-W-N.

Eva: Thanks. And do you email the photo?

David: You have to print it yourself, so you can't send it by email. You have to post it.

Eva: Right. And when do they need to receive the photos?

David: You haven't got that long. They need to get the photos before 15th July, and today is 2nd July, so hurry up!

Eva: OK! What does the winner get?

David: Some money. And if I win, I'm going to spend it on a new camera!

PART FIVE

 **Questions 21–25**

Teacher: Good morning everyone. I want to tell you about the quiz which we're going to have next week, on the last day of term – that's 2nd April.

The quiz is for all of year five, so that's two classes. We'll have ten teams, with six people in each team. You can choose your own teams.

There are too many of us to fit in one classroom, so we'll use the library. The hall is too big.

There'll be questions on four subjects; history, maths, science and geography. As I teach languages, I wanted some questions on my subject, but the other teacher didn't agree!

There'll be a prize for everyone on the winning team – a pen. But don't worry if your team doesn't win – all of you will get a sweet at the end too!

I've put a list on the wall, and when you've chosen your teams, I want you to write your team name and members on the list. Please do that by Thursday. Today is Monday, so you've got a few days.

Test 6 Audioscript

LISTENING PART ONE

Example.

Which kind of ice cream does the girl buy?

Girl: Hello, I'd like a chocolate ice cream, please.

Man: I'm sorry, that's all gone. We've only got these two kinds left. We've been busy today.

Girl: Oh! OK, I'll have a banana one, then. I don't like coffee ice cream.

One

Where is the bank?

Man: Excuse me. I'm looking for the bank. Someone told me it's near this roundabout.

Woman: It was, but it's moved. You need to turn right just over there.

Man: Is it at the end of that road?

Woman: No, about halfway down. It's not far.

Two

What will the weather be like today?

Woman: Aren't you going to wear a jacket today, Josh?

Josh: Why, is it going to rain?

Woman: On the TV this morning they said it's going to be windy. It'll be sunny too, but cold.

Josh: Oh, OK. I'll take it then.

Three

How much will the girl have to pay to swim?

Girl: How much is it going to cost us to go swimming?

Boy: Well I'm a member at the sports centre, so for me it's only £5.60. People who aren't members pay £7.75.

Girl: So I have to pay £2.15 more than you?

Boy: Yeah. Sorry!

Four

Where is Luc's father?

Woman: Luc, do you know where your dad is?

Luc: I saw him in the garden a few minutes ago, Mum. Isn't he there?

Woman: I've just been out there. Maybe he's in the garage. I'll try there.

Luc: Oh, yes, he is! I remember now. He's looking for something to repair the cupboard in the kitchen.

Five

What did Sara do last weekend?

Boy: How was your weekend, Sara? Did you go to the cinema? There was a film you wanted to see, wasn't there?

Sara: Yes, there was. I'll have to see it next weekend instead. I had a lot of studying to do. I didn't even go swimming.

Boy: But you always do that at the weekend!

Sara: Not this one!

PART TWO

 Questions 6–10

Grandmother: You're always so busy, Andres. Do your friends do lots of activities too?

Andres: Yes. My friend Marcus goes to the pool every morning. He wants to get onto the national team.

Grandmother: And what about that tall girl, Tanya. She's always on her bicycle!

Andres: Not any more, Grandma. She prefers running now – most evenings after school.

Grandmother: And that boy who lives near me – Steven. He takes a camera everywhere he goes!

Andres: That's right. That's his hobby. And my friend Lina makes necklaces. She made one for Mum. She was wearing it at the tennis match last week. You asked about it.

Grandmother: Yes, I remember. She's Paolo's sister, right? What does Paolo do?

Andres: Well, he's a great footballer, but he doesn't play anymore. He does a lot of cycling in his free time now.

Grandmother: And your sister's friend Jenny. She and your sister seem to go shopping all the time! I asked them to come for a walk with me, but they weren't interested!

Andres: I'll come for a walk with you, Grandma. Let's go to the park.

Grandmother: Good idea.

PART THREE

 Questions 11–15

Tamsin: Hi Ryan.

Ryan: Hi, Tamsin. Do you want to come to my house after school? Mum's picking me up at 3:15.

Tamsin: Sure, but I'll come round around 4 o'clock. I have to go to the dentist at 3 o'clock.

Ryan: Great. I'll get the games consoles ready.

Tamsin: I've got a great new video game. I could bring it.

Ryan: Sure, what's it called?

Tamsin: It's got a strange name – Visitor. But it's not about a journey or anything like that. It's about a city.

Ryan: And what do you have to do?

Tamsin: Well, those games where you have to collect something or race against other players aren't my favourites. In this one you answer questions. It's really fun.

Ryan: Great. Did someone give it to you?

Tamsin: Yes. I've wanted it for ages – I played it at my friend's house. But my mum said it was too expensive. But then my cousin gave me hers because she didn't like it.

Ryan: Wow, that's really nice! How many levels are there?

Tamsin: I completed four at the weekend. The highest is twelve. My brother tried too and he got to level six.

Ryan: It sounds interesting. How much does it cost?

Tamsin: Mm. That's the problem. It's £25. Most of the other games I have were only about £15. If you wait for a sale you might get it for £20.

Ryan: Yeah. Or I could just come and play on yours!

PART FOUR

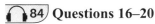 **Questions 16–20**

Jon: Laura, I heard that your brother's selling a guitar. Is that right?

Laura: Yes. It's a Kosman. They make good guitars.

Jon: How much is he selling it for?

Laura: Well, at first he said £50, but no-one wanted to buy it, so now he says he'll take 40. Are you interested?

Jon: Yes. My mum says she'll buy me a guitar if it's not too expensive. What colour is it?

Laura: It's a great colour, actually – purple! I've got a similar one, but mine's white.

Jon: I'd really like to see it. What's your brother's phone number?

Laura: Yes. It's 0154 566 0148. But why don't you just come round. I can show it to you if he's not at home.

Jon: OK. Thanks. Where do you live?

Laura: 16 Litten Road. That's L-I-double T-E-N.

Jon: Thanks. I know where that is. Are you free at the weekend?

Laura: Well, I'll be out on Sunday, but Saturday will be fine. Can you come about two o'clock?

Jon: Yes. Thanks, Laura. See you then.

PART FIVE

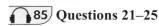 **Questions 21–25**

Rosa: Hello everyone. I'm going to tell you about the race I did last weekend – on Saturday. It's called a triathlon, which is a race where you do three different sports, first swimming, then cycling and finally running.

In an adult triathlon you swim in a lake or sea, but because this was for children, we swam in a pool. For the cycling we had to ride 1km. The path was only half a kilometre long, so we went round twice. Then for the running it was four times around the same path.

I was really pleased with my time, which was 14 minutes for the whole race. My friend was even faster – 12 minutes – but he's done a triathlon before.

At the end of the race everyone got a T-shirt. My dad also bought me a special water bottle that I can use next time.

The next triathlon is on 18th May. If you want to do it with me, your parents need to complete a form online. You have to do that before 30th March.

Task type:
Matching – reading for main message

Topic focus:
sport and leisure

Training

1 In this exercise, students look for synonym pairs. Synonyms often appear in Part 1 sentences and notices. Students look at each item and write its synonym from the box on the line. Tell students to cross out each word from the box as they use it.

> 1 door   2 woods   3 class   4 coach   5 competition   6 price
> 7 mobile   8 photo   9 guest

Encourage students to think of other synonyms. Prompt them using other nouns and adjectives, e.g. *money* (*cash*), *food* (*meal*), *little* (*small*).

2 Before doing this exercise, revise the words *children*, *teenagers* and *adults*. Elicit the age ranges from the students (0−12, 13−17, 18 +). Explain that the notices all say that only one age-group can do each activity. Students write on the lines the two age groups which CANNOT do each activity.

> 1 teenagers, adults   2 children, adults   3 children, teenagers
> 4 teenagers, adults

Some *Key* candidates make mistakes by following modals like *must* with *to*-infinitives or the *-ing* form, e.g. *Children must to use the small swimming pool. Adults can entering after 8 p.m.* Revise all the modals of permission, obligation, prohibition and necessity (they often appear in notices) and make sure students know they are followed by the infinitive without *to*.

3 Before doing this exercise, revise the modals which appear in it: *must, might, will, can, should, may* and *need*. Focus on the meaning of each modal, and how they are different from each other. Tell students that the task of Part 1 is to find the sentence which correctly explains the notice. In this exercise, students must make sentences which explain the notices by crossing out the incorrect modals.

> 1 should not   2 must not   3 cannot   4 need to have   5 will

Exam practice

Go through the advice quickly to check students have the necessary vocabulary and get them thinking about the topic. Tell students to quickly read the notices and say what topic connects them all (they are all leisure activities). Encourage students to underline the key words in both the notices and the sentences. Pay particular attention to the modal verbs in the sentences.

Students do the activity.

> 1 G   2 E   3 D   4 A   5 F

Ask students to look at the wrong notices and say why they are tempting but wrong, e.g.

Notice B – mentions bikes like sentences 1 and 3 – but neither of those sentences talk about keeping bikes safe.

Notice C – mentions animals like sentence 5, and is a prohibition, but it is about feeding animals in the zoo, not bringing them anywhere.

Extension

Students work in pairs or in groups. Tell them to design some more examples of signs that they might see in parks, forests, leisure centres, etc. When each has at least two examples, present them to the class and work together to paraphrase them.

Task type:
Identify appropriate missing word from a sentence – three-option multiple choice – lexical

Topic focus:
work, money

Training

1   In this exercise, students begin to practise Part 2 by thinking about which word best fits each sentence and crossing out the wrong one. These word pairs are often found in Part 2. Point out that the options are always the same part of speech.

> *1 noisy   2 favourite   3 moved   4 clothes   5 yet   6 alone*
> *7 grows   8 packed*

2   Use the **Remember!** box to revise the verbs. Note that the first two verbs, *think* and *want*, often appear in Part 2 because of the words that follow them (*about*, *of* and *to*). The remaining verbs are about financial transactions (*buy*, *pay for*, *spend*, *borrow*, *lend*), and the difference in meaning is quite subtle. Make sure students understand the meanings, and elicit some further examples of their use in sentences.

Students then do the exercise.

> *1 B   2 B   3 C   4 A   5 A   6 C*

You can extend the exercise be asking students to rewrite the sentences in a way which makes the wrong answers work, e.g. *I've decided everyone can come to my party on Friday. I want everyone to come to my party on Friday.*

 Key candidates often make mistakes with the verb *look*, as it combines with several prepositions to make different phrasal verbs. Revise *look for*, *look after*, *look out*.

3   Students can work alone or in pairs to look at each of the five sentences and decide why each one is wrong, then write the correct versions.

> *1 I'm helping to look after my baby brother.*
> *2 Look out! You're going to fall!*
> *3 You look nice today.*
> *4 Look at that beautiful painting.*
> *5 I love looking out of the window on planes.*
> *6 I'm looking forward to seeing you.*

Exam practice

Tell students to quickly read through the sentences and identify the topic (farm). Do the example together as a class.
Use the advice boxes and work through the items together as a class.
Students then complete the task, circling the correct letter (A, B or C).

> *6 B   7 A   8 B   9 A   10 C*

Go over each item. Talk about what make the answers correct, and what makes the distractors wrong, e.g. focus on the meaning of the words in 6 to explain why the wrong answers are meaningless; look at collocations for item 7 (*get lost*, *be alone*, *go missing*).

Extension

Students imagine they recently spent a day on a farm and write a short email to a friend telling them about their day. They should tell their friend:

- **how** they got to the farm
- **what** they did or saw there
- **when** they got home.

Test 1 Reading and Writing Part 3a (Questions 11–15)

Task type:
discrete three-option multiple choice – verbal exchange patterns (functions)

Topic focus:
n/a

Training

Part 3a tests understanding of functional language. Write some examples on the board of functions such as requesting, offering, making a suggestion, complaining, saying *yes*, e.g. *Can you help me? Would you like a drink? Let's go to town. I don't like this food. What a great idea!*
Get students to identify what each speaker is doing.
In pairs, students think of appropriate responses to the statements.

1   Students do the exercise on their own. Tell them that some answers from the box must be used twice.

   1 d   2 a   3 c   4 c   5 b   6 d

2   Students get closer to the task in Part 3a by matching prompts with responses. Ask students to imagine where each of the conversations is taking place, and why. This helps with focus and understanding: 1 in the classroom (needs a pen), 2 anywhere, 3 indoors / at home (they're bored), 4 in a shop (they've seen something they want), 5 outside (someone is carrying something heavy), 6 at home (bored)

   1 Here you are.   2 That's great!   3 Where shall we go?
   4 Do you need to borrow some?   5 Thanks very much.
   6 Great idea!

3   Students now move to choosing between three options, as in the test. Again, tell students to imagine where the exchange is taking place.

   1 That's a pity.   2 Yes, of course.   3 Nice to meet you.
   4 You're probably right.   5 I'm afraid I can't.   6 Thank you!

Extension

Choose some of the incorrect responses from Exercise 3 and ask students to work in pairs to suggest appropriate first sentences.

Exam practice

Cover up the options and tell students to think of their own responses to the sentences. Draw students' attention to the advice box. Tell them to read and refer to it if they are having difficulty with an item. Tell students to underline the words in the first and second sentences that helped them find the answers.

   11 C   12 A   13 B   14 A   15 B

Extension

Write a list of functions up on the board, e.g. asking for something, suggesting something, saying sorry, giving an invitation. In pairs, students write an example of each function. They then write response to each sentence but list them in the wrong order. They exchange their work with another pair and try to match the sentences with the responses. Walk round and help with this if necessary.

Test 1 Reading and Writing Part 3b (Questions 16–20)

Task type:
continuous dialogue – matching exercise – five gaps / eight options

Topic focus:
leisure time

Training

1   Before doing this exercise, brainstorm different ways of saying yes and no to a question, e.g. *Right, Fine, OK, Of course, I think so, I do / will / did, Not really, I don't, I don't think so, Of course not, Not yet*. Write students' suggestion on the board. Then students do the exercise.

> *1 Only for a few hours.   2 OK – at the cafe.   3 I think so.*
> *4 It's fine.   5 I was out.   6 Of course! It's on the corner.*

Yes, No in response to auxiliary questions. (e.g. Did you like the film?).
Students should begin short-form or extended answers with *Yes* or *No* followed by a comma, e.g. ***Yes**, I did. **No**, I didn't. It was boring.*

2   Explain that pronouns often provide good clues about which answer is correct in the Part 3 section of the exam. If necessary, quickly revise subject pronouns, object pronouns, and possessive pronouns and adjectives.

Then students match each sentence with the correct response. When they have completed the exercise, tell them to underline the pronouns which helped them get the correct answers.

> *1 g   2 a   3 b   4 c   5 e   6 f*

3   Students now focus on looking at the parts both before and after the gaps in Part 3b. In this exercise, they choose one option from six possible responses, making sure that the response makes sense with the sentences both before and after the gap.

> *1 C   2 A   3 G   4 E   5 D   6 B*

Exam practice

Tell students to read through the whole dialogue quickly and say what it is about (two boys arranging a bike ride). Tell them to underline any Yes / No questions in the dialogue and in the options. Note that there is one information question option *C Fine. Where's a good place?* Ask students to identify it.
Tell students to cross out the example option, and to cross out the other options as they use them.
Students can do this guided practice is pairs, discussing their answers as they work through the conversation. Remind them of the advice boxes, which are there to help them with some items. When they finish, they can role play Paolo and Freddie.

> *16 G   17 A   18 H   19 E   20 C*

Extension

Put students in pairs. Tell them to look at the two unused options from the practice test (options B and D) and to construct a short dialogue using them. For example:

A: That new café looks great.
B: My brother went there on Saturday.
A: Do you want to meet there this afternoon?
B: Yes, I'll bring some money.

Students read out their dialogues to the rest of the class.

Task type:
Right/Wrong/Doesn't say or three-option multiple choice –
magazine-type factual input text – approximately 200 words
long (230 for multiple-choice type).

Topic focus:
education

Training

1   Quickly read through the words in the box to make sure
    students know what they mean. Elicit examples if necessary.
    Then students do the exercise. Tell students to cross out the
    words in the box once they have used them.

| 1 best | 2 nothing | 3 large | 4 enter | 5 before | 6 start |
| 7 heavy | 8 sad | 9 same | 10 love | 11 always | 12 alone |

2   Tell students to read the short text about Ethan. Explain
    that their task is to find out whether each statement is
    Right, Wrong, or if they don't have enough information
    to say. Before they do this, tell them to read each item and
    underline the key words in each sentence. Point out that item
    3 contains an opposite which they covered in Exercise 1
    (*alone/together*).
    Students now do the task in pairs. There is another item
    which relies on recognising opposites (not listed in Exercise 1)
    – check if students can spot it (item 5, *inside/outside*).

| 1 C   2 C   3 B   4 C   5 B   6 C   7 A |

 Key candidates often forget to add *to* to the verb *belong*,
e.g. *This house belongs my grandfather*. Quickly revise
belong to and possessives with objects in the classroom,
e.g. *This pen belongs to Danielle*. It's Danielle's pen.

Exam practice

Tell students to read the whole text and ask some concept
question to ensure they get the gist (e.g. *Where do they live?
Does Ethan go to school? Where do they learn?*). Then tell them
to read the questions and underline the key words.
Explain that in the type of multiple-choice exercise found
in Part 4, the question always occur in the same order as the
information in the text.
Go through the example and the Advice box to get students
started. Then students do the task.
When you are going through the answers, encourage students
to underline the parts of the text which show the answers for
As and Bs (Cs don't exist in the text). Tell them to do this in the
exam, as it helps when checking over their work when they have
finished.

| 21 B   22 A   23 B   24 C   25 A   26 A   27 C |

Extension

Put students into groups to discuss the advantages and
disadvantages of being taught like Ethan. Tell them to list two
good things and two bad things about home-schooling. Make
a list on the board and take a class vote on whether or not they
would like to learn in this way.

Task type:
multiple-choice cloze – gapped factual text – eight gaps / three optional answers (content and function words)

Topic focus:
entertainment, media

Training

1   Briefly revise verb forms – present, past, past participle, -*ing* form, by going over when they are used and eliciting examples from students. Explain that the correct verb form is often needed to answer Part 5 items, and that it is important to understand how they work.
Look at some of the items in the exercise as a class, and tell students to look for clues in each sentence which can help decide which verb form to use, e.g. time references (*when she was little, yesterday*), the tense of other verbs in the sentence etc.

Then students do the exercise in pairs.

| 1 seen   2 loved   3 growing   4 was   5 swimming   6 live |

Extension

Play 'verb tennis' to revise irregular verbs. Divide the class into two teams and write a list of irregular verbs on the board. Teams take turns to 'serve' one of the verbs by reading out the infinitive form. One player from the opposite team says the past form, then a player from the first team says the past participle. If anyone makes a mistake, the other team gets one point. Continue until all the verbs or the board are used. Add up the points to find the winning team.

 Key candidates often make mistakes with prepositions of time. Revise the prepositions *at*, *in* and *on* in relation to time.

at – a particular time, night, the weekend, festivals e.g. New Year

in – months, the morning / evening / afternoon, seasons

on – days of the week, dates

2   Explain that all of the sentences use the wrong preposition. Put students in pairs to try to find the correct one. Go over the answers in class, taking note of any common mistakes to target for revision.

| 1 on   2 from   3 with   4 of   5 in   6 By |

3   Go over the adverbs in the box with the class, eliciting examples of correct use from the stronger students (note that *well* in the box is part of the phrase as *well as*). Then students do the task alone. Encourage students to cross out the word in the box when it is used.

| 1 even   2 yet   3 well   4 just   5 quite   6 before |

Extension

As homework, you could ask the students to write a new example of each of the seven adverbs tested in this exercise.

Exam practice

Ask students if they read cartoon and comics. What are their favourites? Which are the most popular?
Tell them that the text is about a famous cartoonist. Ask students to read the whole text quickly, but not to look at the options. Ask a couple of general comprehension questions to ensure the text has been understood, e.g. *What did Schultz do with his father when he was a boy? How old was he when his first cartoon was printed?*
Then put students in pairs. Cover up the options, and tell them to try to guess what word goes in each gap. Go through each item as a class before doing the task properly.
Students do the task alone. Remind them to pay attention to the words before and after each gap when choosing the correct answer.

| 28 A   29 C   30 C   31 A   32 C   33 C   34 B   35 A |

Extension

In the next class, show them a copy of the text again without the options. Can they still remember which words go in the gaps?

Teacher's Notes
Test 1 Reading and Writing Part 6

Task type:
word completion – five definitions – five spellings. The first letter and the number of letters given.

Topic focus:
the natural world

Training

1   Students read the text and decide where the family are walking. Tell them to underline the words which helped them decide the answer. C in the forest.
2   Write the letters *e* and *a* on the board. Ask the class to come up with English words which contain these letters together. Point out the it is very rare to see these vowels together in the opposite order (*ae*).
    Before doing the exercise, remind students that in the actual Part 6 they will be given only the first letter of each word. Then students do the exercise.

> 1 beautiful   2 jeans   3 pears   4 bread   5 near   6 great

 Key candidates often make the mistake of adding an extra *l* to words ending in *-ful*, e.g. *beautifull, wonderfull*

3   Write the letters *oo* and *ee* on the board. Again, ask the class to come up with English words which contain these double vowels. Point out that it is rare to see other vowels double up in this way.
    Students underline the double vowel words in the text, then move on to Exercise 4.

> school, woods, took, food, needed, cook, boots, good, see, woods, see, green

4   This is a step closer to an actual Part 6 task. Students match the definitions with the words they underlined in Exercise 3. Remind them that in an actual Part 6 task, the first letter is given.

> 1 cook   2 green   3 good   4 school   5 boots   6 food

5   Another step closer to an actual Part 6 task, with definitions and the first letter given. Tell students to underline the verbs or activity in each definition. Then students complete the task.

> 1 (swim, go fishing) lake   2 (climbing) tree   3 (walk) path
> 4 (play) hockey   5 (collect, make a fire) wood   6 (eat) picnic

6   Write the words *wood* and *would* on the board. Ask students what is unusual about them (they sound the same, but are spelt differently and have different meanings). Students can complete the task in pairs.

> 1 meat   2 pair   3 see   4 too   5 buy   6 there

 Other common spelling confusions at *Key* level are *prize / price, quite / quiet, then / than*. Make sure students understand what these words mean and know how to spell them correctly.

7   Now we move on to a model Part 6 task. Before doing the task, elicit as many animals from the class as possible and write them on the board. Then erase the animals and tell students to do the task. Point out that two of the items require plural nouns. Can they identify which ones? (2 and 4)

> 1 horse   2 insects   3 bear   4 rabbits   5 duck   6 chicken

8   Remind students of the two items in Exercise 7 which required plural answers. Ask them to identify the words which indicated the plural. Then students complete this exercise in pairs, underlining the parts of the definitions which reveal the number.

> 1 singular   2 singular   3 plural   4 singular   5 plural   6 plural
> 1 This   2 one of these   3 these   4 this   5 these   6 these/them

9   Students now write the correct words for each definition in Exercise 8. They should take care to write the plural form where necessary.

> 1 river   2 fire   3 flowers   4 sun   5 clouds   6 fields

10 To revise some key vocabulary in this unit, students now write their own definitions using the key words.

> 1 borrow these from the library   2 walk over this to cross a river
> 3 keep this type of animal in your house   4 find this food growing on trees   5 wear these when the weather is hot   6 see these in the sky at night

Exam practice

Remind students that the answers in Part 6 are usually singular nouns, but can be plural, and that they must be spelt correctly. Ask students to read the sentences and identify the theme (outdoor life). Brainstorm things you can find in the forest and write the words on the board.
Go over the example in class, then point out the advice for items 38 and 40. Students then complete the task alone.

> 36 bear   37 lake   38 wood   39 tent   40 insects

Extension

In pairs, students think of two or three other things you can find in the forest. They then write definitions of them, and give the first letter plus spaces for the remaining ones. When this is done, they swap papers with another pair and attempt to complete the exercise.

Test 1 Reading and Writing Part 7

Task type:
open cloze – structure and vocabulary. Texts are types that a student might write.

Topic focus:
travel, cities

Training

1   Revise the use of auxiliaries *be* and *have*, in the passive voice and present perfect, as these often appear in Part 7. Students choose the correct form of *be* or *have* to complete the sentences.

| *1 have   2 am / 'm   3 is / 's   4 are   5 is / 's   6 has*

Extension

This is also a good place to revise Yes / No questions with *be* and *have*. Tell students to look again at the items in this exercise and construct Yes / No questions based on them, e.g. 1 *Have you lived in this town for long?* 2 *Are you pleased that I can come and stay with you?* 3 *Is the city tour expensive?* 4 *Are your friends going to come round ... ?* 5 *Is there a big park near your house?* 6 *Has the new sports centre got a swimming pool?*

2   In Part 7, the missing words often form part of a longer phrase. Look at the example with the class – *a lot of* is the phrase used here. Students now look at the sentences and circle the word which correctly completes each phrase in the sentence.

| *1 Let   2 How   3 if   4 for   5 wait   6 would*

 Key candidates often make mistakes with the would love / like + to infinitive structure to express desire, e.g. I would love visiting your country. I'd like come to your house. Revise the structure by asking students simple questions like, Which country would you like to visit? What would you like to do now?

3   Revise subject and object pronouns before attempting this exercise. Write them in two columns on the board. Get students to produce their own examples of their use. You can use prompts like *I like her BUT* to elicit *she doesn't like me, She likes him, but he doesn't like ...* etc.
Ask students to read the text. What is it about? Students then complete the text. Point out that one of the pronouns is possessive (*mine*).

| *1 She   2 we   3 him   4 us   5 they   6 mine*

Extension

In pairs, students write an email to a friend about their own plans and inviting them to join them. Write on the board:

> *I'm going to ... on ... . Do you want to come? Let's meet ... . I'll bring ... . Don't forget ... is coming too.*
>
> *Bye for now!*

Exam practice

Tell students to read the whole text once – this is good practice in the actual test too. Ask a stronger student: *Who wrote the email?* and *Who it is for?* Look at the example together and point out the advice for items 45, 46 and 47.
Remind students that they must write only one word in each space, and that contractions such as *can't, don't,* etc. count as two words. Also emphasise that the correct spelling is important in this part of the test.
Then ask students to do the task alone.

| *41 me / us   42 if   43 It   44 to   45 there   46 For   47 near   48 has   49 forget   50 of*

When complete, tell students to go back and underline all the answers which are parts of phrases, as in Exercise 2 of the Training.

Extension

Tell students to imagine they are going to have a visitor from abroad staying with them over the summer. Tell them to write an email saying:

- what they will do
- where they can go together
- what they should bring with them.

Encourage them to refer to this Part 7 for ideas and sentence structures.

Task type:
non-sequential information transfer: using input text/s to complete a form

Topic focus:
leisure time, hobbies

 Part 8 is often about transport, and candidates often make mistakes with prepositions relating to transport, e.g. *I will travel with train. We'll get there with a bus. I'm going in car.*
Revise *by* with forms of transport. Remind them of the exception *on foot.*

Training

1 In this exercise, students are introduced to the type of information they are typically required to take note of in Part 8. Explain that the words in the box are examples of what they see in the form they must fill in, and the words in the items are what can be read in the emails.
Look at the example together to make sure they know that they have to match the words and phrases.
Students then do the task in pairs.

1 how we'll travel 2 bring 3 date 4 place 5 start time
6 phone number 7 level 8 number of people

2 Explain that in Part 8s there are nearly always two examples of the type of information required for each item – but only one of these examples is the correct answer. So candidates must read the texts carefully in order to complete the task successfully.
This exercise practises choosing the correct answer from two possibilities.
Look at the example together. Get students to explain why £8 is the correct answer. Ask, who has to pay £10? (non students)
Students do the task in pairs. Make sure they cross out the wrong answer.

1 Friday 2 June 13th 3 £4 4 sandwiches 5 My Life
6 2 7 4.30 p.m. 8 sports club

Extension

Get students to concentrate on the wrong answers in Exercise 2. In pairs, they take turns to ask and answer questions about why the answers is wrong, e.g. 1 *Why don't they go on Tuesday?* Because she has football on Tuesday. 2 *Why don't they go on 21st July?* Because he is going on holiday in July. 3 *Why doesn't it cost £8?* Because £8 is the price for two people. 4 *Why not bring water?* Because they sell drinks there. 5 *Why not see Places?* Because he's seen Places. 6 *Why not meet at the station?* Because they're meeting at the sports club. 7 *Why don't they finish at 3.30?* Because that's when they're starting. 8 *Why isn't there one boat?* Because there are eight of them and only four fit in a boat.

Exam practice

Tell students to read the both texts and the notes before attempting the task. Point out that some of the answers are to be found in the notice, some in the email, and some will require a careful reading of both texts.
Students complete the task alone. Tell them to use the advice box to help them find the answers if necessary.

51 (on) Friday   52 (by) car   53 (at) 9 p.m.   54 3.00   55 cooking

Ask students to identify the item which requires a reading of both the notice and the email to answer (54).

Extension

In pairs, students go over the task and identify the wrong answers. They work together to say why the answers are wrong. Check back with the rest of the class when finished.

Training

Task type:
guided writing – write a short message of 25–35 words in response to a short input text or rubric

Topic focus:
celebrations

Training

1 This is an example of a Part 9 task in which candidates are asked to reply to an email. In this exercise, students identify the information they are required to give in their reply. Tell students that they must include all the information asked for. Students should underline the questions in the email. Ask stronger students to give example answers to the questions.

2 Students can work in pairs to match the messages with the questions in the original email.

> 1 How shall we get there? 2 Which day are you free?
> 3 What do you want to see?

3 This exercise targets a common problem with *Key* level writing tasks. It focuses on getting students to identify the correct tense to use in their answers.
Look at the example together. What is the question asking about – the present, past, or future? (future). What is the answer talking about – the present, past, or future? (past). Put the students in pairs to complete the rest of the task.

> 1 ✔ 2 ✘ 3 ✔ 4 ✔ 5 ✘ 6 ✘ 7 ✔ 8 ✔

4 Quickly go over the uses of *-ing* forms of verbs (present continuous, future, gerunds, *go* + *-ing*). Tell students to look in the ***Remember!*** box to remind themselves of the spelling rules for this form.
Look at the example together, then students do the task alone.

> 1 swimming 2 getting 3 driving 4 shopping 5 starting
> 6 playing

5 Revise the days of the week and the months on the board. Then erase and tell students to do the exercise alone. Identify any common errors and correct them.

> 1 August 2 Monday 3 September 4 Wednesday 5 Saturday
> 6 July 7 Thursday 8 February 9 May 10 March

6 This exercise focuses on common errors with prepositions of time. Draw students' attention to the ***Remember!*** box. Then write some other examples of each on the board and do them together as a class.

> 1 on 2 at 3 on 4 at 5 in 6 on 7 on 8 [no preposition]

7 This exercise focuses on prepositions of place. This time students must cross out the wrong word.

> 1 to 2 from 3 to 4 with 5 by 6 in 7 to 8 at

8 Now students focus on errors commonly made in constructions with verbs describing the actions of bringing and taking. Each item has two sentences – one is correct, and the other contains a mistake. Students do the task pairs.

> Correct sentence indicated by a tick:
> 1 a 2 b 3 b 4 a

9 In this exercise, we look at some actual Part 9 answers. Focusing on the errors of others helps students avoid making the same ones. Remind students that to get full marks in Part 9 task, they must:

- **answer** all 3 questions clearly
- **make** few spelling and grammatical errors
- **write** between 25 and 35 words

First, read the three pieces of information candidates are asked to include in their email. Then, put students in pairs and get them to give a mark out of 5 for each of the answers. Using the following mark scheme:
5 – three parts of message, very minor spelling or
   grammatical errors
4 – three parts of message, some spelling and / or grammar
   and / or punctuation errors
3 – three parts of message, some confusion due to spelling
   and / or grammatical errors
3 – two parts of message, minor spelling and / or
   grammatical errors
2 – two parts of message, some confusion due to spelling
   and / or grammatical errors
1 – one part of message
Check with the class to see if everyone agrees which is the best and worst.
Then ask students in their pairs to answer questions 1–8.

> 1 C 2 B 3 C 4 A 5 B 6 A 7 B/C 8 C

Exam practice

Read through the task in class. Remind students of the requirements: 25–35 words, three pieces of information, start and end the text correctly. Go through the advice and then tell students to complete the task alone.
When students have completed the task, ask them to swap their work with a partner for checking.

> *Sample answer*
> *Hi Danni*
> *Monica's having a party at her house tomorrow.*
> *She wants us to bring party food such as crisps, pizza, or a drink.*
> *I think Ben and Marco are going too.*
> *Bye for now,*

Teacher's Notes
Test 1 Listening Part 1

Task type:
three-option visual multiple choice to answer focus question –
two-speaker short conversations

Topic focus:
n/a

1 Tell students they will hear a short conversation between
two people. Students read the questions and underline the
key words.

> **1** Her Dad   **2** Her grandmother   **3** By train

Play the recording again if necessary.

2 Quickly revise months and dates before doing this task. Tell
students they will hear all three dates shown in the pictures,
but only one is the correct answer. Students should underline
the key words in the question (*When* and *flying to Australia*).

> **Picture A**

3 Part 1 sometimes includes a question which has a day of the
week as an answer. Tell students to underline the key words
in the question (*Which day* and *practise*). Then play the
recording and tell students to answer the questions alone.

> **Picture A**

4 Ask students to underline the key words in the question
(*What* and *now*). What tense is the question?
Tell students to read and role play the dialogue in pairs, and
then answer the question. Point out that, once again, the
activities in all three pictures are mentioned in the text, but
only one is the correct answer.

> **Picture C**

5 This continues the focus on tense, this time modelling an
actual Part 1 listening question. Ask students to underline
the key words in the question (*What* and *this afternoon*), and
to identify the tense.
Students then look at the three pictures and say what is
happening in them. Tell students it is always a good idea to
say the words in the pictures to themselves before listening,
as this prepares them for what's coming.

> **Picture B**

6 Tell students to underline the key words and to identify the
tense in the question (*What* and *lost*; present perfect). Then
ask them to look at the pictures and identify what they show.

> **Picture B**

7 Part 1 often includes questions about where something
is. Revise the rooms in a house, and identify them in the
picture. Tell students to underline the key words and identify
the tense in the question (*Where*, *at the moment*; present tense).

> **B (bathroom)**

 The words *sitting room*, *living room* and *kitchen* are
often misspelt as *seating room*, *leaving room* and *kichen*.
Revise the spellings of rooms in the house.

8 This exercise focuses on numbers, using four short dialogues.

 Key candidates at this level often confuse the pronunciation
of the *-teen* and *-ty* numbers. Revise and practise the
difference in stress between the two, e.g. *fourteen* / *forty*, etc.

Tell students that although these dialogues are shorter than
standard Part 1 dialogues, they will still hear all three numbers
and only one of them is correct.

> **1** B   **2** C   **3** A   **4** C

9 Ask students to read the question and underline the key
words (*How much*, *decide*). Then students look at the
pictures and say the numbers. Students complete the task.

> **1** C

Exam practice

Before doing the test, remind students to:

- **underline** the key words in each question
- **identify** the tense of each question
- **look** at all the pictures and 'say' what they see in English
- **always** pick an answer even if they aren't sure!

Go over the example in class. Draw attention to the advice.

> **1** B   **2** B   **3** A   **4** B   **5** C

Extension

Play the recording for question 5 again. Ask students to work in
pairs and write questions to go with the other two answers. For
example, 1 *What was on TV last night?* (A) *What is on TV next
week?* (B)

Task type:
matching – informal dialogue – listening for key information –
matching five items (plus example) – eight options

Topic focus:
holidays, activities

Training

1 Listening Part 2 often involves recognising paraphrases. Use
the example in this task to explain the concept to students.
Point out that the sentences on the right are the words they
hear in the test, and the words on the left are the words they
read.
Students draw lines to match the sentences and activities.

1 *visiting a classmate*   2 *packing*   3 *learning a sport*
4 *doing homework*   5 *shopping*   6 *cooking*

Extension

Divide students into small groups and ask them to think of other
ways to describe. For example:
emailing   (writing a message on a computer)
exercising   (going to the gym)
eating   (having lunch / dinner / a sandwich)

2 This exercise helps students learn the importance of
listening carefully to what is said before deciding on the
answer. They have to pick out the correct answer from two
options. Emphasise that they should not choose a word just
because they hear it in the recording (although sometimes
that is the right answer)!
Do the example in class, then let students complete the task
in pairs.

1 *maths*   2 *looking at photos*   3 *eating dinner*   4 *playing football*
5 *swimming in the sea*   6 *making biscuits*

Listen to the recording again. Stop the recording after each
person's comment and ask why the other option is the wrong
answer.

  Some *Key* candidates misspell *interesting* (*interessting*,
intresting). Check that students can spell it correctly.

3 Students do further practice with this using a simpler and
shorter version of the exam Part 2.
Go over the activities in the right-hand column and ask
students to think of other ways of expressing them. This will
help them when listening for paraphrases.

1 E   2 A   3 B   4 C

Exam practice

Go through the advice boxes with the class. Tell students to
cross out the example in the 'BEST THINGS' column – this
prevents them from being distracted by it when listening to the
recording.
In pairs, students look at the answer column and try to think of
different ways of expressing the activities.
Tell students that the questions 6–10 are in the same order as
the recording, i.e. George will talk about Tuesday first, then
Wednesday, etc.
Students complete the task.

6 D   7 F   8 H   9 E   10 B

Extension

Put students into groups and ask them to write a list of as many
activities ending in *-ing* as they can remember from this section.
See if any group can remember 20 different *-ing* words. (Could
include: *cooking, learning a sport, shopping, packing, looking
at photos, watching a film, eating dinner, playing tennis /
football, lying in the sun, swimming, making biscuits / a cake,
preparing food, moving furniture, looking for something, going
on a boat ride, visiting a classmate, doing homework, visiting
a farm, working on a computer, sending texts*) Check spellings.
In groups of four or five, students can take turns to mime one of
the activities. The other students try to guess what it is, and spell
the word correctly.

Task type:
three-option multiple choice, question / answer or sentence completion format, – informal or neutral dialogue – five items plus an example

Topic focus:
school, homework

Training

1   This exercise practises questions about numbers, as there are often one or two number items in Part 3. Before doing the exercise, elicit from the class as many 'number contexts' as possible, e.g. room number, house number, age, height, length, price, weight, time, date, frequency (with per), etc. Write them up on the board.
Listen to the example question and find the room number answer.
Look at the options in the box and talk about what kind of number each is.
Then students listen to the recording and complete the exercise.

1 *an hour and half*   2 *ten of us*   3 *fifteen pounds*   4 *five metres wide and four metres long*   5 *three times a week*   6 *six forty five*

Key candidates often confuse (*How*) *much* and (*How*) *many*, e.g. *How much people came to the party? How many money do you have?* Revise these words and explain about the countable / uncountable difference.

Extension

In pairs, students write a number questionnaire to ask other pairs. They should think of five questions, e.g. *What number is your house / flat? How much were your trainers? What time do you go to bed?*

2   Explain that some of the items on Part 3 are often sentence completions. This exercise practises this type of question. Ask students to read the questions carefully before playing the recording. Students then listen and cross out the wrong answers.

1 *Mr Walters*   2 *Emma*   3 *45 minutes*   4 *soup and bread*
5 *quarter to four*   6 *Thursdays*

Play the recording again, stopping after the answer to each question. Students say what the wrong answers refer to, e.g. 1 Mrs Taylor is a teacher at Rachel's old school. 2 Jane is another girl with long red hair. 3 An hour is how long Rachel first thought the lunch break was. 4 Salad is what Rachel will eat tomorrow. 5 Three-thirty is when school usually finishes. 6 Tuesday lunchtime is football practice.

3   Students read through the sentences. Revise / teach vocabulary if necessary. Tell students to listen to the recording and tick only the correct sentences.

1 *and* 3 *are correct*

Ask students what the correct answers for 2 and 4 are (where water comes from and goes, an empty bottle). Play the recording again if necessary.

4   Students now practise a short version of a real Part 3, with listed A, B and C options. Remind students that they will hear all three options spoken, but that only one is correct. Play the recording twice.

1 *C*   2 *A*   3 *C*

Play the recording one more time, stopping after each question is answered. Ask students what the wrong options in each question refer to.

Exam practice

Tell students to read all the questions and options, and revise / teach any vocabulary if necessary. Ask them to identify the type of answer in each item (11 a place 12 a thing 13 a number 14 a day 15 a time). Tell them to underline the key words in each question. Go through the advice with students.
After the first listening, students check answers with each other in pairs. Allow them to discuss any differences, and then play the recording again.

11 *C*   12 *A*   13 *C*   14 *C*   15 *B*

Extension

Play the recording one more time, stopping after each question section is answered. In pairs, students write down what each wrong answer is referring to.

Test 1 Listening Part 4

Task type:
gap-fill – two-speaker short conversation – writing down specific information to complete a form (names, numbers, places, times etc.)

Topic focus:
entertainment

Training

1 Elicit vocabulary related to entertainment and write examples up on the board, e.g. *theatre, cinema, concert, exhibition, ticket, television* etc. Tell students that Part 4 conversations are not between friends or relatives.
As in Parts 1, 2 and 3, you will often hear more than one possible answer. This exercise practises picking out the correct one in a choice of three.
Students listen to the recording and circle the correct answers.

B

2 In this exercise, students practise listening to spellings. There is usually a dictated spelling item in Part 4 and/or Part 5. The words are usually less than six letters long. Students listen to the recording and put a tick next to the correct spellings and a cross next to the wrong ones.

1 ✘ 2 ✔ 3 ✘ 4 ✔ 5 ✘ 6 ✘

Check answers, then play the recording again and tell students to write down the correct spellings for 1, 3, 5 and 6 (*Alsopp, Telus, Aqinto www.japes.com*).

 Some *Key* candidates have problems distinguishing vowels *a, e* and *i*, and consonants *g / j*. they might also have problems understanding half-vowels *w* and *y*, and consonants *t / d, b / v, p / b*. Identify where your students' problem areas are and focus practice on those.

3 Students continue spelling practice using short dialogues. Note that some of these spellings are of longer words than they will hear in the exam. Allow students to listen to the dialogues a third time if they are having difficulty.

1 Draycott 2 Radisson 3 Johnston 4 Constantinou
5 Dialhex 6 Ubangi

4 Before doing this exercise, write the word *start* on the board. Ask students for another word which means the same (*begin*). Then ask for two words which mean the opposite (*finish, end*). A time is often an answer in Part 4 – frequently in the context of when something starts and / or finishes. If one of the start or finish verbs is used in the question, it is likely that a synonym will be used in the recording.

Also, revise times, particularly *a.m.* / *p.m., a quarter to / past, half past.* Different ways of writing the time are acceptable in Part 4, but you should encourage students to write it in numbers, as it is quicker and they are less likely to misspell it. Students listen to the recording and put a tick or a cross next to each answer, as in the example.

1 ✔ 2 ✘ 3 ✔ 4 ✔ 5 ✘ 6 ✔

Check answers, then play the recording again and tell students to write down the correct answers for 2 and 5 (2 10.00 a.m. 5 9.00 p.m.)

5 Students continue to practise times in the context of short dialogues. You could ask the students to write down all times they hear for each item (sometimes there are two, sometimes three) on the first listening. Then on the second listening, they cross out the incorrect time.

1 9.30 2 9.45 3 4.10 4 11.40 5 1.00 6 8.20

Play the recording one more time. What do the other times mentioned refer to?

Exam practice

Ask students to read all the questions before listening. What kind of answers are they looking for? (About a dancer in a show.) In pairs, students can try to predict the actual questions asked, e.g. *Where were you born? When did you begin dancing?* Remind students that the answers come in the same order as the recording.
Look at the advice with students, then do the task.

16 3 17 Winter 18 Aldhurst 19 8.30 20 painting

Task type:
gap-fill – one speaker – writing down specific information to complete a form (names, numbers, places, times, etc.)

Topic focus:
education

Training

Note: The only difference between Part 4 and Part 5 is the number of speakers. Part 5 has only one.

1   The exercise revises the spellings of days of the week. All of the items in this exercise are spelt wrongly. Ask students to look at the exercise is pairs and correct the spellings.

> 1 Monday   2 Wednesday   3 Saturday   4 Tuesday

 Key students often forget to capitalise days of the week and months. Certain days and months cause particular difficulty when it comes to spelling. Make sure you practise days and months at the start of every lesson by asking a student to write the day and date on the board.

2   Students now move on to listening for days. Remind students that they will often hear more than one possible answer. On the first playing of the recording, ask students to write down both days that they hear. On the second playing, tell them to cross out the incorrect answer.

> 1 Tuesday   2 Sunday   3 Saturday   4 Friday   5 Wednesday

   Play the recording one more time and ask students to say what the wrong day refers to.

3   Students now move on to the spelling of months. Quickly revise the 12 months orally before doing this exercise. Students complete the task alone and then check their answers with a partner.

> 1 December   2 May   3 March   4 August   5 February   6 June
> 7 October   8 April   9 July   10 November

4   Revise ordinal numbers with students. Remind them that although they may hear ordinal numbers in dates in Part 5, they do not have to write numbers as ordinals.
   Listen to the example and explain that students have to put a tick next to each correct answer and a cross next to each wrong one. Students listen and complete the exercise.

> 1 ✗   2 ✔   3 ✗   4 ✗   5 ✔   6 ✗

Play the recording again and ask students to explain what the wrong answer in each item refers to.

5   Students continue to practise dates. Encourage them to write the dates in the simplest form: number + month. On the first play, tell students to write both dates they hear. Then, on the second play, tell them to cross out the wrong one.

> 1 4 July   2 22 August   3 18 March   4 10 September
> 5 6 February   6 15 November

Exam practice

Ask students to read all the questions before listening. What kind of answers are they looking for? Encourage students to guess some sensible answers.
Go over the advice and then do the task.

> 21 Tuesday   22 12   23 game   24 9.15   25 27.50

Extension

Ask students if they would like to do this course. Why? Why not? Students write a short text to a friend inviting them to do the course with them. Say
- **what** the course is about
- **where** the course is
- **why** you think it will be interesting.

Task type:
a conversation with the examiner. The examiner asks the students questions about themselves in turn, and they answer. The interview last for about six minutes.

Topic focus:
personal information: family, friends, school and study, home town, hobbies

Training

1   Ask students some questions about themselves, for example, *Where are you from? How old are you? What are your favourite hobbies?*
    Explain that they will hear Pablo asking Marianne some questions and that they should decide whether each statement is true or false. Play the recording. Students listen and tick the statement if it is correct and put a cross if it is incorrect. Play the recording again and ask students to correct the false statements.

> 1 ✔ 2 ✘ (She is from France) 3 ✘ (She has a brother and a sister) 4 ✔ 5 ✔ 6 ✘ (Her favourite sport is football) 7 ✘ (Her favourite subject is science) 8 ✔

Extension

Ask students to think about what the questions are that she has been asked (*What is your surname? Where are you from? Have you got any brothers or sisters? How old are you? Do you like your (new) school? What's your favourite sport? What's your favourite subject? Do you like studying English?*). Students then interview each other, using Marianne's information in Exercise 1.

2   This exercise will help students familiarise themselves with what happens at the beginning and during Part 1 of the Speaking test. Students read the stages of the test and put them into the correct order.

> 1 You will get a mark sheet with your name on it.   2 Someone will take you to the room where you will do the Speaking test.
> 3 Your partner will go to the room with you.   4 There will be two examiners there.   5 They will say hello and you will sit down.
> 6 You will give the first examiner your mark sheet.   7 This examiner will ask you questions.   8 The second examiner will fill in your mark sheet.

3   Students read the questions and consider the missing words. Explain that these are the kinds of questions they will be asked in Part 1 of the Speaking test. Play the recording. Students listen to the interview and complete the missing words.

> 3 1 surname, 2 old, 3 come from, 4 student, 5 school, 6 subject, 7 languages, 8 classes

4   Students practise answering the questions in pairs. Ask them to think carefully about their answers and think about what

they would like to say in the exam. Monitor and offer help as they are working. Then ask pairs of students to ask and answer the questions.

Extension

Role play Part 1 of the Speaking test. Students work in groups of four where possible (alternatively, choose one group of four to role play Part 1 for the rest of the class to watch). Assign each student in the group a different role: the two examiners (one speaking, one non-speaking) and the two students. Students act out entering the examination room and completing Part 1 of the test, using the questions from Exercise 3. Ask the non-speaking 'examiner' to listen and decide whether the 'candidates' answer the questions well. They can give feedback at the end if they wish. Students swap roles and repeat the activity until all students have had a chance to answer the questions.

5   Students read the questions and complete the answers. Encourage them to think carefully about using accurate grammar. Check the answers by asking different students the questions and asking the rest of the class to say whether the answer is grammatically accurate and correcting it where necessary.

> 1 I come from / I'm from, 2 I like (going/to go), 3 I go (shopping), 4 I'm going (to go) (swimming) on Saturday, 5 My favourite hobby is / I like / I love, 6 I do.

6   Explain that at the end of Part 1, the examiner will ask a question which begins *Tell me about ... .* These will not always be the same and will vary from student to student. Ask students to read the three *Tell me about ...* questions and complete the answers. Remind them that they should try to give longer answers to this question, rather than just one or two words. Monitor and offer help as they are working.

7   Students listen to the recording and say which question the candidate is answering (question 1). Play the recording again and ask students to note down how many sentences there are in the candidate's answer (four). Remind them to answer this part of the test with similar extended answers them. Students then practise asking and answering the *Tell me about* questions in Exercise 6 with a partner.

> Tell me about your home.

Exam practice

Make sure you have drawn students' attention to the Tips for this section before playing the recording for Exercise 7. Then ask them to listen carefully to Andrei's answers. Play the recording again, encouraging students to answer the questions. At this point, encourage the whole class to speak, without choosing individuals to answer.
You could play the recording a third time and ask individuals to answer each question.

Teacher's Notes
Test 1 Speaking Part 2

Task type:
candidates take turns to ask and answer five questions about two situations (events) which the examiner provides on prompt cards

Topic focus:
sports and exercise

Training

1 Review / Teach sports and exercise vocabulary. Ask students what kind of sports and exercise they enjoy.
Students look at the information. Explain that they will hear a conversation between two students who are talking about one of the activities. They should listen and decide which activity the students are talking about. Play the recording and check the answer.

B

Extension

Ask students to listen again and write down the questions they hear (*Can you tell me about the classes? Are the classes at the weekend? Are the classes at the weekend? How long are the classes? What should I wear? What do you do at the classes?*). They then work in pairs to role play the questions and answers for Activities for teenagers.
Work as a class to produce questions for Activity Days (*Can you tell me about the activity days? When are they? What time are they? What can you do? What do you need to wear?*). Ask the questions for different students to answer.

2 This exercise will help students familiarise themselves with what happens in Part 2 of the Speaking test. Students read the stages of the test and put them into the correct order.

1 The first examiner gives each student a question and information booklet. 2 One student (A) gets some questions. 3 The other student (B) gets some information. 4 Student A asks five questions, using the question words in their booklet. 5 Student B answers each question, using the information in their booklet. 6 The examiner gives each student a new booklet with a different task. 7 Student B asks questions about the new topic. 8 Student A finds the information in their booklet and answers the questions.

3 Tell the students that the box containing the information about the swimming classes is similar to the kind of thing they will see in the exam. Explain that in this part of the test they should think carefully about how to form questions from the prompts they are given.
Students then work in pairs to form the questions. Draw their attention to the question words which are used in each case (*where* for places, *when* for dates, *who* for people and so on).

1 When are the classes? 2 How long are the classes? 3 Where are the classes? 4 What can you do every week at the classes? 5 Who can/should/do you call to book a place?

4 Students take turns to ask and answer the questions in Exercise 3, using the information given in 3 and the appropriate words and phrases. Remind them not to add anything which isn't stated in the information and to keep their answers short and clear.

The classes are on Tuesday evenings. They are an/one hour long. They are at Hall Bank Swimming Pool. You can do races every week. You can call Daniel to book a place.

5 Elicit students' ideas before completing the task. By now, they should be aware that they only need to ask the five questions from the prompts on their card. They should also know that they should answer each of their partner's question using only the information they have been given.
Play the recording for the students to listen and answer the questions.

Student A asked five questions. Yes, she did.

Extension

Students work in pairs. They prepare one set of prompt cards: one with information about an event, and the other with five prompts for questions (they can use five different question words for this, as in Exercise 3).
The pairs then exchange their cards with another pair of students, giving one student the information card and the other student the question prompts. Students practise the task. Monitor as they are working and offer help if necessary. Choose pairs of students to role play their dialogues.

Exam practice

Divide the class into pairs and assign them a role (A or B). Ask them to look at the first scenario and check that there is no unknown vocabulary. Then ask them to think about what they will say. Give them one minute to do this.
They then complete both exam tasks. Monitor and note down any difficulties as they are working. Feed back to the class about any improvements they should aim to make.

Students can listen to the model questions and answers after their practice by going to:
www.cambridge.org/elt/keyforschoolstrainer/audio.

Test 2 Reading and Writing Part 1

Task type:
Matching – reading for main message

Topic focus:
leisure, cinema

Training

Before doing the exercises, remind students what they need to do in Part 1. With books closed, ask them

- **How** many sentences do they have to match? (5 plus 1 example)
- **How** many notices are there? (8)
- **How** many notices don't match a sentence? (2)

1   In this exercise, students look for synonym pairs. Synonyms often appear in Part 1 sentences and notices. Students look at each item and write its synonym from the box on the line. Tell students to cross out each word from the box as they use it.

1 passenger   2 closed   3 seat   4 bigger   5 gift   6 movie

   Encourage students to think of other ways of expressing some of the words, e.g. *someone who is travelling – tourist, traveller*; *place to sit – chair, sofa*

2   Before doing this exercise, revise the time words *morning, afternoon, evening, weekend, week*, etc. Students have to say whether or not the sentence matches the notice. Go over the example in class.

1 yes   2 no   3 no   4 yes   5 no

   Explain that a dash (–) between two dates includes the two dates and all dates in between. Point to items 1, 2 and 5 to illustrate this.

 Key candidates often make mistakes with the word weekend. *I'll see you in weekend*. Remind students that it usually takes the definite article the (*weekend*) and the preposition *at*: *I'll see you at the weekend*.

3   Quickly revise *this / these*, reminding students that one is singular and the other plural. Elicit some example sentences. Explain that these words can give an important clue about which sentences match which notices. Note that *this / these* will usually appear in the sentences, rather than the notices. This exercise practises matching notices with *this / these* sentences.

1 these   2 this   3 this   4 these   5 this

Extension

You can take this opportunity to practise the pronunciation of /iː/ and /ɪ/. Test students can hear the difference between *this / these*, *chip / cheese*, *ship / sheep*, *bin / bean* etc.

Exam practice

Ask students to read the notices and then the sentences. What is the topic of this Part 1? (cinema). Go through the advice to help them find matching notices for 1, 3 and 5. Then get students to do the task. Make sure students underline the words in the sentences and notices which match or help them find their answers.

1 G   2 C   3 F   4 B   5 H

Ask students to look at the wrong notices and say why they are tempting but wrong, e.g. Notice A mentions food (like sentence 3) Notice D mentions opening hours (sentences 5).

Extension

Students write a short email about a trip to the cinema. They should say

- **who** they went with
- **what** they saw
- **what** they thought of the film.

Teacher's Notes
Test 2 Reading and Writing Part 2

Task type:
Identify appropriate missing word from a sentence – three option multiple choice – lexical

Topic focus:
sport

Training

1   In this exercise, students begin to practise Part 2 by thinking about which word best fits each sentence and crossing out the wrong one. These word pairs are often found in Part 2. Remind students that the options are always the same part of speech.

> 1 pilot   2 advertisement   3 groups   4 free   5 shared
> 6 spends   7 way   8 mind

Go through the answers with the class. Pay attention to the wrong answers and try to elicit examples of correct usage.

2   This exercise focuses an commonly confused verbs. Tell students to read through the items and try to say what the verbs have in common. (They are all to do with possession or holding / taking.) Read through the **Remember!** box to revise those verbs. Make sure students have a good grasp of these verbs before doing the task.

> 1 carry   2 receive   3 hold   4 got   5 takes   6 collects

Extension

Students take one wrong option from each sentence and write a new sentence illustrating its correct use, e.g. 1 Shall I hold your bags? 2 Did you collect the post card I sent you from the post office?

3   Revise usage of the -ing and infinitive forms after certain verbs: *want, decide, like, love, enjoy, prefer*. Although Part 2 is mainly lexical, it often includes such verbs, and these can give candidates a clue to the correct answer, so it is important to know.

> 1 going   2 to see   3 going   4 playing   5 playing

 Key candidates often make mistakes with the -ing form and infinitive after certain verbs: *I'd prefer meeting you on Tuesday. He decided bought it. I will enjoy to see you next week.* Revise other verbs which also take either form, e.g. *hope, would like, stop,* etc.

Encourage students to keep a list of these verbs and learn them. They are also useful for other parts of the *Key* exam, especially Part 5.

Extension

Students write true or false sentence about themselves. They should say something they

- hate doing
- love doing
- hope to do soon
- decided to do recently.

Exam practice

Tell students to quickly read through the sentences and identify the topic (horse-riding competition). Do the example together as a class. Look at the advice and work through items 6, 7 and 10 with the class.
Students then complete the task, circling the correct letter (A, B or C).

> 6 B   7 A   8 A   9 C   10 C

Go over each item. Talk about what make the answers correct, and what makes the distractors wrong.

Extension

Write these sentences on the board. Students can complete each sentence using the same distractors in each item of this exam practice.
1 Sonja .... to get to the competition by 10 a.m.
2 The journey was so .... that she fell asleep.
3 There was a big .... of about 20,000 people watching the competition.
4 Sonya .... she did quite well, but she wasn't sure.
5 Sonya .... a silver cup home with her.

> 1 needed   2 boring   3 crowd   4 thought   5 brought

Test 2 Reading and Writing Part 3a (Questions 11–15)

Task type:
discrete three-option multiple choice – verbal exchange patterns (functions)

Topic focus:
n/a

Training

Part 3a will often include opening statements which contain question words. Write *What, Why, Which, When, Where, Who, Whose* on the board. Then write these answers:

1 At the bus stop
2 Tomorrow evening
3 The red one
4 Because it's cold
5 I think it's Daniel's.
6 Our new teacher
7 It's a book.

Students match each answer with a question word.

1 Where 2 When 3 Which 4 Why 5 Whose 6 Who
7 What

Elicit full questions that could match the answers.

1 Students do the exercise on their own, then check their answers with a partner.

1 whose 2 Why 3 Where 4 When 5 Who 6 What

 Key candidates often make mistakes with who's and whose. Revise the difference in meaning. Point out that the pronunciation is exactly the same.

2 Students now move on to matching prompts with responses. After completing the task, students role play the exchanges. Encourage them to extend each conversation by two turns.

1 Me too! 2 It is, isn't it? 3 It's mine. 4 That's great.
5 I hope so. 6 I'd rather not.

 Key candidates often make mistakes with I think and I hope by omitting the final so or not. Explain that so carries the meaning of yes, and not carries the meaning of no.
Can you do this exercise? I think so. / I hope so.
Will you fail the test? I hope not.

3 Now students move on to choosing between two responses. The focus is on meaning. Explain to students they have to choose the option which makes most sense.
Students work in pairs and role play the exchanges, choosing the answer which sounds best to them.

1 a 2 b 3 b

Extension

Students work together to write appropriate first sentences for the incorrect responses in Exercise 3, e.g. *When are you getting your new jeans?* 1 *I'm never going to Canada again.* 2 *My picture is really good.* 3 *Did you get into trouble today?*

Exam practice

Write these functions up on the board: *asking a question, giving instructions, giving an opinion, making a suggestion*. Students match each item with the correct function. (N.B. There are two questions.) Tell students to cover up the options and work in pairs to think of responses. Then look at the advice box with the class. Students do the task then check their answers with a partner.

11 B 12 C 13 B 14 C 15 A

Extension

Put students in pairs and tell them to think of positive and negative responses to the following prompts. Encourage them to use expressions from this section, and avoid simple *Yes, okay / No thanks* answers.
I love this film!
Let's got a taxi into town.
I think you're very funny.
Whose bag is that?
Why are you laughing?
I just ran a marathon!

Test 2 Reading and Writing Part 3b (Questions 16–20)

Task type:
continuous dialogue – matching exercise – five gaps / eight options

Topic focus:
leisure time

Training

Remind students what they have to do in Part 3b. Ask *How many gaps are there? How many option to choose from? How many wrong options are there?*

1   In this exercise, students focus on whether an item is talking about time or place. Tell students to underline the words in each sentence which helps them get the correct answer.

> 1 time   2 place   3 place   4 time   5 place   6 time
> 7 place   8 time

2   Revise the difference between Yes / No questions and information questions. This will help students make the correct links in the conversation gap. Tell students to look at the example in this exercise. Is it a Yes / No or an information question? (Yes / No). Then tell students to identify the other questions in this exercise (1 and 3 are statements).
Point out that for this task, there is only one wrong answer. This shows that there are different structures possible to answer a question appropriately. Emphasise that in the exam there is only one correct answer.

> *Wrong answers:*
> *1 I think so   2 They were in my room!   3 Yes, she's too busy*
> *4 No I'm not   5 We're not going   6 At 7 o'clock.*

Extension

In pairs, students think of questions / statements the 'wrong answers' would work with, e.g. *Did you get that for free? No, but it wasn't expensive. Is Maria coming? I think so.*

3   Students move towards practising the test format by choosing one answer from eight options in a conversation. Emphasise the importance of looking at the sentence before and after the gap – the answer must make sense in both cases.

> 1 C   2 A   3 B   4 H   5 D   6 E

Ask students to identify the extra option (f). Encourage them to underline the words which link together.
In pairs, students role play the entire conversation.

Exam Practice

Tell students to quickly read the whole conversation, without worrying about what goes in the gaps. What are they talking about? (a school trip).
Ask them to underline the Yes / No questions and the information questions in the conversation and the options.
Remind students to always cross out the example option, and to cross out the other options as they use them.
Go over the advice as a class. Then students complete the task in pairs.

> 16 B   17 H   18 A   19 D   20 G

Extension

Put students in pairs. Tell them to look at the two unused options from the practice test (options C and F) and to construct a short dialogue using them. They can completely change the situation for the dialogue if they want. For example:

A: When did you start work on your art project?
B: Last week. Here, have a look at what I've done.
A: These are excellent pictures.
B: Thanks!

Students read out their dialogues to the rest of the class.

Task type:
three-option multiple choice – magazine-type factual input text – approximately 200 words long (230 for multiple-choice type).

Topic focus:
animals, natural world

Training

Remind students about the three-option multiple choice exercises in Part 4 by writing this up on the board.
In three-option multiple choice tasks:

- *there are 5 / 7 items*
- *all / some of the items are questions*
- *none / some of the items are incomplete sentences*
- *the order of the questions is / isn't the same as the order of information in the text.*

There are 7; some of the items are questions, some of the items are incomplete sentences; the order of the questions is the same as the order of information in the text.

1   Ask students what they know about pandas. Where are they from? What do they look like? What do they eat?
    Explain that this exercise focuses on where in the text the information you are looking for is. Remind students that it is good practice to underline the key words in the questions and the parts of the text which provide the information. Students complete this task alone.

> 1 4   2 2   3 2   4 1   5 5   6 6

Check the answers and clear up any vocabulary questions.

 Key candidates often confuse *its* and *it's*. Remind them that *its* is the possessive adjective and *it's* is short for *it is*. You can note that this is also a very common mistake among native English speakers!

2   In this exercise, students are presented with a short text which contains the information needed to answer the question. The text also contains references to the wrong answers (distractors). This help students identify the correct answer among three possibilities. They should beware of choosing an answer just because the same word appears in both the text and the question.
    Note that this exercise includes examples of sentence completion and question items – two of each.

> 1 C   2 B   3 A   4 B

Go over the answers. Ask the students to tell you why the distractors are wrong in each case.

Exam practice

This is an example of a single text multiple choice Part 4. Note that in this type of Part 4, the questions are in the same order as information in the text. (They are not in multiple-text Part 4s.) Tell students to read all the text first, and clear up any vocabulary questions if necessary. Remind students of the advice box and look at the example together.
Then put students in pairs to read the questions. Students underline the key words in each question. As students answer the questions, tell them to underline the parts of the text which contain the answers.
Go through the answers together as a class. Ask each pair of students to choose one response and explain their answers.

> 21 B   22 C   23 A   24 A   25 C   26 A   27 B

Extension

Ask students if they have a favourite animal. Students do the task below telling their friends about their animal. They should write 25–35 words.
You have a favourite animal. Write a short description.

- **What** is the animal?
- **Where** does it live?
- **What** does it eat?
- **Why** do you like it?

Task type:
multiple-choice cloze – gapped factual text – eight gaps / three optional answers (content and function words)

Topic focus:
natural world, rainforests

Training

Remind students what they need to do in Part 5.
To introduce the topic focus, write *rainforest* on the board. Ask *What is a rainforest? Where are they? How many types of rainforest are there? What kind of animals can be found there?* Make a list of words associated with rainforests.

1   Look at the **Remember!** box, and elicit examples of the use of those determiners. Go over the example in class. Students can do this exercise alone or in pairs.

| 1 Both   2 several   3 the   4 One   5 A   6 an |

2   Revise modal verbs *need, must, can, could, would, will, may* and *might*. At least one item in Part 5 is usually a modal verb. Focus on the meaning of each.
Look at the example, and ask students to explain why *may* is the correct answer and the other two are wrong. Students complete and task then check their answers with a partner. Then go through each item in class.

| 1 could   2 can   3 need   4 can   5 should   6 must |

 Key candidates often make mistakes with modal verbs. As well as following a modal with the *-ing* form, they frequently use an inflected verb. *Sorry I couldn't came to your party. I can met you next Saturday.*

Extension

As homework, you could ask the students to write examples of each of the modal verbs practised here.

3   This exercise practises expressions with numbers which require prepositions or adverbs. Before doing the task, write the words in the box on the board and elicit correct examples of their use from the class. Students then complete the task.

| 1 of   2 a   3 under   4 than   5   about / under / over
6 between |

 Key candidates generally use *than* correctly in comparative sentences but misuse it in other contexts, e.g. *I did my homework than I went to bed. I got one than is new. My bike isn't as new than your bike.* Go over these examples with students and correct them.

Exam practice

Tell students to quickly read through the whole article. Ask two or three comprehension questions, e.g. *Where can you find temperate / tropical rainforests? How many different types of plants are there in the rainforests? Why are rainforests important?*
Go through the advice. Students then complete the task.

| 28 A   29 B   30 C   31 B   32 A   33 B   34 C   35 A |

Go through the answers in class. Ask students to identify what items correspond to the exercises in the Training section. (Ex 1 – 29, 34, Ex 2 – 30, Ex 3 – 29)

Extension

In pairs, or for homework, students do some more research into rainforests to find out why they are important. The reason given in the text is that they are useful for medicine. Students should find three more reasons. (They are a home for animals and plants. They are important for stabilising the climate / weather. They are home to a lot of people.)

Task type:
word completion – five definitions – five spellings. The first letter and the number of letters given.

Topic focus:
weather, leisure, camping

Training

Before doing the exercises, remind students what they need to do in Part 6.

1   Write the word *Camping* on the board. Ask What do you take with you when you go camping? Elicit as many words as possible and write them on the board. Follow up by eliciting why you take each of these things.
Look at the exercise. Explain that there is nothing grammatically wrong with the sentences, but some of them do not make sense. The example item is one of those which does not make sense.

> 1 ✔   2 ✗   3 ✗   4 ✔   5 ✗   6 ✔

Go over the answers. Ask students to correct the wrong sentences.

2   This exercise models one in Part 6 with one difference. Ask students if they can spot it (in Part 6 only the first letter is shown). Ask, *What is the weather like today?* Elicit some more weather words from the students.

> 1 windy   2 ice   3 snow   4 sunny   5 warm   6 cloudy

3   This gets students thinking about definitions. Students choose a word from the box and write it next to the definition.

> 1 barbecue   2 field   3 knife   4 umbrella   5 beach   6 chair   7 fire

4   This exercise draws students' attention to time clues in the definitions which could help them find the answer.

> 1 lunch   2 dress   3 moon   4 light   5 dinner   6 stars

5   Students revise clothing vocabulary through reading and underlining.

> T-shirts, hat, sweaters, jumpers, trainers, sunglasses, jeans, boots

Extension

Students sort the clothes in Exercise 5 into things you wear 1 on your head 2 on your upper body 3 on your lower body 4 on your feet. Tell them to add items which do not appear in the text.

6   Students practise recognising spelling errors. Point out that when the wrong words are read out loud, they sound the same as the correct words. This is because the mistakes are due to silent letters. Students complete this exercise in pairs.

> 1 autumn   2 Listen   3 guitar   4 build   5 guide   6 stomach
> 7 comb   8 biscuits   9 scissors

 Another thing which you might take camping with you is also one of the most common spelling errors made by *Key* candidates: *a mobil* (*mobile*). You can talk about whether or not you should take your mobile with you when you go camping – what are the advantages and disadvantages?

7   Here the focus is on how similar sounds can be made in different ways. Explain what *rhyme* means
Make clear that students have to read each word aloud in order to determine which word rhymes with it.

> 1 break   2 go   3 white   4 free   5 they   6 bought
> 7 foot   8 shoe

Extension

Play 'rhyming tennis'. Divide the class into two groups. Start the game by serving the first word, e.g. coat. Any student from Group 1 says a word which rhymes with it (e.g. boat). Then any student from Group 2 says another. When one group fails, the other gets a point.

8   This exercise tests students' understanding of the meanings of the words which appeared in the previous exercise.

> 1 sort   2 bought   3 free   4 white   5 shoe   6 break
> 7 they   8 foot

9   Here students revise jobs. Go through the words in the box and make sure they are all known.

> 1 doctor   2 teacher   3 mechanic   4 cleaner   5 pilot   6 guide

Exam practice

Go through the advice for items 38 and 40. Look at the example together. Tell students to underline the key words in the definitions. They are all words which have appeared in this unit.

> 36 windy   37 fire   38 boots   39 lamp   40 guitar

Extension

Ask students how many clothes, types of weather, jobs, and camping accessories they can remember from this unit. In pairs, they make four separate lists. When they have complete the words from this unit, ask them to expand their lists. Check spellings!

Task type:
open cloze – structure and vocabulary. Texts are types that a student might write.

Topic focus:
music, communication

Trainer

Before beginning the exercises, remind students of what they need to do in Part 7. Ask them what this part of the exam mainly tests (grammar). *Key* candidates typically find Part 7 one of the hardest parts of the paper, so it is worth spending time on it.

1   Write the connecting words on the board: *and, or, so, but, because, when, if, as.* Ask stronger students to give some examples. Point out that *because* and *as* mean the same. Look at the example in class then students do the task.

| 1 but   2 because   3 so   4 if   5 or   6 as |

Point out that items 1–6 contain two complete sentences each, separated by the connecting word.

The most common spelling mistake that *Key* candidates make is with *because*, which is often spelt *becouse*. Make sure students know how to spell it correctly.

2   In this exercise, students revise some common prepositional phrases. Look at the ***Remember!*** box. In pairs, students think of one example for each phrase. Students complete the task.

| 1 at   2 in   3 about 4 of   5 at   6 to |

Check the answers, then tell students to underline the words immediately after the prepositions. What kinds of word are they? (1 and 2 (article +) noun 3 and 4 (possessive adj+) noun 5 and 6 pronoun). Ask what other kind of word often follows a preposition (-*ing* form).

3   This exercise gives students practice with questions words. Question words often appear in Part 7. Tell students to read the whole email. Ask, *What is Hana talking about?* (music exams) Quickly go through the question words in the box, eliciting examples from students.

| 1 Where   2 Who   3 Which   4 When   5 Why   6 What |

Point out that item 3 is *Which* rather than *What* because the question is about a limited number of alternatives (as in exam levels in this case). We use *what* when there isn't a limit.

Extension

Tell students to underline the sentences in the first paragraph which are not questions. In pairs, they write questions to which the sentences could be answers, e.g. *Where do you do your music exams?*

Exam practice

Tell students to read the whole text quickly. Ask some general comprehension questions about it first, like *Who is Bea? How many times has Sali written to Bea?* (It's her first email.) Go over the example and point out the Advice for items 43, 46 and 50. Students complete the task alone or in pairs.

| 41 from   42 about   43 What   44 Have   45 are   46 far
  47 but   48 much   49 ago   50 for |

Check the answers. Point out the most of them are grammatical. Ask students to identify the prepositions (41, 42 50) and the connector (47). Only two of the answers test vocabulary (46, 49).

Extension

Students write a short reply to Bea's email. They should answer her two questions (*What is your school like? Have you got any brothers or sisters?*) and give one more piece of information, e.g. how they get to school, what's their favourite subject, do they play a musical instrument?

Test 2 Reading and Writing Part 8

Task type:
non-sequential information transfer – using input text/s to complete a form

Topic focus:
leisure time, sport

Training

Remind students what they need to do in a Part 8. Ask how many items they need to fill in (5), and what a Part 8 tests (reading and writing information).

1   In this exercise, students practices the cross-referencing between the notice/advert and the email. Explain that the items on the left are sentences from the email, and the options on the right are from the notice/advert.
Look at the example. Which word in the sentence indicates the correct option (shorter).
Tell students to read the sentences and underline the key word in each. Students complete the task.

> 1 12th July 2 £40 3 5.30 p.m. 4 12 – 17s 5 Beginners
> 6 1420

Extension

In pairs, students look at the items again and write sentences so that the other options are the correct answers, e.g. *Let's do the longer run*, 1 *I think we should do the last date*, etc.

> *Key* candidates often make mistakes with *o'clock*, e.g. *3 o'clock p.m.*, *3 oclock*, *3 hour o'clock*, *3 o'clok*, *13 o'clock*, *08.00 o'clock*. Write these on the board and explain why they are wrong. Explain that centuries ago, people would say *It's five of the clock!* instead of *It's five o'clock*. *o'* is the modern abbreviation meaning *of the*.

2   In this exercise, students practise looking for answers in two texts. In Part 8, some answers will come from the first text and some from the second. Sometimes you need to cross reference both of them to get the answer.
Point out that these texts are longer than Part 8 in an exam. Tell students to cover the questions so that they can't read them. Then students read the two texts. In pairs, they try to anticipate what kind of information they will be asked to write in the notes.

They write their prompts, but not the answers. Then students swap with another pair, and they attempt to complete the other pair's notes.
When they have finished, they check each other's answers. Students now do the task.

> 1 077 5345 7867 *(Text 1)* 2 climbing *(Text 2)* 3 6 p.m. *(Text 1)*
> 4 3 *(Text 2)* 5 £2 *(Text 1)* 6 playground *(Text 2)* 7 (on) foot *(Text 2)*

Ask students to identify the two questions which require them to have read both of the texts. (3 and 5)

Extension

In pairs, students look again at the task. For each correct item, they find a distractor. Point out that two items don't really have a distractor. (1 077 4754 2280 2 badminton 3 4 p.m. 4 none 5 £3 6 none 7 bus)

> Some *Key* candidates mistakenly make the pronoun agree with the plural noun, e.g. *theirs classes*. Tell students that *mine*, *yours*, *ours* and *theirs* are never followed by a noun.

Exam practice

Tell students to read both text and the notes before attempting the task. Remind them that correct spelling is important, as all they have to do is copy words and numbers from the texts. Students complete the task alone. Point out the advice box which they can use to help them find the answers if necessary.

> 51 14 August 52 (£)25 53 (warm) jacket 54 sailing 55 bike

Extension

As homework or in class, students write another email based on the notice. They use the email as a model but use their own ideas about the time, date, means of transport and what to take.

Test 2 Reading and Writing Part 9

Task type:
guided writing – write a short message of 25–35 words in response to a short input text or rubric

Topic focus:
communication

Training

Remind students of what they need to do in Part 9. Ask how many words they need to write (25–35), how many pieces of information they need to include (three), and if they have to start and end their messages properly (yes).

1 Sometimes a Part 9 takes the instruction format. This exercise looks at possible instructions.

> *1 Why don't we play badminton on Tuesday? 2 Thanks for booking the tennis court 3 Would you like to play tennis with me tomorrow? 4 We need to be at the sports centre by about five 5 The new sports centre opened last weekend 6 I can't come swimming, because I have to visit my grandad 7 I'm sorry I lost your football. I'll buy you another one.*

2 In this exercise, students focus on expressions for suggesting. Go through the ***Remember!*** box eliciting examples. Make notes about which expressions take *-ing* form, to infinitive and bare infinitive.
Explain that students have to say what the writer is doing in each sentence.

> *1 suggesting 2 inviting 3 suggesting 4 thanking 5 suggesting 6 suggesting*

3 Here students practise spotting errors in sentences which are explaining something or saying sorry for something. Explain that they have to underline the error and write the correction in the right hand column. Students do this task alone or in pairs.

> *1 call, to call 2 while, because 3 than, that 4 and, but 5 except, so 6 don't, 'm not 7 but, that 8 if, but*

4 This exercise revises the verbs *play*, *go* and *do* with sports and other activities. Look at the ***Remember!*** box and make sure students understand when each should be used. Students do the task.

> *1 go 2 did 3 goes 4 play 5 go 6 play*

 One of the most common past simple spelling errors made by *Key* candidates is *playd*. Make sure they know how to spell this correctly!

5 This exercise focuses on frequent preposition errors at *Key* level, with *at*, *by* and *on*. To illustrate the usage of these prepositions, ask students how they get to school, what time they leave home, and what's the latest time they get home again (to elicit by + latest time).

> *1 at 2 by (at) 3 at 4 by 5 on 6 on 7 by 8 at*

6 Go through the spellings of some of the more common irregular verbs.

> *1 came 2 cost 3 flew 4 left 5 put 6 brought*

 Costed is another very common irregular verb spelling error at *Key* level, as is *payed*. Make sure students know the correct past forms are *cost* and *paid*.

7 The task gives students practice in error correction. Emphasise that spotting one error can make a big difference to the final grade!

> *1 Saturday 2 of 3 Would 4 something 5 Maybe 6 food 7 don't 8 Could 9 address*

Extension

8 Sometimes *Key* candidates forget that they have to start and end their messages properly. This exercise provides nine examples of good starts and endings.

> *1 end 2 end 3 start 4 end 5 end 6 end 7 end 8 start 9 start*

9 Now students look at a complete Part 9 task with three example answers. In pairs, or groups of three, students read the first message and identify the three pieces of information necessary to give a complete answer.
Then they read the example answers and answer the questions.

> *1 Christophe 2 Alfredo 3 Brad 4 Brad 5 Christophe 6 Christophe*

Ask students to give each example answer a mark out of 5, using the marking scheme on page 193.

Exam practice

Tell students to read the email. Get them to identify what three pieces of information they need to include in their answer. Go through the advice and tell students to complete the task alone.

> *Sample answer*
> *Hi Frankie*
> *Let's go to the sports centre on Wednesday. It's not far so we can ride there on our bikes. I think we should play badminton.*
> *See you soon,*
> *Mark*

Test 2 Listening Part 1

Task type:
three-option visual multiple choice to answer focus question –
two-speaker short conversations

Topic focus:
n/a

Training

Before beginning the exercises, remind students what they have
to do in Listening Part 1.

1   Tell students to look at the three pictures. Elicit a description
    of each of the girls, focusing on hair (long, short, dark) and
    what she is wearing (glasses). Remind students that it is
    always a good idea to try to say what they can see in each of
    the pictures to themselves in English, as it prepares them for
    what they are about to hear.
    Students listen to the recording and tick the box which
    shows the correct answer.

    B

    Play the recording again. Check if any students chose the
    distractor (C), and get a stronger student to explain why
    it is wrong (Eva says *that's not her* and gives the correct
    description).

2   This exercise builds on Exercise 1 by giving further practice
    on descriptions of people. Ask what the men in pictures
    B and C have on their faces (a beard) and then elicit
    descriptions of the men in the three pictures. Make sure the
    adjectives *tall*, *slim* and *fat / large* are used.
    Students listen to the recording and choose the correct answer.

    A

3   This exercise revises clothing items. Warm up by asking
    students what they are wearing today. Then put students into
    groups and tell them to list the clothes they can see in the
    pictures.
    Students listen to the recording and tick the boxes which
    show the correct answer. Remind them that they will hear all
    of the items in the pictures mentioned in the dialogues, but
    that only one answer is correct.

    1 C   2 B   3 C   4 A

4   This provides further revision of clothing items. Ask students
    what they usually wear to parties. Then ask them to describe
    what they can see in each picture. Then play the recording.

    C

Extension

For homework or in class, ask students to cut out pictures from
magazines and create a poster which illustrates the clothes words
they need to know at *Key* level (*bathing suit, belt, blouse, boot,
cap, coat, dress, glove, hat, jacket, jeans, jumper, raincoat, scarf,
shirt, shoes, shorts, skirt, suit, sweater, swimming costume/
swimsuit, tie, tights, trainers, trousers, T-shirt*).

5   Students now move on to revising prepositions of place. Part
    1 often has an item which requires students to say where
    something is. In pairs, students look at the picture and say
    where each book is. Write the words *on, under, next to,
    between, on top of* to help if necessary.

    *1 next to bag   2 on the floor between two chairs   3 on the table
    with a glass on top of it   4 on the floor under the table*

6   In this exercise, students revise weather words and practise
    with a Part 1 style task. Write *sunny, cloudy* and *rain* on the
    board. Elicit as many other weather words as possible.
    Point out that we can make adjectives by adding *-y* to
    weather nouns (*sunny, windy, cloudy, foggy*). Add that for
    sun and *fog* we double the final consonant. Ask them to
    describe the weather today.

    B

7   This exercise focuses on telling the time, something which is
    often tested in Part 1. Students read the times in the box and
    match them with the clock faces.

    1 nine thirty   2 five past eight   3 ten o'clock   4 twenty to twelve

    Tell students that we usually write *a quarter to five* or *a
    quarter to seven*, but in spoken English the article *a* is often
    not included. The article *a* is never used with half past.

Exam practice

Before doing the test, remind students to:
- underline the key words in each question
- identify the tense of each question
- look at all the pictures and 'say what they see' in English
- even if they don't know the answer, always pick one!

Go over the example in class. Draw attention to the advice.

1 B   2 B   3 C   4 B   5 A

Extension

Play the recordings for items 1–3 again. What do the two wrong
answers refer to?

Teacher's Notes
Test 2 Listening Part 2

Task type:
matching – informal dialogue – listening for key information – matching five items (plus example) – eight options

Topic focus:
people, entertainment

Training

Before beginning the exercises, remind students what they have to do in Listening Part 2 by asking questions: *How many questions are there?* (five plus example) *How many options?* (eight) *How many conversations?* (one)

1   Before doing the exercise, brainstorm as many personality adjectives from the class as possible. Write them on the board and make sure students know what they mean.
    This exercise uses paraphrasing to indicate the answers. Go over the example as a class. Ask: *How do we know Britt is musical?* (She can play three instruments.)
    Students listen to the recording and connect the name to the adjective with a line. Point out that, as in the exam, the names in the left hand column appear in the same order as in the recording.

> 1 *Ada – kind,*   2 *Nicole – clever,*   3 *Sara – funny,*   4 *Katy – quiet,*
> 5 *Serena – brave,*   6 *Esther – tidy*

Key candidates often confuse the words *quiet* and *quite*, *It's quiet a big book.* Make sure students understand the difference between the two words.

Extension

In pairs, students look at the list of personality adjectives you wrote on the board at the start of this exercise. Tell them to write down the ones they think apply to themselves. Then ask them to write down the ones they think apply to their partners. Students then compare their lists – did they choose the same words?

2   This exercise practises both paraphrasing and choosing between two possible answers. In Part 2, you often hear a distractor mentioned alongside the answer, so it is necessary to decide which is correct. Note that this exercise consists of separate items, unlike the test which has a full dialogue.
    Go over the example and ensure students understand why *being with other people* is the correct answer (The girl says: 'study' is 'great', but 'the best thing is spending time with friends').
    Students do the task – remind them to cross out the wrong answer.

> 1 *being outside*   2 *seeing new places*   3 *snowboarding*
> 4 *the music*   5 *the presents*

Extension

Note the pattern of these recordings – how both options are mentioned, but only one is correct. In pairs, students construct their own sentences saying what they like about
– computers
– holidays
– eating out
– their bed.
First they think of two options, then they write a short statement in which both options are mentioned but only one is correct (the one they really like).

3   This as a shorter version of an actual Part 2 type task. Before doing the task, put students in pairs and ask them to come up with paraphrases which suggest a person is in the places in the right hand column – but without actually mentioning those places by name e.g. *He's picking up some books* (library), *She's gone to collect her friend whose plane lands at 4 o'clock* (airport).
    Students do the task. You should play the recording twice, as some of these are quite tricky!

> 1 B   2 E   3 D   4 C

Go over the answers and play the recording one more time. Stop after each answer and ask students to explain how they know each answer is correct.

We can say *I'd like to go shopping* but not *I'd like to do shopping*. To *go shopping* is more of a leisure activity, while *to do (the) shopping* is a task. Make sure students spell *shopping* with a double *p*!

Exam practice

Before doing the task, make sure students understand all the words in the right-hand Reasons column. Play the first part of the recording which contains the example. Remind students to always cross out the example option before they listen.
Play the recording twice.

> 6 A   7 H   8 B   9 E   10 C

Extension

Play '20 questions' in groups. One student thinks of a famous person. The other students can ask Yes / No questions about that person to try to find out who it is. They are limited to 20 questions. If they don't get the answer after 20 questions, the student who thought of the person wins. This practises not only personality adjectives, but a wide range of other vocabulary such as jobs.

Task type:
three-option multiple choice, question / answer or sentence completion format, – informal or neutral dialogue – five items plus an example

Topic focus:
school, travel

Training

Before beginning the exercises, remind students what they have to do in Listening Part 3. Ask students: *How many questions are there?* (five plus example), *How many options per question?* (three), *How many dialogues are there to listen to?* (one)

1   Before doing this exercise, introduce the topic by asking: *What's your favourite school subject? What's your least favourite?* Try to elicit the names of all the other school subjects and write them on the board. Ask students to describe what is taught in each of the subjects. Students do this exercise in pairs.

1 art   2 maths   3 history   4 biology   5 geography
6 chemistry

Extension

Use the list you wrote on the board to do a class survey about what the most and least popular school subjects are. Ask students what they like or dislike about each of them.

2   In this exercise, students do further practice in discerning the correct answer from two options. The recording is slightly longer than a standard Part 3. Tell students to read all the questions before playing the recording. Then play the recording and tell them to decide whether or not the answer is right or wrong.

1 ✔   2 ✘   3 ✘   4 ✔   5 ✔   6 ✘

Extension

Play the recording again, and tell students to correct the wrong answers. (2 18 days, 3 27 degrees 6 a book). You could also ask them to explain what the original wrong answers are referring to (2 – ten hours, 3 the August temperature 6 a necklace she wanted).

   Key candidates generally know that the names of countries must begin with a capital letter, but they often forget to capitalise nationalities and languages, e.g. *american*, *spanish*. Make sure they understand that these too must be capitalised.

3   This exercise provides further practice in choosing between two possible answers. Introduce the topic by writing *Tourist Information Office* on the board and eliciting what kind of information you can find there.
   Play the first part of the recording which contains the example. Ask students to explain why *Castle Street* is the wrong answer (The man recommends starting at River Gardens).
   Play the whole recording, making sure students know they have to cross out the wrong answer.

1 24 hours   2 £20   3 9.30   4 15th century   5 When it's windy.
6 clothes

   The word information is the most common uncountable noun that *Key* candidates make plural. *I need some informations.* Make sure students know that this word is always singular. Other very common uncountable errors are *music*, *paper* and *homework*.

Exam practice

Tell students to read all the questions and options, and revise / teach any vocabulary if necessary. Then ask them to identify the type of answer in each item (11 a school subject 12 a century 13 a price 14 a place 15 a type of weather). Tell them to underline the key words in each question. Go through the advice with students.
After the first listening, students check answers with each other in pairs. Allow them to discuss any differences, and then play the recording again.

11 C   12 A   13 A   14 C   15 B

Extension

Play the recording one more time, stopping after each question section is answered. In pairs, students write down what each wrong answer is referring to.

Teacher's Notes
Test 2 Listening Part 4

Task type:
gap – fill – two-speaker short conversation – writing down specific information to complete a form (names, numbers, places, times etc.)

Topic focus:
prices, trips

Training

Before beginning the exercises, remind students what they have to do in Listening Part 4. Ask questions: *How many questions are there?* (five plus example) *What do they have to do?* (fill in information). *Is it a dialogue or a monologue?* (dialogue).

1 Students practise listening to prices. Check that they know the currencies necessary at *Key* level – dollar, pound, euro, cent. Write the symbols on the board. Tell students that although they should know these currencies, they will probably only be tested on pounds in the exam. Ask *How much does a ticket to the cinema cost?*
Listen to the example dialogue. Is the answer given right or wrong? What does the wrong answer refer to?
Play the rest of the recording. Make sure students understand that they need to say whether the give answer is right or wrong.

> 1 ✔ 2 ✔ 3 ✘ 4 ✘

Play the recording again and ask students to correct the wrong answers.

2 In this exercise. students are now asked to write the answers. Remind them that they will hear at least two prices in each dialogue, but only one of them is correct.
Listen to the example. Ask, *How much is the full adult price?* (£4.50)
Now play the whole recording. Students complete the task.

> 1 £2 2 $4 3 £28 4 $35.50 5 5 pence 6 $1.20

Play each item again, asking students to write down every price they hear. In pairs, they should identify what each 'wrong' price is for. (1 £5 = actual cost; 2 $2 = extra needed for photo exhibition; 3 £25 = what the ticket appears to say; 4 $50 = cost of bag in shops, £14 = amount less online; 5 no price; 6 90 cents = how much boy has, 30 cents = how much boy needs)

Extension

Give further practice with prices if necessary by dictating random prices for students to write down. You can also ask for approximate or average prices for such things as a can of cola, a burger, a pair of trainers, a notebook, etc.

3 Students keep the focus on numbers, but move from prices to ages. Play the recording once and tell students to write down every number they hear in the space. Then on the second recording, tell them to cross out the wrong numbers, leaving only the correct answer.

> 1 15 2 10 3 3 4 8 5 3

4 Students try to predict what kind of answers they need to write in the test. In pairs, they look at the exercise and write their guesses in column A.
Go over their guesses and make sure they have properly understood the kind of answers required. Then play the recording. Students complete the task. Remind them that spelling is important in this part of the test.

> A: 1 name 2 type of transport (coach) 3 time (o'clock / a.m. / p.m.) 4 clothes (warm, rainproof) 5 a price (£5)
>
> B: 1 Kendall 2 coach 3 12.45 4 raincoats 5 £4.50

Exam practice

Go through the advice with students before they listen. Tell students to read all the questions before listening. In pairs, students try to guess what kind of answer they need to write. Ask them to guess which question is the spelling question (19). Play the recording twice.

> 16 8.70 17 9.30 18 lions 19 Wilton 20 Sea

Extension

Students write a short email about a school or family trip they have been on.
Say

- **Where** they went
- **What** they saw
- **Why** they liked / didn't like it.

Test 2 Listening Part 5

Task type:
gap – fill – one speaker – writing down specific information to complete a form (names, numbers, places, times etc.)

Topic focus:
entertainment, television

Training

Before beginning the exercises, ask students what the difference is between Part 4 and Part 5 listenings (the number of speakers).

1   Here students have further practice with numbers, both long and short. Listen to the example. Ask students: *Why the answer is wrong. What is the answer?* Play the whole recording once and tell students to complete the task in pairs.

> 1 ✔   2 ✘   3 ✔   4 ✘   5 ✔

Play the recording again. Ask students to write the correct answers to items 2 and 4 (4 and 67).

2   This exercise continues to practise numbers. Play the example. Make sure students understand why 15 is the correct answer, and 425 is wrong. Then play the recording once and tell students to write down every number they hear in the space. Before playing the recording a second time, tell them to cross out the wrong numbers, leaving only the correct answer.

> 1 14   2 353   3 500   4 20   5 0163 564 7885   6 3

Extension

Ask students to guess some very expensive prices, e.g. of an aeroplane, a castle, a Ferrari, a space trip.

3   This exercise gives further practice of spelling of school subjects. Students do the task alone, then check answers with a partner.

> 1 history 2 science 3 biology 4 chemistry 5 physics 6 geography

4   In this final exercise, students revise the meanings and spelling of sports, hobbies, places in a town, possessions, ways to travel and animals. Before starting each section, elicit as many examples of the word sets as possible. You can turn it into a game by putting students in pairs and asking them to try to guess what items they will hear. Count up the number of correct guesses at the end. If someone guesses all three in one set, maybe you could offer a special prize!

> Sports
> 1 cricket 2 fishing 3 golf
> Hobbies
> 1 listening to music 2 watching films 3 photography
> Places in a town
> 1 theatre 2 university 3 café
> Possessions
> 1 pen 2 coat 3 book
> Ways to travel
> 1 plane 2 boat 3 train
> Animals
> 1 monkeys 2 elephants 3 rabbit

Exam practice

Ask students to read all the questions before listening. What kind of answers are needed? Go through the advice before they listen to the recording.

> 21 Science   22 63   23 5.40   24 15th October   25 insects

Extension

Write a sample Part 5 form on the board:

X's Favourite programme

Name of Programme	....
Day(s) it's on	....
Channel	....
Time	....
About	....

In pairs, students interview each other about their favourite TV programme and fill in the form with the information. Go through each item first to make sure students are asking the correct questions. What is the most popular TV programme in the class?

Task type:
The examiner asks both candidates questions about themselves. This part lasts for about six minutes.

Topic focus:
personal information: family, friends, school and study, home town, hobbies

Training

Students answer the lead-in questions.

There will be two students and two examiners. You have to speak to an examiner.

1   Elicit some of the personal information questions that the students may be asked in the exam. Then ask them to read the questions and answers before completing the activity. When you have checked the answers, elicit the missing question (*Have you got any brothers or sisters?*).

1 d   2 c   3 a   4 f   5 b

2   Ask different students to spell their surnames. Practise any difficult or confusing pronunciations of letters (for example, G and J). Go through the English alphabet: ask students to call out the letters in turn. If the pronunciation is correct, write each letter in sequence on the board. If not, repeat the correct pronunciation several times before writing it up. Students look at the spellings, listen and choose the correct name. Check the answers by asking different students to spell out the name they chose. Play the recording again to confirm if there are any disagreements.

1 b   2 a   3 a   4 b

3   Students read the questions and answers. Play the recording for them to tick or cross the information. Check the answers. Then play the recording again and ask them to correct the incorrect information.

1 ✔   2 ✘ (a town called Alanya), 3 ✘ (He has classes after school.),   4 ✔   5 ✘ (three hours)

4   Draw students' attention to the Tip. Tell them that they will become more confident about the test the more they practise giving information about themselves.
Students take turns to ask and answer the questions about themselves.

5   Point out the Tip and explain that they will not lose marks for asking the examiner to repeat a question, but they should listen carefully to everything the examiner says.
Play the recording for students to check.

four

6   Students close their books. Elicit ways of asking for a question to be repeated and write any correct phrases on the board. Students then open their books and compare the phrases with the ideas on the board.
Students listen to the conversation again and tick the phrases they hear. Then ask them which of the phrases is not polite.

Can you say that again, please? Sorry? I'm sorry, what did you say? I don't understand.
What? is not a polite way to ask for repetition.

7   Students read the information about Evgeni. Elicit the questions they think he has been asked. Then play the recording for them to check their ideas. Play the recording a second time for them to correct the incorrect information.

1 Evgeni's surname is Petrov.   2 He's from the east of Russia.
3 He goes to school in Scotland.   4 His favourite subjects are maths and English.   5 He has two English classes at school.
6 He has a big family.   7 His sister is studying at university.
8 She likes dancing.

8   Students read the ***Remember!*** box. They then take turns to ask and answer the *Tell me about ...* questions. Remind them to give three or four pieces of information per question. Monitor as they are working and note down any particularly good answers. Write these on the board and ask students to say what is good about them.

Exam practice

Go through the Tips with the students.
Play the recording, pausing after each question for the students to answer. It may help them to concentrate if they close their eyes during this part of the activity. They can say their answers aloud or whisper them as they prefer.
Play the recording again. This time ask individual students to answer the questions during the pauses.

Test 2 Speaking Part 2

Task type:
candidates take turns to ask and answer five questions about two events which the examiner provides

Topic focus:
school events

Training

Students read and answer the lead-in questions.

> *Your partner (another student). You ask five questions and give five answers.*

1   Elicit the kinds of activities that school students might do together outside of the classroom (for example, have a party, do a play and so on).
   Students read the conversation and complete it with the missing words. Point out that they should write only one word per space.
   Check answers by asking a pair of more confident students to read out the dialogue.

> *1 on   2 Where   3 in   4 eat   5 food   6 time   7 evening   8 How   9 per*

2   Ask the students to look at the information and elicit what they think the play is about (a boy and his horse). They then complete the questions, using the information to help them.

> *1 When is the play?   2 What time does the play start? Where is the play? How much are tickets for students? What is it/the play about?*

3   Remind the students to answer questions in this part of the test using the information on the card only. They will not get extra marks for trying to add information, but they may lose marks if they do not use the information on the card.
   Students then complete the answers.

> *1 It's on Monday 3rd May.   2 It starts at 7 p.m.   3 It's at Canton Theatre   4 They are £4 (for students)   5 It's about a boy and his horse.*

Extension

Students practise asking and answering the questions using the information in Exercise 2.

4   Students look at the prompts and example. Explain that these are the kinds of prompts they will see in the exam and they should think carefully about question formation.
   Students write the questions. Monitor as they are working and offer help if necessary.
   Elicit the answers and write the questions on the board. Revise the formation of present simple questions if

necessary, paying particular attention to questions which begin without a question word (such as 4 and 5).

> *2 What day are the quiz nights?   3 What time do they start?   4 Is there a prize?   5 Do you need to book a place?*

Extension

As a class, make an information card on the board for the quiz nights in Exercise 4. Ask the questions, and elicit ideas from the students. Students then work in pairs to ask and answer about the quiz night.

5   Ask students to read the **Remember!** box Then ask them to read the information and prompts for the skiing competition. Ask them whether the question prompts and information are in the same order (No, they aren't). Explain that this is the kind of task they will see in the exam.
   Play the recording and ask them to look at the question prompts as they listen. Ask which question the girl forgot to ask.

> *No, they don't.*

6   Play the recording again for students to make a note of what the girl says. They should also note the phrases used to express interest (*Oh! Great!*).
   Point out that the students would get full marks for this part of the test because they asked and answered all of the questions accurately.

> *Oh, I forgot a question!*

Extension

Students take turns to ask and answer the questions using the information and question prompts in Exercise 5. Encourage them to respond to what their partner says using phrases such as *Oh!* and *Great!* and remind them to thank their partner for the information at the end.

Exam practice

Give the class instructions for the speaking based on Test 3 Speaking Part 2, but use substitute *School camping* trip for beach party and *School barbecue* for new dance club. Then allow one minute for the students to read through the tasks. Make sure students understand all of the vocabulary before completing the task.
Note: In the exam, each candidate is given a separate booklet with their information and prompt questions. It is likely that they will be able to see each other's booklets, but this is fine.

Students can listen to *the* model questions and answers after their practice by going to:
www.cambridge.org/elt/keyforschoolstrainer/audio.

Key

Test 3

Paper 1 Reading and Writing

Part 1

1 B   2 G   3 C   4 E   5 A

Part 2

6 C   7 B   8 C   9 B   10 A

Part 3a

11 A   12 B   13 B   14 C   15 A

Part 3b

16 D   17 B   18 F   19 A   20 H

Part 4

21 C   22 A   23 B   24 A   25 A   26 C   27 B

Part 5

28 C   29 B   30 C   31 B   32 A   33 C   34 B   35 A

Part 6

36 camera   37 poster   38 bike   39 money   40 chocolate

Part 7

41 live   42 than   43 lot / number   44 and   45 to
46 every / each   47 is / 's   48 me   49 would / 'd / always / really
50 my / our

Part 8

51 31st (any convention)   52 7 / seven
53 £3.00 (any convention)   54 10.00 (any convention)
55 cinema ticket(s)

Part 9

56 Sample answer

> Hi Marco,
>
> We studied rivers in geography yesterday. We have to choose a river in Africa to write about for homework. We have to give it to Mrs Wales on Thursday.
>
> Bye

Paper 2 Listening

Part 1

1 C   2 B   3 A   4 B   5 A

Part 2

6 E   7 F   8 H   9 C   10 B

Part 3

11 C   12 B   13 C   14 A   15 B

Part 4

16 Bauckhan   17 sea   18 6 / six   19 websites   20 Friday

Part 5

21 pet(s)   22 3 / three   23 T-shirt   24 16 / sixteen
25 24th (any convention)

Key

Test 4

Paper 1 Reading and Writing

Part 1

1 G   2 E   3 H   4 A   5 D

Part 2

6 B   7 C   8 B   9 C   10 A

Part 3a

11 B   12 A   13 A   14 B   15 C

Part 3b

16 B   17 E   18 H   19 C   20 D

Part 4

21 A   22 B   23 B   24 A   25 C   26 A   27 A

Part 5

28 C   29 B   30 A   31 B   32 C   33 C   34 B
35 A

Part 6

36 pool   37 lamp   38 mirror   39 lift   40 desk

Part 7

41 Do   42 've / have   43 at   44 Can / Could   45 the
46 Of   47 Why   48 we   49 be   50 she

Part 8

51 Red Fox   52 10 June   53 7 p.m.   54 3
55 £10 / £15 at the door

Part 9

56 Sample answer

> *Hi Kathryn*
> *We have to write about the Romans in Britain. When they came and what life was like. We have to write 200 words and give it to Mrs Graham next Wednesday.*
> *Bye*

Paper 2 Listening

Part 1

1 C   2 C   3 A   4 B   5 B

Part 2

6 F   7 B   8 H   9 G   10 C

Part 3

11 B   12 B   13 C   14 B   15 A

Part 4

16 Oberleigh   17 33 / thirty three   18 bus / by bus / on the bus
19 £65 (any convention)   20 bread

Part 5

21 Reynolds   22 car   23 8.30 (any convention)   24 purple
25 056 700 14783

Key

Test 5

Paper 1 Reading and Writing

Part 1

1 F   2 A   3 C   4 G   5 E

Part 2

6 B   7 C   8 A   9 A   10 B

Part 3a

11 A   12 B   13 C   14 A   15 C

Part 3b

16 B   17 H   18 A   19 F   20 D

Part 4

21 A   22 B   23 B   24 C   25 A   26 A   27 C

Part 5

28 C   29 B   30 A   31 B   32 C   33 A
34 C   35 A

Part 6

36 sink   37 fridge   38 cupboard   39 bowl   40 cooker

Part 7

41 in   42 have / 've   43 he   44 if   45 at   46 are
47 each / every   48 of   49 to   50 who / that

Part 8

51 Memory   52 4.45 p.m.   53 £3 (all conventions)
54 money (for snacks)   55 (in the) car

Part 9

56 Sample answer

> *Hi Kim,*
>
> *We're in Ravello, in Italy. We've been on the beach all day and swum in the sea every day! The weather's great. It's really hot.*
>
> *See you soon.*
>
> *Jade*

Paper 2 Listening

Part 1

1 B   2 A   3 B   4 B   5 C

Part 2

6 A   7 D   8 E   9 B   10 H

Part 3

11 C   12 A   13 C   14 B   15 B

Part 4

16 14 / fourteen   17 Hagerstowne   18 post
19 15th July (any convention)   20 (some) money

Part 5

21 6 / six   22 library   23 science   24 (a) pen
25 Thursday

Key

Test 6

Paper 1 Reading and Writing

Part 1
1 H   2 C   3 F   4 D   5 G

Part 2
6 A   7 B   8 C   9 B   10 A

Part 3a
11 C   12 A   13 A   14 B   15 C

Part 3b
16 C   17 A   18 G   19 D   20 H

Part 4
21 A   22 B   23 A   24 C   25 B   26 C   27 B

Part 5
28 C   29 A   30 B   31 C   32 A   33 C
34 A   35 B

Part 6
37 pilot   38 passport   39 shop   40 suitcase   5 restaurant

Part 7
41 but   42 with   43 If   44 me   45 are   46 'll / will / can
47 it   48 Why   49 my   50 at

Part 8
51 £10 / ten pounds   52 23rd July (all conventions)
53 0121 496 0691   54 (by) train   55 (Perfume) T-shirt(s)

Part 9
56 Sample answer

> Hi Sandy,
>
> The basketball game is at Newlands School. It's quite a long way but we can go with the rest of the team on the bus. The game starts at 5:30.
>
> See you,
>
> Josh

Paper 2 Listening

Part 1
1 B   2 B   3 C   4 B   5 C

Part 2
6 F   7 C   8 B   9 A   10 G

Part 3
11 B   12 B   13 A   14 C   15 C

Part 4
16 £40 / forty pounds   17 purple   18 0154 566 0148
19 Litten   20 Saturday

Part 5
21 pool   22 1 / one   23 14 / fourteen   24 T-shirt
25 18th May (all conventions)

(5–6 minutes)

Greetings and introductions

At the beginning of Part 1, the examiner greets the candidates, asks for their names and asks them to spell something.

Giving information about place of origin / school

The examiner asks the candidates about where they come from / live, and for information about their school / studies.

Giving general information about self

The examiner asks the candidates questions about their daily life, past experience or future plans. They may be asked, for example, about their likes and dislikes, recent past experiences, or to describe and compare places.

Extended response

In the final section of Part 1, candidates are expected to give an extended response to a *'Tell me something about ... '* prompt. The topics are still of a personal and concrete nature. Candidates should produce at least three utterances in their extended response.

Test 1 Exam practice
Speaking Part 2

CANDIDATE B – your questions

CANDIDATE B – your answers

Table tennis competition

♦   where / table tennis competition?

♦   what / win?

♦   only for beginners?

♦   competition finish? 🕐

♦   phone number? ☎

Join our new gym!

Open 7 days a week

8 a.m.–10 p.m.

All the latest machines!

Staff always happy to help

Students – only £10 a month!

Adults – £30 a month

www.gym.com

Test 2 Exam practice
Speaking Part 2

CANDIDATE B – your questions

School camping trip

Bring your friends and family

♦ when / camping trip?

♦ expensive?

♦ where / sleep?

♦ travel by train?

♦ what / need?

CANDIDATE B – you answers

School Barbecue

at Blue Park

from 4 p.m.–7 p.m. on Saturday

Enjoy great sausages, burgers and salads

Football and basketball matches!

Tickets £2 – available from school office

Introductions

Good morning!
What's your name?
And what's your surname?
And how do you spell that?

Do you like your school?
What is your favourite subject?

Where you are from / your studies

Where do you come from?
Are you a student?
What do you study?
Do you like your studies?

Do you study English at school?
What other subjects do / did you study?

Information about you

Do you like watching films?
What kind of films do you like watching?
Did you watch a film yesterday?

Tell me something about ...

Tell me something about the last film you saw.

Speaking Part 2
(3–4 minutes)

Activity with prompt material

Note: Test 3 questions and answers for Part 2 are on pages 228 / 230 and 232 / 234.

The examiner says 'In the next part, you are going to talk to each other.'

The examiner introduces the activity as follows:

Examiner: Candidate A, here is some information about a **beach party**.

         (Examiner shows Task 3A on page 228 to Candidate A.)

         Candidate B, you don't know anything about the **beach party**, so ask Candidate A some questions about it.

         (Examiner shows Task 3B on page 230 to Candidate B.)

         Use these words to help you.

         (Examiner points to the question prompts.)

         Do you understand?

         Now, Candidate B, ask Candidate A your questions about the **beach party**, and Candidate A, you answer them.

When the candidates have asked and answered their questions about the beach party, they then exchange roles and talk about a different topic.

The examiner introduces the activity as follows:

Examiner: Candidate B, here is some information about a **new dance club**.

         (Examiner shows Task 3C on page 232 to Candidate B.)

         Candidate A, you don't know anything about the **new dance club**, so ask Candidate B some questions about it.

         (Examiner shows Task 3D on page 234 to Candidate A.)

         Use these words to help you.

         (Examiner points to the question prompts.)

         Do you understand?

         Now, Candidate A, ask Candidate B your questions about the **new dance club**, and Candidate B, you answer them.

Introductions

Good morning!
What's your name?
And what's your surname?
And how do you spell that?

Where you are from / your studies

Where do you come from?
Are you a student?
What do you study?
Do you like your studies?

Do you study English at school?
What other subjects do you study?

Do you like your school?
What is your favourite subject?

Information about you

What kind of books or magazines do you like reading?
How often do you read?
What are you reading at the moment?

Tell me something about ...

Tell me something about your favourite book or magazine.

Speaking Part 2
(3–4 minutes)

Activity with prompt material

Note: Test 4 questions and answers for Part 2 are on pages 228/230 and 232/234.

The examiner says 'In the next part, you are going to talk to each other.'

The examiner introduces the activity as follows:

Examiner: Candidate A, here is some information about a **Museum of music**.

(Examiner shows Task 4A on page 230 to Candidate A.)

Candidate B, you don't know anything about the **Museum of music**, so ask Candidate A some questions about it.

(Examiner shows Task 4B on page 228 to Candidate B.)

Use these words to help you.

(Examiner points to the question prompts.)

Do you understand?

Now, Candidate B, ask Candidate A your questions about the **Museum of music**, and Candidate A, you answer them.

When the candidates have asked and answered their questions about the **Museum of music**, they then exchange roles and talk about a different topic.

The examiner introduces the activity as follows:

Examiner: Candidate **B,** here is some information about a **school show**.

(Examiner shows Task 4C on page 234 to Candidate B.)

Candidate A, you don't know anything about the **school show**, so ask Candidate B some questions about it.

(Examiner shows Task 4D on page 232 to Candidate A.)

Use these words to help you.

(Examiner points to the question prompts.)

Do you understand?

Now, Candidate A, ask Candidate B your questions about the **school show**, and Candidate B, you answer them.

Introductions

> Good morning!
> What's your name?
> And what's your surname?
> And how do you spell that?
> Where you are from / your studies

Where are you from / your studies

> Where do you come from?
> Are you a student?
> What do you study?

> Do you like your studies?
> Do you study English at school?

> What other subjects do you study?
> Do you like your school?
> What is your favourite subject?

Information about you

> What kind of books or magazines do you like reading?
> How often do you read?
> What are you reading at the moment?

Tell me something about ...

> Tell me something about your favourite book or magazine.

Speaking Part 2
(3–4 minutes)

Activity with prompt material

Note: Test 5 questions and answers for Part 2 are on pages 229/231 and 233/235.

The examiner says 'In the next part, you are going to talk to each other.'

The examiner introduces the activity as follows:

Examiner:	Candidate A, here is some information about **cooking classes**.
	(Examiner shows Task 5A on page 229 to Candidate A.)
	Candidate B, you don't know anything about the **cooking classes**, so ask Candidate A some questions about it.
	(Examiner shows Task 5B on page 231 to Candidate B.)
	Use these words to help you.
	(Examiner points to the question prompts.)
	Do you understand?
	Now, Candidate B, ask Candidate A your questions about the **cooking classes**, and Candidate A, you answer them.

When the candidates have asked and answered their questions about the cooking classes, they then exchange roles and talk about a different topic.

The examiner introduces the activity as follows:

Examiner:	Candidate B, here is some information about a **cycling race**.
	(Examiner shows Task 5C on page 233 to Candidate B.)
	Candidate A, you don't know anything about the **cycling race**, so ask Candidate B some questions about it.
	(Examiner shows Task 5D on page 235 to Candidate A.)
	Use these words to help you.
	(Examiner points to the question prompts.)
	Do you understand?
	Now, Candidate A, ask Candidate B your questions about the **cycling race**, and Candidate B, you answer them.

Introductions

Good morning! What's your name? And what's your surname? And how do you spell that?	Do you like your school? What is your favourite subject?

Where you are from / your studies

Information about you

Where do you come from? Are you a student? What do you study? Do you like your studies?	Can you cook? Who do you usually eat with? Which food don't you like eating?

Tell me something about ...

Do you study English at school?
What other subjects do you study?

Tell me something about your favourite meal.

Speaking Part 2
(3–4 minutes)

Activity with prompt material

Note: Test 6 questions and answers for Part 2 are on pages 229/231 and 233/235.

The examiner says 'In the next part, you are going to talk to each other.'

The examiner introduces the activity as follows:

Examiner: Candidate A, here is some information about a **film club**.

(Examiner shows Task 6A on page 231 to Candidate A.)

Candidate B, you don't know anything about the **film club**, so ask Candidate A some questions about it.

(Examiner shows Task 6B on page 229 to Candidate B.)

Use these words to help you.

(Examiner points to the question prompts.)

Do you understand?

Now, Candidate B, ask Candidate A your questions about the **film club**, and Candidate A, you answer them.

When the candidates have asked and answered their questions about the film club, they then exchange roles and talk about a different topic.

The examiner introduces the activity as follows:

Examiner: Candidate B, here is some information about a **zoo visit**.

(Examiner shows Task 6C on page 235 to Candidate B.)

Candidate A, you don't know anything about the **zoo visit**, so ask Candidate B some questions about it.

(Examiner shows Task 6D on page 233 to Candidate A.)

Use these words to help you.

(Examiner points to the question prompts.)

Do you understand?

Now, Candidate A, ask Candidate B your questions about the **zoo visit**, and Candidate B, you answer them.

3A

Beach Party

– Long Beach –

June 23rd

7 p.m.–11 p.m.

Bring food to share!

swimming, games, dancing

4B

Museum of Music

- ◆ open every day?

- ◆ address?

- ◆ student tickets? £ ?

- ◆ what / do at the museum?

- ◆ buy gifts?

5A

Cooking classes

Learn to cook simple meals!

Hall Park School – in the kitchen

Every Tuesday 6 p.m.–7 p.m.

Classes are free!

All ages welcome

6B

Film club

◆ when?

◆ where?

◆ what / see?

◆ tickets / £?

◆ what / bring?

3B

Beach Party

- ◆ date ?
- ◆ where ?
- ◆ what / do ?
- ◆ time / starts ?
- ◆ food ?

4A

Museum of Music

at 21 Station Road

Come and play 15th-century
guitars and drums!

Open Tuesday – Sunday

10 a.m.–5 p.m

Tickets – adults £3.00
– students £1.50

Shop selling gifts and snacks

5B

Cooking classes

- ◆ for teenagers?

- ◆ when?

- ◆ what / cook?

- ◆ cost / £?

- ◆ where?

6A

Film club

Watch films with your friends!

See a different film every week

7 p.m.–9 p.m. every Wednesday

Roxy Cinema

Tickets cost £2.50 per film

Bring your own snacks

3C

Dance Club

King's Theatre
Every Saturday afternoon
1–3 p.m.
Come and learn to dance!
£2.50 each
Dance teacher – Tessa Jones – ☎ 435612

4D

School Show

♦ when / meeting?

♦ for everyone?

♦ where / meeting?

♦ need musicians?

♦ who / see at the meeting?

5C

Cycling race

20-kilometre race

For 13–15 year-olds

Meet in front of the theatre at 1 p.m.

Race starts 2.15 p.m.

Book your place – ☎ 67431

6D

Zoo visit

- ♦ what / see?

- ♦ give food / animals?

- ♦ cost / children ?

- ♦ when / open?

- ♦ more information?

3D

Dance Club

- ◆ day ?

- ◆ how much / cost ?

- ◆ where ?

- ◆ who / telephone ?

- ◆ time ?

4C

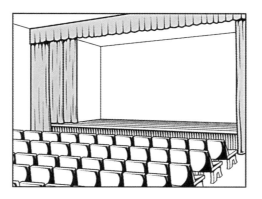

School show

Can you dance, sing or play an instrument?

Come to a meeting about the School Show

with Mr Black

at 4 p.m. on Wednesday

in music room

11–14 year-olds only

5D

Cycling race

- ◆ who for?

- ◆ book / place?

- ◆ how far?

- ◆ when / start?

- ◆ where / meet?

6C

Zoo visit

See baby animals!

Adults £9 Children £5

Open 10 am–4 p.m. every day

Give food to the elephants

See the website to find out more

CAMBRIDGE ENGLISH
Language Assessment
Part of the University of Cambridge

Candidate Name		Candidate Number	
Centre Name		Centre Number	
Examination Title		Examination Details	
Candidate Signature		Assessment Date	

Supervisor: If the candidate is ABSENT or has WITHDRAWN shade here ○

KET Reading and Writing Candidate Answer Sheet

Instructions
Use a PENCIL (B or HB).
Rub out any answer you want to change with an eraser.

For Parts 1, 2, 3, 4 and 5:
Mark ONE letter for each answer.
For example: If you think A is the right answer to
the question, mark your answer sheet like this:

0 [A● B○ C○]

Part 1

	A	B	C	D	E	F	G	H
1	○	○	○	○	○	○	○	○
2	○	○	○	○	○	○	○	○
3	○	○	○	○	○	○	○	○
4	○	○	○	○	○	○	○	○
5	○	○	○	○	○	○	○	○

Part 2

	A	B	C
6	○	○	○
7	○	○	○
8	○	○	○
9	○	○	○
10	○	○	○

Part 3

	A	B	C
11	○	○	○
12	○	○	○
13	○	○	○
14	○	○	○
15	○	○	○

	A	B	C	D	E	F	G	H
16	○	○	○	○	○	○	○	○
17	○	○	○	○	○	○	○	○
18	○	○	○	○	○	○	○	○
19	○	○	○	○	○	○	○	○
20	○	○	○	○	○	○	○	○

Part 4

	A	B	C
21	○	○	○
22	○	○	○
23	○	○	○
24	○	○	○
25	○	○	○
26	○	○	○
27	○	○	○

Part 5

	A	B	C
28	○	○	○
29	○	○	○
30	○	○	○
31	○	○	○
32	○	○	○
33	○	○	○
34	○	○	○
35	○	○	○

Continues over ➡

For Parts 6, 7 and **8:**

Write your answers clearly in the spaces next to the
numbers (36 to 55) like this:
Write your answers in CAPITAL LETTERS.

Part 6	Do not write below here
36	36 1 0 ○ ○
37	37 1 0 ○ ○
38	38 1 0 ○ ○
39	39 1 0 ○ ○
40	40 1 0 ○ ○

Part 7	Do not write below here
41	41 1 0 ○ ○
42	42 1 0 ○ ○
43	43 1 0 ○ ○
44	44 1 0 ○ ○
45	45 1 0 ○ ○
46	46 1 0 ○ ○
47	47 1 0 ○ ○
48	48 1 0 ○ ○
49	49 1 0 ○ ○
50	50 1 0 ○ ○

Part 8	Do not write below here
51	51 1 0 ○ ○
52	52 1 0 ○ ○
53	53 1 0 ○ ○
54	54 1 0 ○ ○
55	55 1 0 ○ ○

Part 9 (Question 56): Write your answer below.

Examiner's use only
0   1   2   3   4   5
○   ○   ○   ○   ○   ○

CAMBRIDGE ENGLISH
Language Assessment
Part of the University of Cambridge

Candidate Name		Candidate Number	
Centre Name		Centre Number	
Examination Title		Examination Details	
Candidate Signature		Assessment Date	

Supervisor: If the candidate is ABSENT or has WITHDRAWN shade here ○

KET Listening Candidate Answer Sheet

Instructions
Use a PENCIL (B or HB).
Rub out any answer you want to change with an eraser.

For Parts 1, 2 and **3:**
Mark ONE letter for each answer.
For example: If you think **A** is the right answer to the question, mark your answer sheet like this:

0 A B C

Part 1

	A	B	C
1	○	○	○
2	○	○	○
3	○	○	○
4	○	○	○
5	○	○	○

Part 2

	A	B	C	D	E	F	G	H
6	○	○	○	○	○	○	○	○
7	○	○	○	○	○	○	○	○
8	○	○	○	○	○	○	○	○
9	○	○	○	○	○	○	○	○
10	○	○	○	○	○	○	○	○

Part 3

	A	B	C
11	○	○	○
12	○	○	○
13	○	○	○
14	○	○	○
15	○	○	○

For Parts 4 and **5:**
Write your answers clearly in the spaces next to the numbers (16 to 25) like this:
Write your answers in CAPITAL LETTERS.

0 EXAMPLE

Part 4

		Do not write below here
16		16 1 ○ 0 ○
17		17 1 ○ 0 ○
18		18 1 ○ 0 ○
19		19 1 ○ 0 ○
20		20 1 ○ 0 ○

Part 5

		Do not write below here
21		21 1 ○ 0 ○
22		22 1 ○ 0 ○
23		23 1 ○ 0 ○
24		24 1 ○ 0 ○
25		25 1 ○ 0 ○

Acknowledgements

Our highly experienced team of Trainer writers, in collaboration with Cambridge English Language Assessment reviewers, have worked together to bring you *Key for Schools Trainer 2*. We would like to thank Helen Chilton (writer and reviewer), David McKeegan (writer), Susan White (writer), Helen Garside (reviewer) and Diane Reeve (reviewer) for their work on the material.

The authors and publishers acknowledge the following sources of copyright material and are grateful for the permissions granted. While every effort has been made, it has not always been possible to identify the sources of all the material used, or to trace all copyright holders. If any omissions are brought to our notice, we will be happy to include the appropriate acknowledgements on reprinting and in the next update to the digital edition, as applicable.

Photographs

All the photographs are sourced from Getty Images.

p. 10: gradyreese/iStock/Getty Images Plus; p. 13: Echo/Juice Images; p. 14: wundervisuals/iStock/ Getty Images Plus; p. 16: pepifoto/iStock/Getty Images Plus; p. 19, p. 94 (Dora): Hero Images; p. 22: Petro Feketa/Hemera/Getty Images Plus; p. 24: Andreas_Zerndl/iStock/Getty Images Plus; p. 26, p. 130: Westend61; p. 28: Val Corbett/VisitBritain; p. 30: Jupiterimages/liquidlibrary/Getty Images Plus; p. 38: David Sacks/DigitalVision; p. 40: PeopleImages/DigitalVision; p. 53: Sally Anscombe/Moment Open; p. 58: GoodOlga/iStock/Getty Images Plus; p. 60: Christopher Hope-Fitch/Moment; p. 61: Ramdan_Nain/iStock/Getty Images Plus; p. 63: asiseeit/iStock/Getty Images Plus; p. 64: Peter Dazeley/Iconica; p. 66: Inti St Clair/Blend Images; p. 91: Claudia Viegas Schröder/ EyeEm; p. 94 (Farah): PeopleImages/DigitalVision; p. 94 (Isabel): Roberto A Sanchez/E+; p. 96: tzahiV/iStock/Getty Images Plus; p. 109: Jose Azel; p. 112: Andy_Oxley; p. 114: thehague/iStock/ Getty Images Plus; p. 123: PeopleImages/iStock/Getty Images Plus; p. 127: Seb Oliver/Cultura; p. 130: Westend61; p. 132: ANNECORDON/iStock/Getty Images Plus; p. 145: Rayman/Photodisc; p. 148 (Klaus): amazingmikael/iStock/Getty Images Plus; p. 148 (Luiz): Jbryson/iStock/Getty Images Plus; p. 148 (Andre): albert mollon/Moment; p. 150: Alessia Izzo/Moment.

Illustrations by Cambridge Assessment, Celia Hart, Stephen Dew and QBS Learning.

Commissioned Photographs on pages 7, 46, and 48 by Trevor Clifford Photography.

Audio recordings by: DN and AE Strauss Ltd. Engineer: Neil Rogers; Editor: James Miller Producer: Dan Strauss. Recorded at: Half Ton Studios, Cambridge

Cambridge English

OFFICIAL EXAM PREPARATION MATERIALS

CAMBRIDGE.ORG/EXAMS

What do we do?

Together, Cambridge University Press and Cambridge English Language Assessment bring you official preparation materials for Cambridge English exams and IELTS.

What does *official* mean?

Our authors are experts in the exams they write for. In addition, all of our exam preparation is officially validated by the teams who produce the real exams.

Why else are our materials special?

Vocabulary is always 'on-level' as defined by the English Profile resource. Our materials are based on research from the Cambridge Learner Corpus to help students avoid common mistakes that exam candidates make.